Albert Augustus Gore

The story of our services under the Crown

A historical sketch of the Army Medical Staff

Albert Augustus Gore

The story of our services under the Crown
A historical sketch of the Army Medical Staff

ISBN/EAN: 9783337269319

Printed in Europe, USA, Canada, Australia, Japan

Cover: Foto ©ninafisch / pixelio.de

More available books at **www.hansebooks.com**

THE

STORY OF OUR SERVICES

UNDER

THE CROWN.

A Historical Sketch

OF THE

ARMY MEDICAL STAFF.

BY

SURGEON-MAJOR ALBERT A. GORE,

SANITARY OFFICER ON THE STAFF OF THE QUARTERMASTER-
GENERAL'S DEPARTMENT DURING THE ASHANTEE WAR.

*Author of "A Medical History of Our West African Campaigns,"
"Notes of a Visit to the Military Hospitals of the Continent," &c.*

LONDON:
BAILLIÈRE, TINDALL AND COX,
KING WILLIAM STREET, STRAND.
1879.

Reprinted from "COLBURN'S UNITED SERVICE MAGAZINE."

Dedicated

TO THE

DIRECTOR-GENERAL

SIR WILLIAM M. MUIR, M.D., K.C.B.

AND OFFICERS

OF THE

ARMY MEDICAL STAFF.

CONTENTS.

	Page
Preface	vii
Note	viii

CHAPTER I.
Period of the Greeks and Romans . 1

CHAPTER II.
Under the Crusaders and Normans . 15

CHAPTER III.
During the Early English Wars . 23

CHAPTER IV.
Campaigns of the Sixteenth and Seventeenth Centuries . 38

CHAPTER V.
Early Regimental Reminiscences . 61

CHAPTER VI.
Later Regimental Experiences . 88

CHAPTER VII.
Peninsular, Crimean and Modern Wars . 128

Appendix . , . 187

PREFACE.

The following sketch is the first attempt to bring together the scattered but most interesting History of the Medical Staff of the Army; as such it is necessarily imperfect. It has been compiled under every disadvantage of time, opportunity and surroundings, and has necessitated an amount of research and perseverance few who peruse it can form any idea of. The first two chapters were written whilst under orders for service in India; the third and fourth on board H.M. troop-ship 'Malabar,' and the remaining ones at Ferozepore. I have had, in addition, no opportunity of correcting the proofs previous to publication, which will account for some typographical errors remaining to be expunged in any future edition. These are my apologies for its many faults. Yet I will be amply repaid if I have been the means of preserving to all time, the excellent service and the gallant conduct of the many accomplished men who, forming the great majority of our profession, have hitherto, as they will always, continue to preserve its ancient and honourable traditions intact. Their example may be studied with advantage by all those who make the Medical Service of the Army their profession, and the younger officers will, I hope, find in its pages many facts illustrating the gradual progression in the sanitary history of the soldier about to be committed to their charge.

THE AUTHOR.

Ferozepore, Punjab,
April 9th, 1878

NOTE.

For the following particulars relating to the death of a Medical Officer, I am indebted to the kindness of Lieutenant-Colonel Brockman, 86th Regiment.—A. A. G.

"Dear Sir,

"I trust you will pardon me for venturing to point out an error in your highly interesting paper of 'Services under the Crown,' in 'Colburn's Magazine' for July. I allude to the part where it is stated, that Assistant-Surgeon Stack was killed at Jhansi, whilst attending the wounded of the 84th Regiment.

"This officer joined the 86th Regiment at Bombay, in 1856, as Surgeon of the Regiment, having been promoted from the 84th in Madras, and it was whilst in the very act of dressing a wounded soldier of the 86th, under a hot fire, that he met his death by being shot through the heart.

"He was a man who, in the short time he was with the Regiment, had endeared himself to both officers and men, and his loss was very deeply felt.

"I am, dear Sir,

"Truly yours,

"J. D. BROCKMAN,
"Lieut.-Colonel 86th Regiment.

"Aldershot, 6th July, 1878."

THE STORY OF OUR SERVICES UNDER THE CROWN.

CHAPTER I.

My plea for making the records of the Army Medical Department historical are—its ancient lineage, that its members share with the soldiers, on whose deeds history is founded, the fortunes and vicissitudes of war and pestilence, and that the object of its existence is the alleviating human suffering. I trust that my plea will be justified by the evidence I shall adduce of the good work done by it from time immemorial and by the heroic deeds of so many of its members which have earned for it the motto,
"Semper et ubique fidelis."
As mankind early congregated together for the purpose of mutual aggression and mutual defence, the more simple and obvious means of relieving themselves from the injuries inflicted by an enemy became a necessity. Hence the origin of the medical services of armies, and it is extremely interesting to trace up the gradual rise and progress of military medicine and surgery. In the oldest history extant the Hebrew word physician occurs four times, and it is curious that when translated according to its etymology, denotes "one who stitches a wound," pointing to a military origin. The practice of giving a portion of the spoil to the wounded or maimed soldier dates from an equally remote period being mentioned as early as 2 Maccabees.

Homer's "Iliad" and "Odyssey" are full of descriptions of various kinds of wounds and injuries, and from his writings we infer that the army-surgeons of antiquity united in their own persons the soldier and physician. He mentions Podalarius and Machaon, sons of Æsculapius, who accompanied Agamemnon and the Trojan Army to the siege of Troy, B.C. 1192, "as two excellent physicians," and there are several passages in Zenophon's Cyropaideia which show that the ancients in their military expeditions had always physicians and surgeons attending their camps to take care of their sick and wounded. In the discourse between Cyrus and Cambyses, the former tells the latter that he had taken care to provide military surgeons to attend him on his expedition, to take care of the health of his troops, and after the defeat of the Chaldeans, Cyrus made his people untie the prisoners, and committed the care of the wounded to his surgeons. Again, after the defeat of the Cadusians, this great commander of antiquity went himself round to visit the wounded and see that they were properly taken care of, and upon his getting possession of Babylon, formed in that city a depôt of medicines and surgical instruments for their use and as a reserve in the case of extraordinary sickness.

From Quintus Curtius we learn that physicians constantly attended the camps of Alexander the Great, and that in the hour of action, the wounded were carried off the field to be taken care of. In his account of the first battle of Alexander with Darius, he mentions that the wounded could not be carried off the field as usual, the enemy pressing so before and his own people behind. "Nec vulnerati (ut alias solent) acie poterant, excedere, cum hostis induret a fronte, a tergo fui urgerent." When Alexander was wounded at the assault of the town of Oxydraca, Cytobolas dilated his wound and extracted the dart, and in the history of these campaigns we find that he lost more of his soldiers on their arrival at the Oxus heated, enfeebled and fatigued after their toilsome march of forty-six miles across the scorching sands of the desert, after they had drank profusely from the waters of that river, than in any one of his battles. So early as the siege of Troy had the probe and bandage been used in the diagnosis and treatment of wounds, but it would appear from the following passage in Celsus that the Greek military physicians should have been rather termed surgeons, as they only treated wounds. "Sed vulneribus tantummodo, ferro et medicamentis, mederi solitos esse." Machaon himself was wounded by Paris, upon which occasion, so great was the affection of the soldiers for their surgeon, that the whole army is represented by Homer as interested in his recovery; Achilles inquired anxiously after him, and Nestor, to whose care he was entrusted, was exhorted to unwonted exertion in his behalf, " for such like him, who knows how to cut out darts and relieve the smarting of wounds by soothing unguents, is to armies more in value than many other heroes," wrote the great poet. Podalarius, on his return from Troy, was cast by a tempest on the shore of Coria and rescued by a shepherd, who upon learning that he was a physician, conducted him to the king of the country, Damitus, whose daughter he was the means of rescuing from apparent death (the symptoms following upon a violent concussion) by bleeding her from both arms, the first example of the operation being practised for the purpose of a cure. To the ancient Greek military surgeons then, are due our first knowledge of modes of treatment and diagnosis still in use in the nineteenth century. The simple extraction of darts and other offensive weapons, the checking of hæmorrhage by styptics or pressure, and the application of soothing or healing salves, appear, however, to have been the extent of their surgical knowledge. Weapons were extracted by evulsion or traction, by protrusion or by enlarging the wound and cutting them out.

So important and high was regarded the study of medicine at this time, that the Athenians had a law that no slave or woman could study it. Pythagoras, Democritus and Aristotle, the greatest philosophers of antiquity, devoted themselves to the acquisition of its doctrines. The inhabitants of Smyrna associated upon their coins the names of their celebrated physicians with the effigies of their gods, and in the time of Julius Cæsar, the Greek physicians who came to Rome were complimented with the freedom of the Eternal City. Democedes was so welcome to King Darius, that he had to use all his arts to escape from Susa.

In his celebrated account of the retreat of the 10,000 Greeks, Xenophon relates how that on the conclusion of the fifth day of their march, and after considerable skirmishing with the troops of Tissophernes, " they appointed eight physicians, as there were many persons wounded." In this march the cold and snows of Armenia "caused the blood to congeal and the toes to rot off, which was the case of a great many." " With respect to health, (says Cyrus,) having observed that commanders, for the sake of their soldiers, take physicians, so when I was placed in this command I immediately attended to this point, and I believe that I have now with them, men that are skilful in the art of physic." Quintus Curtius speaks of Philip of Arcania, one of the physicians who accompanied Alexander the Great in his march towards India as one "inter nobilis medicus," and Arrian speaks of him, not as medical attendant upon the King, but as one " in whose extraordinary skill in physic Alexander had great confidence, because of his success in the camp." Proving that in their onward march to the rivers of the Punjaub the Greek Army was not unprovided with military surgeons of skill and eminence in their profession for this early date.

It is certain that soon after men began to destroy each other, the agency of fire was employed. We gather this from the following passage in the " Æneid" :—

" Hi facilis, illi certant dependere taxis
Molirique ignem, nervoque aptare sagittis."

This must have added much to the suffering of the wounded. To Judaism belonged the honour of so humane an institution as the lazar-house, where the leper dwelt alone without the camps of this martial people.

The original and most renowned of the Æsculapial temples had been founded at Epidaurus in Greece, from whence the worship of the God of Medicine was introduced into Rome at the commencement of the Delphic Oracle, 293 B.C. These temples were resorted to by numbers of sick who received treatment in them, and were therefore to be compared to our hospitals. The Greeks had derived their earliest knowledge from the Egyptians. Homer speaks of the Egyptian art of healing. According to Herodotus and Diodorus Siculus, Egypt was always famed for its physicians, and in the Memoirs of Larrey, allusions may be found to the delineations of surgical instruments upon the walls of their ancient buildings. Even at this early time the inhabitants seemed to have suffered at certain seasons from that ophthalmia which proved so serious a cause of inefficiency to our troops in after years. Egypt had her state-paid physicians, who exercised their profession in accordance with written medical treatises long before the art of medicine had attained any scientific development among the Greeks. At first the priesthood had been the chief practitioners, but were forbidden to attend to more than one disease. A papyrus in the Library of the University of Leipsig reckoned to date from the middle of the sixteenth century B.C., is supposed to contain one of the six books on medicine mentioned by Clemens of Alexandria. Of the forty-two hermetic books, six treated on the structure of the body, on illnesses, on surgical instruments, on medicaments, on eyes, and on female complaints. From the following incident, referred to in history, in which an Egyptian king, when thrown from his horse in battle, wounded and speechless from an injury to the head, was trepanned by his surgeons on the field, it would appear that their armies were not unattended by medical officers. The incident refers to Ptolemy Philometer, who defeated Alexander Pinlas, 146 B.C. In those days only the slave, the priest, children and old men were exempted from obeying the summons to arms, some of these armies were immense. Darius led 500,000 men into Greece, but was repulsed with a loss of 6,300 men at Marathon by 10,000 Athenians, with a loss of only 190. At Issus 400,000 infantry and 100,000 cavalry were pitted against Alexander the Great, but the superior discipline and organization of the Macedonians enabled them to defeat the Persians and slay 110,000 of them with a loss of only 450.

For upwards of 600 years after the Trojan War, medicine and surgery made little progress. Pythagoras (B.C. 600) first brought philosophy to bear upon the practice of the healing art, and led the way in raising it to the dignity of a science. It was still, however, a rude, imperfect, and uncertain one, little more than the binding up of wounds and the mere elements of military surgery. Hippocrates, a contemporary of the illustrious Socrates, born 460 B.C., soon freed medicine from the absurdities with which ignorance and superstition had invested it, and through a long, honoured and glorious life he set a splendid example of persevering industry and philosophical research. So correct was his observation and so faithful his chronology of diseases, that many of his descriptions may be fairly quoted in our modern works although more than two thousand years old. His name is associated with the great plague which visited Athens, the contagious inroads of which are stated to have been arrested there, as in other places, by kindling fires. This plague had got among the army of Artaxerxes about the period of the third Peloponessian War, and we find the King writing to the Persian Governor of the Hellispont desiring the presence of Hippocrates in aid of the Persian physicians, who were dying faster than their patients.

An early record, repeated in many a campaign, and showing how great is the risk to the medical attendants from the deadly contagion of the sick. Hippocrates must have been no mean military surgeon, as evidenced by his description of wounds received at the siege of Datus from engines constructed to throw darts or stones. One of his kinsmen, taken prisoner by Artaxerxes Mnemon, in a battle fought against his brother Cyrus, was successful in curing his captor of a severe wound, and thus obtained favour and rewards.

On the dismemberment of the vast empire of Macedonia after the death of Alexander the Great, learning took up its chief abode at Alexandria, under the protection of Ptolemy Soter, (B.C. 300,) and here it was that popular prejudice gave way and permitted the examination of the dead by human dissection—the importance of which to the military surgeon was self-evident. After the conflagration of Alexandria in the reign of Julius Cæsar, the arts and sciences followed the seat of empire in its transfer to Imperial Rome. It was after the establishment of the Alexandrian School, that the separation of medicine into the departments of dietetics, pharmacy and surgery commenced, a measure which essentially tended to the improvement of the different branches of the profession and the advancement of knowledge.

For a long time after the foundation of the Roman Empire the pursuit of science gave way to the love of warlike affairs. Rome had subdued most of her rivals before she turned her attention to the arts and sciences. According to Pliny for 600 years she was without physicians, no individuals being especially trained to the exercise of medicine and surgery, which were replaced by spells and incantations to the gods. In their subsequent efforts they readily copied from the Greeks, who had had permanent armies from the days of Philip of Macedon, previously to which the forces of Greece had been a sort of unpaid militia, composed of rich citizens, drawn by ballot, and who returned to their homes after a summer campaign. Philip had introduced a standing army, a portion of which had consisted of mercenaries, who were not only constantly ready for war but were perfect in the tactics and organization of the day. When the Greeks were expelled from Italy by the Romans, the law which banished them exempted by name those who followed the profession of medicine.

Under the Roman Republic the armies were formed by liability to personal service of all citizens paying not less than £20 a year taxes. The Roman forces were therefore numerically weak, but well trained and armed. Shortly after the birth of Hippocrates she had commenced the conquest of the world with only 45,000 men, little better than a militia, who returned to their homes and civil occupations in the intervals between the campaigns. Under Marius, the lower orders and freed men were allowed to serve, and a class of professional soldiers instituted. Augustus established a permanent army as a regular institution by exacting, instead of twenty campaigns with long intervals of repose at home, twenty years continuous service in camp. He also enrolled in the legions none but provincials and the poor of the city, which led to the loss of the military spirit, a decline in discipline, and a retrogression in tactics. In proportion as the army became more mercenary its qualities decreased, and in compensation therefore, its quantity had to be augmented. The largest armies of the Republic never exceeded 83,000 men, but at the close of the reign of Augustus there were 173,000 men permanently under arms, and in the reign of Constantine over 450,000.

About 200 B.C. the first professor of medicine, Archagathus, a Peloponnessian, settled at Rome as a practitioner of surgery. A century later Archipiades of Bythenia, acquired a considerable degree of popularity, relying principally upon the effects of exercise, diet, bathing, and other hygienic measures. In the reign of Augustus and Tiberius, Celsus, the contemporary of Horace, Virgil and Ovid, gave a further impulse to medicine by his treatise remarkable for the purity of its style, and the description of those febrile diseases which ever have been the curse of armies in the field. He is the first native Roman physician whose name is transmitted to us. Before his time all who had risen to eminence had been either Greeks or Asiatics. This was in the first century of the Christian era. From at least two Latin contemporary writers it would appear that in this century were established the first hospitals among the Romans. According to Cooper the *Thesaurus* or *Valetudinarium*, was "a place where men lie being sick." Andromachus, who lived in the reign of Nero, was the first individual on whom the title of Architer or principal physician was bestowed by the Emperors, a title continued for several centuries. Seneca, who died under Nero, refers in at least three passages to early hospitals. Celsus had laid down distinct and practical precepts for the extraction of warweapons, such as arrows, spears, leaden bullets, &c., from the bodies of the wounded. Galen, born A.D. 131, and the author of no less than 200 distinct treatises on subjects directly or indirectly connected with medicine, was the last original writer for some centuries. For more than 1,300 years after his death his doctrines were regarded almost in the light of oracles. Literature was now rapidly declining, various moral and political causes suspending the progress of science and learning for many centuries, producing what has justly been denominated the dark ages. Medicine, although not allowed to remain as stationary as other sciences, felt its paralysing influences declining with the Roman Empire.

Undervalued at the beginning as calculated for the effeminate and feeble, when temperance of living and perseverance in regular and impressive discipline, which had hitherto kept the Roman legions in the greatest state of efficiency and health, had given rise to ease and effeminacy, it was found necessary to correct these evils—inseparable from such a state of society as existed at the period of the decline of the Roman Empire—by recourse to the medical art, which we have already seen had by this time made rapid strides.

From the commentaries of Cæsar we find that the Romans were in the habit of sending their sick and wounded to the nearest towns whenever their armies moved, and that the invalids who were rendered incapable of further service were provided for at the public expense. Hygenus Gromaticus, who is supposed to have been a servant of Augustus, and to have been made a freeman, and to have written in the reign of Trojan his treatise "De Castramatitione," tells us that the sick and wounded soldiers were laid in tents, pitched in a place of the camp appropriated for that purpose, called the Valitudinarium, of which Schellius has given a figure in the plan of a Roman camp. The inspection and good order of this, as well as of all the economical concerns of the encampment, were placed under the immediate superintendence of an officer denominated "Prefect of the Camp." As late as the third century Lampridius speaks of the Emperor Alexander Severus visiting his sick soldiers in their tents.

Tacitus alludes to the fact that among the ancient Germans the women followed the armies to the field, and dressed the wounds of the combatants. "Ad matres, ad conjuges vulnera ferunt; nec illæ numerare aut exigera plages pavent." From other passages in the history of this author as well as in Livy and Justin, it would appear that the greater part of the care of the sick in these early times, fell as a tax upon the neighbouring people, or as a duty assumed by the patriotic and humane of the Roman state. These writers also inform us, that after great battles near to large cities, the wounded Romans and Greeks were received into the homes of the nobility, had physicians to attend them, and were furnished with fomentations and other remedies. Titus Livius says, "that after the victory obtained over the Veii and Etruci, Fabius, the general, distributed the wounded amongst the nobility. According to Justin the same practice was followed by the Spartans after their defeat at Sallustra; and Cæsar, when his army moved, sent his sick and wounded in waggons to the neighbouring towns to be taken care of. In fact the Roman generals seemed to have followed very much the same practice as is carried out in the present day About this time Vegetius, in his work "De re Militari," embodies a chapter containing directions how to preserve the health of soldiers, and tells us that it was the duty of the Præfectus Castrorum (quartermaster-general) to superintend the conduct of the physicians and surgeons, and to provide everything that was wanted for the sick, and it was a common practice of the Roman generals, in order to gain the affection of the soldiers to go round among the wounded, to inquire if they were well taken care of, and to give them every assistance in their power. Livy, Tacitus, and Pliny, mention Pipirius Curzon, Germanicus and Trojan respectively as having followed this practice, showing that great attention was paid to prevent diseases, and keep the armies in health, and that equal care was taken of the sick and wounded soldiers.

The Romans also were very attentive to the preservation of the health of their soldiers in the time of service, for we learn from Vegetius that they took great care that they should be well supplied with good water and provisions, and firewood, and their horses with forage; and that a sufficient quantity of wine, vinegar and salt, should always be provided for their camps, and that they endeavoured to keep their armies in good health by due attention. 1. To situation. 2. To the water. 3. To the season. 4. To medicine. 5. To exercise.

1. *To situation.*—In not encamping near to unwholesome marshes, or on dry uncovered ground in summer; or without tents; or to remain too long on the same ground in summer or in autumn.

2. *To the water.*—By taking care that the army did not use bad or unwholesome water of marshes, for bad water was very productive of disease.

3. *To the seasons.*—By not beginning the marches of the army too late in the summer, and exposing the men to the scorching heat of the sun; but setting out so soon as to get to the end of the day's march by day-break; and in winter, by not marching the men in the night in time of frost and snow; and taking particular care that the men never were in want of fire-wood, or of clothing.

4. *To medicine.*—By the officers seeing that the sick had their regular meals, and were well looked after by the physicians.

5. *To exercise.*—By keeping the troops during the day time in constant exercise; in dry weather in the open air; and in the time of rain or snow, under cover; for exercise did a great deal more for the preservation of health than the art of physic.

These precepts of Vegetius may be remembered in the nineteenth century with advantage.

The powers of the engines used by the ancients in war, catapultæ, balistæ, &c., were, according to the Chevalier Folard, little inferior to the instruments of destruction used at the commencement of the present century, and the effect of the leaden balls and stones projected by them were well known to Celsus and other medical writers who preceded him.

In courage and corporeal strength, the Gauls were at least on an equality with their enemies, to whom they were individually superior in bulk and stature, though deficient in the formation of limb and power of endurance possessed by the Romans, whose habits and discipline had hardened them against the exhalations of the marshes, and the change or deprivation of food, no less against the extremities of heat and cold. The soldiers of the legion appear to have rarely suffered from the cause of mortality which decimates, and in some instances, have almost exterminated modern armies. For the free use of his arms the Roman soldier required a space of three feet on each side of him, having which he was enabled to single out his adversary, to get within his guard, and with the point or edge of his well-tempered sword, to inflict deadly wounds upon his opponent's naked body. The soldier of the Roman legion having armour on the head, breast and shoulders, possessed an immense superiority over the Gauls, who, at all times imperfectly furnished with armour, frequently in action cast it off as unworthy to be employed by a true warrior. Thus when their antagonists had strength and firmness sufficient to enable them to receive unbroken their fierce onset, there was little chance of their proving victorious when engaged in a hand-to-hand combat with troops perfectly armed, both for offence and defence. This will account in great measure for the immense slaughter which always attended the victories over the Gauls.

In most ancient battles the vanquished lost vastly more in proportion to the successful assailant in killed and wounded. At the battle of Pharsalia, Cæsar's loss was only 200 men, whilst Pompey's was 18,000. The cause of this difference was in great measure owing to the arms in use and the capture of prisoners. The lighter projectiles seldom did much execution, but when the opponents met hand to hand it became inevitable that the conquerors would lose but few soldiers, while the broken and routed vanquished would suffer severe slaughter, chiefly from the sword or spear. There were few casualties in the early part of the engagement, the shields being a safeguard against the missiles in use and the sword, and it was not until the commencement of the defeat that they were discharged. Arrows, darts and stones were not destructive to life, shields having been known to have been struck by as many as 200 arrows.

One of the main difficulties of the Romans in campaigning arose from the necessity of providing food and wine for the troops. The latter was not absolutely required, for in its absence they were satisfied with water, slightly flavoured with acid, therefore in their supplies for the soldiers acid was always included instead of wine. Bread was not baked for them in ovens, but flour and lard was issued to each man and cooked together, forming a savoury and strengthening diet. Thus the provisions of the troops merely consisted of flour, acid and lard, and barley for the horses. Droves of cattle and smaller animals generally, however, followed an army, as they required no transport, and caused but slight impediment on the march. Thus provided, ancient armies oftentimes traversed barren and desolate countries for many consecutive days, without suffering from hunger, as they carried with them, without any difficulty, the requirements for the support of men and horses. Wives and female camp-followers were forbidden; and there was not much difficulty in preventing their access to camp, as the soldiers were so constantly engaged in their exercises, sometimes in a body, at other times individually, that they had not time to think of Venus, or of frivolous pursuits, or of other indulgences of the indolent and useless. The value of this was apparent, as the men were healthy in quarters and camp. They were regular, and sober, and victorious in battle. When these precautions were neglected, on the day of trial the troops were found wanting, as for example on the Trebbia, when Sempronius after crossing it in mid-winter, fought against Hannibal (whose men had breakfasted and formed leisurely to meet the enemy) with his army wet, exhausted, half frozen and fasting, and was ignominiously defeated. At Ferozeshah many centuries later, a very similar result was nigh occurring, from the men after a fatiguing march through heat and dust, and while suffering from hunger and thirst being brought on to the attack, the trite military maxim that in war "every possible chance should be enlisted on your side," being for the moment forgotten. It would appear that the ancients laid great stress upon the importance of not fighting upon empty stomachs. The second meal of the Greeks (ἄριστον) was a late meat breakfast, and said to be etymologically derived from ἄριστον, to take pluck or courage, because after partaking of it, the soldiers buckled on their armour, went to battle and were expected to do their duty on the strength of their fighting meal.

The military pre-eminence of the Romans was the result of military training and actual practice in war, for the Roman was of ordinary stature, energetic in action, but not of extraordinary physical force. "In the infancy of the Republic, a sentiment of honor, emulation of power, and love of glory, stimulated the Roman soldier to action. Modesty, a sense of shame, or dread of disgrace, supported him under difficulty, and rendered him in a manner insensible to danger. When completely drilled he was placed in the ranks by tribe. Twenty thousand paces in five hours constituted the ordinary rate of marching, twenty-five thousand the march of alert or exertion. He was practised in leaping and running drill, and carried a load of 60lbs. weight of baggage, placed equally on all parts, so that the sense of fatigue during a steady march was not materially felt. The art of swimming was taught systematically, and practised assiduously. These various exercises were so conducted, that while subservient to the military purpose, they increased the bodily strength, improved health, and steeled the habit against vicissitudes of heat and cold, or the effects of rain or scorching suns."

The exercise of the stake with the Romans was considered the first exercise in the system of training. The recruit was furnished with an osier shield and wooden club, each of them double the weight of the military shield and sword, with which he approached the stake, as he would have neared an enemy, practising all modes of attack, taking care to leave no part of his own body uncovered. He was exercised morning and evening, and principally instructed in the mode of giving point, as wounds inflicted by the edge were then known to be comparatively less mortal than those which were given by the point, particularly when the more vulnerable parts of the body were covered with armour. The most dexterous were rewarded with a double ration and employed as teachers, while those slow in learning were fed on barley instead of wheat, and restricted to that species of food until their proficiency was acknowledged. The earliest record of a punishment diet.

The recruit was next practised in throwing the javalin, the art of shooting arrows, in using the sling, from which in later times leaden bullets were projected instead of stones, also in mounting horses, vaulting, &c. The armour of the infantry soldier consisted of a shield, helmet, coat of mail, and an iron boot or greave for the right leg; the arms, a pike, a javalin, a sword and dagger. Their army consisted of three orders or lines—*hastati* in front line; *principes* directly in rear; *triarii* behind. The first line was compact, the second and third were open with a view to receive the first in the intervals if forced to retire. A certain number of cavalry and bowmen and slingers as skirmishers were upon the flanks. Fully accoutred and armed at all points, the Roman soldiers were obliged three times in the month, with a view that they might be always fit for field service, to march ten thousand paces from the camp, and to return the same distance. The legion was the basis of the army. According to Vegetius it consisted of ten cohorts, the first containing 1,105 infantry and 132 horsemen, was entrusted with the care of the eagle. The second, third and fourth, contained 555 foot and 66 horse each, and constituted the first line, 3,721 officers and men. The sixth, seventh, eighth, ninth and tenth, numbered each 955 foot and 66 horse. The legion in all 6,800 foot and 726 horse.

In the Roman order of battle the cavalry were placed on the wings, when the order of battle was formed, the first and second ranks remained in position, the third rank rested on the knee, the skirmishers provoked the enemy to battle, followed and annoyed his retreat if he retired, and if unequal to resist retired behind their own lines. The heavy armed then took up the combat, remaining in position as a wall of iron, and if the enemy fled, did not follow but committed the pursuit to the light armed and cavalry.

In issuing some peremptory orders regarding the discipline of the army, the Emperor Aurelius enumerated various rigid rules which his soldiers were to observe. He concludes:—"Let each soldier aid and serve his fellow; let them be cured gratuitously by the physicians; let them give nothing to soothsayers; let them conduct themselves quietly in their hospitals; and he who would raise strife let him be lashed." According to Sir James Simpson, the date of this order is about A.D. 270.

The military physicians of the Romans (Medici Militaris) were exempted from some burdens and taxes, because "the office which they fill is beneficial to the public." According to Justinian, the physician of the legion (Medicus Legionis) was exempt from civil duties when absent on the public service. This was in the sixth century. While the prefect of the camps had authority over the sick soldiers, the physician who had the care of them regulated the various expenses. Celsus spoke of the possibility of studying human internal anatomy by looking at the wounds of soldiers, and added, that in consequence of a want of this knowledge the physicians employed in the German wars, and having power of dissecting the barbarians, learned little. The wars he alludes to occurred between A.D. 167 and 175.

About the year A.D. 208 the Emperor Septimius Severus led an army of not less than 80,000 across the Forth to Murray Frith, returning to York. He is stated to have lost 50,000 of his men without having met a single enemy. This was due to his having encountered many difficulties and devastations from the rivers, marshes, woods and stratagems of the Caledonians. He had been obliged to make roads over mountains, mounds across the marshes, and bridges over the rivers. When his wounded could not be brought off, they were, according to Cassius, slain by their comrades, that they might not fall into the hands of the enemy. The Scots were then ignorant of the use of clothes, but painted their naked bodies with various devices. They were described as being very warlike and fierce, and armed only with a narrow shield and spear. The Caledonians who lived at this time, says Cassius, "inhabited rugged passes and dry mountains, and desert places full of marshes, with neither castles or towns, or cultivated ground; they lived on their flocks and hunting, and the fruit of some trees, not eating fish although extremely plenty; they lived in tents, naked and without buskins; they fought in cars, had small and swift horses. Their infantry were remarkable for speed in running, and for firmness in standing. Famine, cold, and all sorts of labour they could bear, for they would even stand in their marshes for many days up to their necks in water, and in the woods would live on the bark and roots of trees. They prepared a kind of food on all occasions, of which, taking only a bit the size of a bean, they felt neither hunger or thirst."

Such were the enemies which the old Emperor failed to conquer. The late Sir James Simpson has proved conclusively, that under the empire at least, the Roman armies were provided with a medical staff, of which the cohort physician was the unit. At Housesteads in Northumberland, the ancient Boscovinis, one of the principal stations on the great defensive wall which the Emperor Hadrian raised in the second century between the Tyne and the Solway, a monumental tablet was discovered with an inscription upon it from the first Tungriac Cohort to the memory of their Medicus Ordinarius. The inscription was—

Diis Mautibus
Anicio
Ingenio
Medico
Ordinario Cohortis
Primæ Tungrorum
Vixit Annis XXV.

Translated by Mr. Bruce as "Sacred to the Gods of the Shades below. To Anicius Ingenius, Physician in Ordinary of Cohort the First of the Tungrians. He lived twenty-five years."

In Gruter's work on Roman inscriptions, there are copies of others in which physicians of cohorts (Medici Cohortis) are mentioned, one as early as A.D. 83. This inscription is dedicated by "Sextus Titius Alexander, Physician of the fifth Prætorian Cohort, to Æsculapius, and the safety of his fellow soldiers." Another is erected by the Physician of the fifth Prætorian Cohort, in conformity with a vow he had taken to the health of his fellow soldiers, showing the interest taken by the Roman surgeons in the men in their care.

Murston, in his "Thesaurus," cites a Roman sepulchral tablet discovered in Viterbi, and containing an inscription by a father to his deceased son, M. Vulpinus Sporus, Physician to the Indian and Asturian Auxiliaries. Most of these tablets refer to one rank of military medical officer, namely, the surgeon of cohorts, (Medici Cohortis,) each cohort consisting of from 500 to 600 men. These officers had the distinctive term of "Ordinarius" and "Clinicus" and "Medicus Cohortis." Whether these terms indicated or no three different grades of the Roman Medici Cohortum, there is, according to Simpson, sufficient evidence for proving that there existed in their army a higher rank of medical officer than these, namely, "Medici Legionum." The Roman Legion consisted of ten cohorts, each of which was provided with at least one medical officer, over whom was placed the medical officer of the Legion, monumental tablets having been discovered dedicated to the Medicus Legionis. Maffei in his Museum Veronense gives the inscription of one raised by Scribonia Faustina to the manes of her very dear husband, L. Cælius Arrianus, Physician to the second Italian Legion, who died, aged 49½ years.

Medical stores were also carried with the Imperial armies. According to Tacitus in the war conducted by Germanicus against Arminius, in one of the contests with the German Army, the Roman troops lost their entrenching tools, tents and remedies or dressings for the wounded (fomenta sanciis.) Subsequently it is related how that Agrippina, the wife of a Roman general, distributed gratuitously amongst the soldiers, clothes to the needy and dressings to the wounded, and after the battle fought near Ruspina, Labienus ordered his wounded to be carried to Adrumentum, bound in waggons, the first mention of a rude ambulance system. Sometimes the exigencies of war converted the stronger soldiers into the only available transport corps for the sick and wounded. Zenophon alludes in his "Anabasis" to the number of Greeks capable of fighting being severely diminished, because some of the soldiers were employed in carrying the wounded, and others in carrying the arms of the latter, a contingency which in modern armies is obviated by the formation of a special hospital corps.

Physicians were also in attendance upon the Roman Senators, Consuls and Emperors during the course of their campaigns. Galen himself was employed in that capacity to attend upon the Emperor M. Aurelius and L. Verus at Apuleia, and Scribonius Largus composed his therapeutical work "De Compositione Medicamentorum" when absent from Rome as surgeon to the Emperor Claudius during his short campaign in England. When the Emperor Severus returned to York from his campaign against the Scots, attempts were made to induce his medical attendants to adopt means to hasten the old soldier's death; refusing, to their undying honour, to accomplish so heinous a crime, they were on his decease doomed to die.

"This retrospect," writes Sir James Simpson, "affords a strange subject of meditation for us in this nineteenth century, to consider; some fifteen hundred years ago, it thus happened in England that a number of physicians were themselves doomed to death for refusing to pervert their profession so far as to become the murderers of the royal invalid; and the modern physician may look back with some degree of pride upon the fact, that in an age and at a court when cruelty and corruption held unrestrained sway, some members, at least, of the medical profession remained so uncorruptible as to endanger and sacrifice their own lives rather than tamper with the life of their patient."

The legions which conquered Britain remained for the most part as its permanent garrison during the whole period of the subsequent occupation. During that long period at least, the 2nd, the 6th, and 20th Legions remained without relief—the Romans, seeming not to recognise the necessity for those constant changes of quarters which prove so serious an item in English Army Estimates. They were not finally withdrawn until A.D. 414, when the Romans found themselves attacked by so many enemies nearer home, that it became necessary to recall the legions in Britain. While in occupation of England, the Roman soldiers, when not drilling or fighting, were occupied in the laborious duty of constructing camps, fortifications or roads, so many remains of which are from time to time brought to light in our own day. The Britons adopted readily the civilization of the Romans, and Britain was extensively colonised by inroads of immigrants from Italy. The women of Britain were then celebrated for their large blue eyes, dazzling complexions, and golden hair, and were eagerly sought in marriage by the colonists and the soldiers. The aboriginal Britons became in turn identified with their conquerors, and the bold and enterprising entered into the ranks of the legions, and were soon drafted from the island to other scenes and climates, to contribute to the Roman triumphs or stem for a while the tide of barbarian conquest, soon to overwhelm the great empire, and with it all that was glorious in art, literature and science.

CHAPTER II.

The Saracens, who succeeded the Romans in power and reputation, were wont to collect their sick and wounded in the rear of their armies, into places of security, where they were provided with medical and surgical assistance in regular form. They captured Alexandria A.D. 640. A few works, among which were the writings of Galen, were preserved during the destruction of that great emporium of commerce which the sagacity of Alexander had placed at the *embouchure* of the Nile; with these, knowledge was gradually communicated to Arabia, where towards the end of the eighth century, was founded at Bagdad a college by the Caliph Almanzar, where medicine obtained a permanent footing. So great was the celerity of this school, that at one time it contained 6,000 students. Hospitals and pharmacies were common, and placed under regular inspection; and it is stated by Sprengel that the General of the Arabian Army visited in person the pharmacies of his troops, in order to ascertain if they were equipped with all the medicines mentioned in his dispensatories. The first of the latter ever published was written by Aboul Hassan, bishop and physician to the Caliph. These Arabian physicians and philosophers represented in their time to Europe the science of the world. They combined the study of mathematics with medicine. With them originated chemistry, which subsequently produced, indirectly, a very important effect on the progress of medicine, and now enters so largely into the ever-varying problems of military hygiene. They added to the Pharmacopæia many useful medicines; but on the other hand, carried with their armies to Egypt some of those contagious diseases, notably variola and leprosy, which exercised for so long a time a pernicious influence upon the health of soldiers; and which between the eleventh and twelfth centuries the Crusaders, returning broken and dispirited from their unequal contest, spread over Europe.

By the settling of the Moors in Spain, Arabic medicine and other branches of learning were introduced into Europe, and Italy especially, where about the middle of the seventh century Hebrew, Arabic and Latin professors of the healing art settled at Salerno, which, from its local situation as one of the great outlets from which the Crusaders passed over to Asia, acquired naturally a great degree of celebrity, and the intercourse thus effected between Asiatics and Europeans led to the knowledge of the philosophical and medical writings of the Greeks being made known to the inhabitants of Italy and France. As yet they were only to be read in their Arabic and Latin versions; not until a decidedly later period were they to be perused in their native language. At this renowned school the returning Crusaders added their experience gained in Eastern battle-fields, which gave a further impetus to the study of military medicine and surgery. Here Charles the Great founded a college in 808, the first of its kind in Europe, and where the student in medicine was obliged to devote three years to the study of philosophy, afterwards five to medicine, and at the same time study surgery, and if admitted a surgeon, anatomy for at least a year. It was also the first establishment in which regular medical degrees were granted to candidates after they had passed through a prescribed course of study, and were subject to examination; and it was not until the close of the fifteenth century that it was eclipsed by the rising reputation of the Universities of Bologna and Paris; before this the influence of its teachings was felt throughout the then embryo medical service of armies.

The celebrity of the Arabic or Saracenic School of Medicine in Spain was ascribed to the comparative condition of the neighbouring countries, which from the eighth to the twelfth centuries in Europe was in a state of the most complete barbarism and superstition. The only remains of a taste for literature and the fine arts being found among the Moors and Arabians. Arabic was the general language of science. The last traces of their intellectual illumination appeared among the Spanish Moors in the thirteenth century, when the Christian arms having become more and more powerful, they were compelled to substitute the field for the study, the sword for the pen; and before an overwhelming opposition, were at length driven from a region whose fields they had tilled, and whose olives they had gathered for a thousand years. With the decline of the Saracenic school, the daylight of science went down over the nations; and an intellectual darkness, which endured for 300 years, enveloped the general form of society. All the fountains of science were dried up; and the world seemed retrograding into the unilluminated chaos of ignorance. Prior to the study of anatomy and the discovery of the circulation of the blood, the mediæval physician had pursued his task by only a feeble glimmer of empirical illumination; but this, such as it was, stood boldly out against the surrounding darkness. Thus the profession of medicine did much to soften the savage aspect of war. For "it was one of the happy privileges," writes Armand, "of the military surgeon to draw from the state of war precepts which served humanity by turning to his profit the observations and the treatment of the maladies which follow in its train."

At the close of the tenth century the Jews, from their knowledge of the Arabic language, had been the chief physicians in Europe, and until a canon law was established at the instigation of the clergy, who were endeavouring to rival them as practitioners of physic, and who claimed the practice of medicine as their peculiar privilege, using it chiefly as a means of personal power and gain, disgraced by ignorance, charlatanism, and imposture. This canon declared that no Jew might be a physician or give medicine to a Christian. Still for a long time there was scarcely a Christian Court where physicians of this nature were not entertained.

Two centuries before the foundation of the College of Medicine at Salerno, the Emperor Mauritius had introduced the custom of carrying along with his army *Despotati*, or " drink-givers," whose duty it was to carry off the wounded in battle, for which purpose they were distributed among the cavalry, and were equipped with two stirrups on both sides of their saddles to take up the wounded behind them with the greater ease. They were also obliged to carry water with them for the refreshment of the sufferers. In the ninth century the Emperor Leo VI. mentions them expressly in his "Tactics," as a necessary appendage to an army, furnished with their field medicines and materials.

According to Aranzoar, about this period, surgery and pharmacy had begun to rank much below medicine, and in his time (eleventh century) was so little esteemed by the physicians (the Medici Honorati et Nobiles) that they thought it below their character to understand them, and therefore left all manual operations to their servants (the Servitores et Ministri). The result was that the practice of surgery, a correct appreciation of which was of so much importance to armies, fell into neglect, and into the hands of unskilful persons for the time, whose farrago of vulnery nonsense took the place of the simple and scientific treatment of wounds advocated by Hippocrates, with a result disastrous to the soldier of the Middle Ages.

Under Louis VII., the Faculty of Medicine of Paris assumed a form of consequence in the University which had been founded by Charlemagne, and the attractions of the profession appear then to have been so great, that the clerical physicians became neglectful of their sacred offices, and spent most of their time in attending the lectures which were then delivered on the works of Hippocrates and Galen. Before this a Roman Council assembled by Pope Innocent II. in 1139, had threatened with the severest penalties those monks and canons who applied to the practice of medicine to the neglect of the sacred object of their own profession. These edicts had to be repeated at the Council of Tours under Pope Alexander III. in 1163, and again in 1177 and 1216. By the first of these, the priests were forbidden to quit their cloisters or to exercise the profession, in consequence of which a few laymen were induced to enter upon the study; but being refused by the University without their having contracted a vow of celibacy, on the completion of their studies, most of them entered the Church.

C

The clergy continued to follow the profession of medicine in their own abodes, and to those of the sick to whom their administration was required they sent their servants or dressers, who undertook the practice of bleeding and other minor surgical operations. In the thirteenth century the Italian Universities admitted the lay students to equal privileges with the clerical, and whilst the latter confined themselves to the practice of medicine, the former undertook the capital operations of surgery. The first incorporation of surgeons took place under Louis IX., commonly known as St. Louis, who himself had been engaged in dressing the wounded. In 1268 he established a College of Surgeons, and dedicated it to the house of St. Cosmos and St. Damian. One of the conditions annexed to the foundation consisted of an obligation to attend Divine Service every first Monday in the month, and after its performance to dress gratuitously the wounded poor. The members of this faculty were called "Master Chirurgeons," a name to be found in very late Army Lists. The servants of the priests still, however, continued to practise surgery until John Petard, surgeon to Louis IX., Philip the Brave, and Philip the Fair, obtained from the latter an *ordonnance*, to assemble all practitioners to undergo an examination as to their qualifications, in order that licenses might be only granted to those fully competent. This edict was enforced by King John in 1352—1355, and subsequently by Charles V., who, while Regent, had enrolled his name in the list of "Master-Surgeons," an example followed as late as 1605 by Louis XIII.

The Princes of the Merovingian race, who early founded abbeys and monasteries, had reserved places in them for their wounded soldiers—a practice imitated by the Carlovingian monarchs. Saint Louis, on his return from the Crusades, where he had ample opportunity for seeing the terrible misery of war, founded the house of "Quinze-Vingts," where were received those unfortunate crusaders whom the bright sun of Asia had struck with blindness. This was the first edifice of its kind consecrated to the use of invalid soldiers in Western Europe, over whose wild and uncultivated districts hospitals had begun to spread subsequent to the sixth century. Built close to churches and monasteries, under the superintendence of the clergy and various brotherhoods, from being places of mixed accommodation for the religious, the aged, the destitute orphan and the sick, they gradually arrived at their present form.

At Constantinople the Emperor Alexius had instituted permanent establishments for invalids in the eleventh century, at which time knights attended the sick and wounded themselves, administering compounds of balsams and vulnery drinks with great spirit and perseverance. The "Domus Dei," or God's House, was the name given to the early hospitals of the Crusaders, who built them in emulation of that which about the middle of the eleventh century had been erected at Jerusalem by the merchants of Amalphi trading to the Levant, as a refuge for Christian traders and pilgrims visiting the Holy City. That hospital was dedicated to St. John; and when the hospitals in Jerusalem were confided to the care of the military in 1099, the knights first called themselves "Hospitallers of Jerusalem," changed to Knights of St. John in 1121, the Knights of Rhodes in 1311, and finally to Knights of Malta in 1530. In France the "Domus Dei" was known as the "Maison Dieu," a name still retained by many hospitals in that country, and which in Paris has been changed to "Hôtel Dieu." A very ancient example of these hospitals in England is the garrison church at Portsmouth—the chancel of the church of the "Domus Dei" finished about the year 1336 by Pierre de la Roche, "a man well skilled in war," a knight and a Crusader who had been in the Holy Land, and who by "a special Providence" had been placed in the See of Winchester in 1205. The Order of St. John was first planted in England in the year 1101. The Order raised the Priory of Clerkenwell, which held a high place in England until despoiled and suppressed in 1540.

In 1314, Marodini, Professor of Anatomy in the University of Bologna, published an anatomical description of the human body, dissected from nature, which must have exercised an immense influence for good on the after-progress of military surgery, just emerging from the superstitious practices with which it was surrounded—the doctrine of the ancient physicians *plus* magic, astrology, and supernatural agency. Chemistry was pursued with ardour by the alchemists in order to obtain the transmutation of metals into gold, and the discovery of a universal medicine combining the property of removing all diseases and preserving life. Vain and illusory idea! Guy de Chauliac, who practised at Avignon about the middle of the fourteenth century, in his "Chirurgie," a history of the surgery of his day, gives an amusing description of the so-called surgeons of this date, who he divides into five classes. The first applied cataplasms indiscriminately to every description of wound and ulcer; the second employed wine only; the third, emolient plasters and ointments; the fourth, chiefly military surgeons, promiscuously employed oils, wool, potions, charms, &c.; the fifth had recourse on all occasions to the saints!

To return to England. After the departure of the Roman legions, and until the introduction of Christianity by St. Augustin in the year 600, few attempts could have been made to treat with any effort at scientific exactness the unfortunate soldiers who, with sword or battle-axe, fought in the military engagements of the Heptarchy, the wars of the Great Alfred in his struggle against the Danes, or the petty feuds of the Saxon Kings who followed him. The science of medicine was again introduced by the monks, to whose monasteries were attached regular infirmaries, where the sick and wounded who were fortunate enough to escape being killed or made slaves of (as was then the custom after the bloody battles of these early days) were received with compassion and treated with kindness. When Alfred granted to the conquered Danes the privilege of their lives and freedom in direct opposition to all established usage, he laid the foundation-stone of humanity in war in Britain, and was the first of our great kings who attempted to assuage its horrors by his Christian philanthropy. The advent of the Normans in the middle of the eleventh century was signalised by the erection of numerous castles as bulwarks against the attacks of their Saxon neighbours. The Norman and foreign soldiers settled on the lands which had been given to their leaders, and became their vassals and tenants. By the Anglo-Saxon laws, every freeholder, if not every possessor, was bound to defend his country against hostile invasion, and to preserve internal peace. These laws continued in force after the Conquest, and upon them was laid the foundation of our Army. In 1154, Henry II. directed every freeman between the ages of fifteen and sixty to hold himself in readiness for the fray, constantly furnished with suitable arms and warlike equipment. At this date commodities were ten to twelve times cheaper than at present, and money fifteen times more valuable—a mark (13s. 4d.) was considered a very large sum.

A little more than a hundred years later (1272, reign of Edward I.), the knight received 12d.; the esquire and constable of cavalry the same rate of pay; a constable of foot, 6d.; a captain of twenty, 4d; a crossbow-man, 4d. and 2d.; an archer, 2d.; an agricultural labourer, who was on a par with the lowest grade of foot-soldier, 1½d. and 2d. The foregoing rates included the subsistence of the individuals. In mediæval England each serf had his share in the common fields of the village which surrounded the manor-house of his lord, and was bound to join in the cultivation of his domain. For the simple farming of that time such forced labour was sufficient; and the lord valued his serf more for military purposes than as an agricultural labourer. A change in the character of war was taking place. The insular condition of England made the feudal arrangement, with its limited tenure of service, inconvenient in the higher ranks; therefore military service was changed to scutage or money payment, and armies were raised by contract with some great lord. The payment was beyond the ordinary agricultural wages, the earl himself receiving a mark a day. At this time the average duration of life of the nobility and knights was less, because the *toga virilis* was assumed at a period which we would designate as that of a stripling The Black Prince was in charge of the van of the English Army at the age of fifteen. So severe was the training of a knight that it had to be commenced thus early.

In England, as we have already seen, the country was overrun with castles, where the barons lived like so many little kings, each with a considerable retinue. No nobleman, let his rank have been ever so high, could be considered a complete soldier until he was knighted. The daughters of the noblemen were usually educated in nunneries till they were married, when they lived in their husbands' castles, and were very often besieged and taken prisoners. One of their occupations was that of surgery, and it was their office to make salves and attend to the wounded, for which their gentle natures peculiarly fitted them.

Ladies figure not unfrequently in the romances of the twelfth and thirteenth centuries, as well as in the poems of Ariosto, Tasso, Spencer, and later bards in their *role* of surgeons. In the following passage in "Ywaine and Gawin," written in the reign of Richard II., may be found probably the earliest mention of this in the quaint language of that day:—

"Twa maydens with him thai laft
That weles war lered of leechecraft;
The lordes doghters both thai were
That war left to kepe hym thore
Thir held him ever il ke wound."

Again in the celebrated "Morte d'Arthur," the Knight Sir Tristram, having been severely wounded with a poisoned spear, King Marke sent "after alle manere of leches and surgeons, both unto men and wymmen, and there was none that would behote hym the lyf." His antagonist having been an Irish knight, he, in pursuance of the advice that he should visit the country from whence the venom came, before he could be healed, repaired to Ireland, where "Kynge Anguy whe fur grete fauvoour made Tramtryet to be put in his daughter's ward and kepying, bycause *she was a noble surgeon.*" This was "La beale Isored," at that time the fairest maid and lady of the world, according to Holinshed. A not uncommon result followed such tender nursing. The valiant knight became enamoured of the fair practitioner in surgery, and ended in becoming her husband. These fair dames of old were not deficient in courage, for we learn from Boccaccio, who wrote on the Plague, or Black Death, which caused such fatality in Florence in the middle of the fourteenth century, that at the Hôtel Dieu the "Sœurs de Charité" were strangers to the unchristian fear of death, devoting themselves to the holy calling of tending the sick with that dread disease. The cities in the Middle Ages were, with few exceptions, narrowly built, kept in a filthy state, and surrounded with stagnant ditches, conditions which favoured the origin and spread of epidemics, and reacted upon the soldiers billeted upon the inhabitants. The sweating sickness, the plague, variola, and spotted fevers decimated thousands. In the year 1489, no less than 17,000 of the troops of Ferdinand, then besieging Granada, were destroyed by the latter diseases, which again in 1552 devastated the army of the Emperor

Charles V. during the siege of Metz; in 1556, under the name of "*Morbus Hungaricus,*" the army of Maximilian; and in 1643, while the Earl of Essex was besieging Reading, the same disease, now known as typhus, committed great ravages. In the days of Froissart, when a knight was hurled to the ground unless he surrendered, he was immediately despatched by sword or dagger; in the reverse, the conqueror tended him most carefully, bound up his wounds, and obtained a handsome ransom on the faith of his knightly word, as in the encounter between the Lord Rokeby and a squire of Picardy, when the latter ran his antagonist through both thighs, on which event happening, we are told that he fell helpless from his horse; upon which the squire raised him gently, saying, "You shall be my prisoner, and I will bring you to a place of safety, and see that you be cured of your wounds." The squire drew out the sword from the knight's thighs, wrapped up and bound the open wounds, and set him on his horse; led him easily to Chatel, where he waited with him fifteen days, when his patient getting somewhat better, he brought him to his own house in Picardy, where he remained more than twelve months, till he was perfectly cured. When he parted he paid his ransom, 6,000 nobles.

The *hauberk*, or chain armour, introduced by the Normans, being found an insufficient defence against the point of the spear or arm, in the fourteenth century, was replaced by plate armour, which was often so heavy, that when a knight was thrown, he lay on the ground immovable until helped up, and there were many instances in hot weather and in the press of an engagement, of persons being suffocated with the heat and weight of their own covering. When knights fell in action, the long shield worn in the fourteenth century was used to convey their bodies from the field. These often extended from shoulder to ankle. In this way was the body of Robert de Damas, who fell at Poitiers, borne to the rear by orders of the Black Prince. Sometimes shorter shields were placed together for the same purpose.

A man harnessed as the knight was in the Middle Ages, had small power of action. The exchange from mail to plate-armour must have proved a relief, for although the latter was more ponderous than the former, yet not fitting so closely to the body, was not so sweltering as the gambesin and other quilted and stuffed garments worn beneath pliable mail. "With such an amount of encumbrance," wrote Father Daniel, "it was only wonderful that in the midst of summer, in the heat of Palestine, amidst the dust and press of an engagement, they were not frequently suffocated."

The cross-bow, which was now in extensive use as a weapon of offence, had been interdicted so early as the Lateran Council in 1139, as unfit for Christian warfare on account of its fatal and cruel effects. Few knights were, as a rule, slain in cavalry engagements, because, as afterwards shrewdly remarked by James I., "Armour not only protected the wearer, but prevented him from injuring others." A knight, alive, owing to his large ransom, was also of more value.

Up to this time military surgeons, although coming into existence as a distinct profession, are seldom mentioned, probably owing to the fact that the poorer soldiers, when severely wounded, were discharged with a small gratuity to find their way home as best they might, a practice founded on the economical principle which prevailed, according to Hart, as late as the sixteenth century, that "it cost more to cure a soldier than to levy a recruit." At this time, medical as well as all other kinds of knowledge in this country was in a state of the lowest degradation. There were no means of public instruction or natural philosophy. The light of science had not yet reached the remote shores of Britain, and it was not until the fourteenth century lived Gilbert, surnamed "Anglicanus," the earliest English physician of sufficient celebrity to entitle him to mention. In Europe the feudal system was beginning to be shaken, in the first instance by the Crusaders. The capture of Constantinople in the beginning of the fifteenth century by Mahomet II. expelled the Greek monks from their retreats; flying into Italy, they carried back with them their classical manuscripts. About thirty years after the destruction of the Byzantine Empire occurred the Reformation, as well as the art of printing, both combined to stir up knowledge of which the science of medicine was not slow to avail itself. The works of Galen and Hippocrates were now read in their original Greek, and the publishing of monographs of particular diseases, of individual cases, and reports of hospitals began to prevail—improving in each succeeding age. During the darker period of medical and surgical knowledge, it was probably the more humane course to pursue to send the wounded soldier to his friends, than leave him to the tender mercy of the charlatans who assumed to themselves the name of surgeon, and who aped the knowledge of a science the first principles of which they were unable to comprehend.

Chapter III.

There were now several reasons why military surgeons should come more to the front as a distinct class. The invasion of Ireland by Strongbow in the reign of Henry II., followed by constant wars in Wales, Scotland and France, especially the latter, which endured with varying fortune for more than thirty-four years, and nourished a spirit of adventurous enterprise, which, from the prince of the blood royal to the peasantry, caused a thirst for fighting fields, and for appropriating to themselves the spoils of war to pervade all classes. When the English forces came in contact for the first time with the kerns, or light armed Irish infantry of the septs, they were astonished to find the abbeys, which they defended, the seats of literature and learning. To the clergy in Ireland had been delegated the duties of clothing the naked, feeding the hungry, and relieving the sick. Every clan, we are told in those quaint Annals of the Four Masters, had its hereditary military commanders, physicians, and *brehons*, as well as historians and bards, who accompanied the kings and chieftains in their predatory expeditions. Thus family interest was engaged in the improvement and preservation of every art and profession, every generation was sedulous to hand down the records containing the rules and improvements of each profession to their posterity. In these charming Annals we read for instance that in 1232 Machada, Abbot of Down, kept a house of entertainment for the learned and the relief of the sick and indigent. In 1245 a hospital house is shewn to have been attached to the Castle of Sligo. A little later (1322) the death of the hereditary or head physician of Fermanagh is specially recorded, and in 1395 that of the chief physician of Tyrconnel, and in an account of a battle between the two septs of O'Connor and O'Donnell, which took place in 1497, among the prisoners taken occurs the name of the physician of the latter sept, and at the battle of Delvin in 1548 was slain Murtagh, described as " the best physician of his age in the surrounding neighbourhood." It is also related that after a nocturnal attack on a castle near Dublin, one of the assailants being wounded in the foot " was carried to a cave in the neighbouring mountains, and put under the care of a young physician of his own tribe, who went every day to the adjacent woods to collect herbs for the treatment of his patient."

During the reigns of Henry III. and Edward I., the kings and chieftains of Ireland received regular writs of summons to attend the wars in Wales and Scotland, and it is only natural to suppose that in such expeditions the septs were accompanied by their regular hereditary physicians. In 1272 Edward I. directed the Viceroy de Clifford to grant English privileges to his Irish subjects, on condition of their holding in readiness "a body of good and stout footmen, amounting to such a number as you shall agree upon with them for this turn only to repair to us when we think fit to demand them." A few of the treatises on medicine of these Irish physicians have been preserved, one of the most interesting of such MSS. being a book of the O'Lees, hereditary physician to the O'Flaherties of West Connaught. It treats of various diseases, wounds, fevers, and bears the date of 1434. A century before this, the Irish Earls of Desmond and Kildare had attended Edward III. in his invasion of France with numerous followers, and contributed in no small degree to the fame of the English arms at the battle of Crecy, when Edward is said to have admired the skill at arms displayed by his Irish auxiliaries, and their agility and strength.

There is also ample evidence to prove that medicine flourished at this time in Wales, and that the Welsh footmen who accompanied the English armies to France and Scotland were in receipt of medical assistance. According to the ancient laws of Cambria, translated by Propert, the King had twenty Court officers, twelve for the King and eight for the Queen. The physician comes twelfth in order. We are told that "he ought to have his land free, and his horse in readiness; and he receives his linen clothes from the Queen, and his woollen clothes from the King. His seat in the hall is at the base of the pillar, that he may be near where the King is, sitting in his border. His lodging is with the master of the household. His protection is from the time the King commands him to *visit a wounded man*, neither in the palace nor belonging to it, until he goes to him, taking away the offender. He must give medicine to all officers in the palace and to the master of the household without fee, unless it be one of three dangerous wounds. These are described as "a blow on the head which penetrates the brain, a thrust in the body which penetrates the bowels, and the breaking of one of the limbs." For everyone of these three dangerous wounds he was entitled to a fee of one hundred and eighty pence with his meals, or one pound without the latter. He is never to leave the King's palace except with the King's permission. The fine for insulting him is six cows and one hundred and twenty silver pennies. His value is one hundred and twenty-six cows. At this time, a tent for a wound cost twenty-four pence, a plaister of red oatmeal twelvepence, and one of medicinal herbs eightpence, very large sums for that date. Many of the Welsh corps had an officer styled "Medicus," but none of them were charged to the English levies, and in the Welsh they bore no proportion to the numbers, a corps of 1,907 men having only one, and another of 968 having two.

The Welsh foot were only clothed in scanty dresses of linen cloth, appearing (according to Barbour) naked in the eyes of "even the Scottish peasantry." At Crecy they got among the disabled of all ranks and butchered them with long knives, or the short swords with which they were armed, at which cruelties the King was much incensed because he had rather that they (the French) had been taken prisoners. This incident is noted by Johnes and Buchan, "Among the Englishmen there were certain rascalls that went on foot with great knyves, they were in among the men at arms, and slew and murderedde many as they lay on the ground."

In England, the first colleges were not founded until the close of the thirteenth century. In the course of the eleventh and twelfth centuries the old system of education—the *trivium* of grammar, logic and rhetoric, and the *quadrivium* of arithmetic, geometry, astronomy and music, was being placed by the scholastic system of theology and philosophy with its dialectical formulists and child-like faith. With this speculative philosophy arose two new practical studies, those of law and medicine. The natural philosophy of the time, the philosophy of Aristotle and the Arabians, was narrowly watched in its general applications, but in its application to medicine it could not be restrained, the physician being a person too indispensable to be under surveillance for his orthodoxy by Church or State. From the new-born knowledge at Oxford, a system evolved itself, consisting of arts, and the then faculties of theology, law and medicine; but every one was obliged to pass through the first before he was permitted to proceed to one of the three last faculties. A residence of about fifteen years with perpetual lectures and disputations was required to attain the doctor's degree in either of the faculties. Thus mediæval Oxford embraced within the circle of her studies all the knowledge of the age, both general and professional. It was the soul and centre of all intellectual life in England, and here graduated many of our Royal physicians. On the foundation of New College in 1386 by Wykeham, permission was given in the statutes to two fellows to follow the "*new study of medicine*," showing how long we were in appreciating the necessity of a study which centuries before had risen into prominence in infidel lands, and it was not until 1305 that the surgeons of Edinburgh had, for the first time, become incorporated, it being required of them " to be able to read and write, to know anatomie, nature, and the complexion of the human bodie ; and likewise to know all vagaries of the surgeon, that he made *flew-bothomie* in due time." The science of healing, then in infancy in England, was beginning to break forth from the relics of barbarism and superstition which surrounded it. As a rule, however, our princes brought over as yet their medical attendants from abroad, and the first medical lectures delivered in Oxford were by a foreigner, Andrew Alayard. He had graduated at Montpelier, and was appointed by the Chancellor to lecture on medicine from tables of his own. Nicolas de Farnham, Royal Physician to Henry III. and his Court, who was elected in 1241 to the See of Durham, had been Rector of Arts in Paris, and afterwards practised medicine in Paris. He obtained great favour by his skill, and conducted himself so well and prudently that he had the peculiar good fortune of being raised to the episcopate—a rich reward. The physician to the King accompanied him in his wars, as evident from contemporary history. When Henry V. was passing his last hours in the Castle of Vincennes, near Paris, we are informed that he asked his physicians how long he had to live, when one of them replied, "That without a miracle he could not survive two hours at most."

In 1445, when Margaret of Anjou arrived in England to espouse his successor, she was detained at Southampton owing to illness, and lodged in the religious hospital " Godde's House," founded for sick travellers by two merchants. She was accompanied by her physician, a certain Master Francis, whose fees were discharged by a precept of the Marquis of Suffolk. When Elizabeth, queen of Edward IV. was, in November 1470, obliged to take refuge in the Sanctuary at Westminster on the eve of her confinement, we find her physician, regardless of the threats of Richard and his myrmidons, attending upon her. Master Terigo, her faithful friend in adversity, was afterwards granted a pension of £40 by Edward IV. on his return—a large sum in those days. Many of the Royal wills contain special mention of the physician as either legatee or one of the executors. Katharine of Arragon, when removed to Bugden, requested the King to allow her to retain her "confessor, her physician and her *potecary*." And on her death-bed bequeathed to her physician's wife a considerable legacy—evidences, among many others, of the intimate relation existing between the sovereigns and their medical attendants in ancient times.

The appointment of sergeant-surgeon to the King is also of great antiquity. One of his duties was to attend the King when he ventured to battle, and was in effect the principal medical officer of his army, in which capacity John de Ardern accompanied Edward III. at the battle of Crecy, 1349. He was described by his contemporaries as one "who wrote with simplicity and honesty, and as the reviver of surgery in that country." He was peculiarly successful in the treatment of some surgical affections, and probably owing to the practical experience gained in the French wars, improved both the use and construction of the trepan, adding the central pin, and limiting the operation to the severe forms of injury to the head. His manuscripts remain in the British Museum as monuments of his industry and research. In the reign of Edward VI. the salary appertaining to the office was forty marks per annum. There were several perquisites attached, such as drawing a certain amount of wine from the King's cellars, and during war to take prisoners, retaining the amount of ransom paid by them. He was twelfth person in rank among the attendants upon the Sovereign, and had precedence accordingly.

The earliest notice of army surgeons occurs in the year 1223, the commencement of the reign of Henry III., shortly before he led his army into France to attempt the re-conquest of Normandy. It was in the form of a recommendation from the Chief Justice to the Bishop of Chichester of "one Master Thomas, an army surgeon, who knew how to cure wounds, a science particularly useful in the siege of castles;" but it was not until two reigns afterwards, *tempus* 15th Edward II., A.D. 1322, that paid medical officers to attend on the Army are mentioned in the wardrobe accounts of that monarch; they entered Scotland with the largest army which had ever marched out of England, and which met with so ignominious a fate at Bannockburn. Philip Beauvais had been surgeon of Edward the First's army in Scotland, A.D. 1300. His pay was equivalent to £841 13s 4d of our present currency. In a later reign (Richard III.) a MS. in the College of Arms gives the camp equipage then deemed necessary for barons and knights and includes a " Chappeleyn that to masse klingett, a chirurgeon, and a purveyor for your slatles and vituals." The large retinues following in the train of the nobles at this time, numbering from 500 to 1500 men, pointed to the necessity of the presence of adequate medical assistance.

The value of infantry was, in the fourteenth century, rapidly rising in estimation, and knights to keep pace with the increasing demands of the time, had more frequently to dismount and serve on foot. The men-at-arms, including horse and equipment, weighed 361 lbs. He was much less bulky than the modern trooper, the severe training to be undergone to enable a man to support the weight of armour, and the constant hard exercise required to keep him in muscular vigour for the *mêlée* with the heat produced by the armour and his underclothing, prevented the acquisition of obesity. According to Froissart, the Scottish soldiers encountered in 1327, were "hardy, long marchers, took no bread or wine, and in time of war took long journeys on sodden flesh and water, boiling the beasts in their skins, carrying a little oatmeal which they tempered in the fire, and eat after the sodden flesh."

The Irish light-armed bodies of horse which accompanied the army were called "Hobillers," from the name of the small horse which they rode. An old chronicler writes that one hundred men-at-arms were equal to at least a thousand of these light-armed troops. At this time the English commonalty were decently nourished and moderately worked, had an aptitude for manly exercises, and were sturdy and muscular—archery requiring a strong arm to make it effective. Our infantry, previous to the use of fire-arms, were divided into two classes, archers and billmen, wearing various portions of armour over short leathern or linen doublets stuffed with cotton or wool, and often a long loose garment called a junk, resembling a smock-frock. Such ill-provided individuals were returned as naked foot. At Agincourt, St. Remy described the English archers as being "without armour in their doublets, their hose loosened, having axes swinging from their girdles, or long swords, some with their feet bare, some with bonettes or caps of boiled leather, and some of wicker-work covered over on the top," whose superior physical strength prevailed over the neglected peasantry of France. Froissart ascribed the superior bodily strength of the English to their living far more on animal food than their Gallic neighbours. From numerous entries in the Wardrobe accounts of Edward II., it appears that it was customary to send disabled soldiers and others in the King's service to a religious house, or to an hospital, to be there supported either for a time, or during life. This was called having "*garisonia*" in a monastery. As the latter had always an "herberie" or physic-garden attached to it, it was a peculiarly appropriate place for the purpose.

The English men-at-arms usually fought on foot, riding to the scene of conflict, and then dismounting. In several instances, men-at-arms would be multiplied by three, as each was attended by a page and a custrel. Sieges then lasted a long time; the artillery of the age was the "furneval" which threw large stones. The siege was usually preceded by an attempt at an escalade. Some of the stones thrown weighed at least 300 lbs. Putrid carcases were sometimes discharged within the walls in the hope of creating a plague. In hot weather this greatly incommodated the garrison. The siege of Calais, where the inhabitants were cut off from all supplies, lasted a year. The men slept in tents. A writer who was present at the siege of Minorca by the Spaniards in 1224, alludes to the medicines supplied:—"Every kind of provision was to be had, drugs into the bargain; the rich could get physicked as well as if they had been at Barcelona or Lerida." The poorer soldier had probably but a meagre quantity, if any, allocated to his use.

Froissart wrote in 1399, that it was almost impossible to carry on the war in Ireland, when Richard II. landed with 40,000 men, in consequence of the impenetrable forests, bogs and lakes; the Irish soldiers being so remarkably strong and active that they could overtake an English horseman at full speed, leap up behind the rider, and pull him off. In this war the English soldier was often reduced to a biscuit a day between four men, "which was thought a good allowance." The clergy, as yet, sometimes attended the battle-field. In 1257 we find Henry III. directing the Bishop of Lincoln and other clergy to attend his expedition to Wales, where they discharged their duties more in consonance with their vocation, "attending the wounded and consoling the dying." Between 1069 and 1355, no fewer than one-and-twenty dearths and famines had desolated the people of England, pestilence going hand-in-hand with war.

In the "Roll of Persons at the Siege of Calais in 1346," only one surgeon is named in the retinue of the Prince of Wales:— "Edwardus Wallæ Princeps. Princeps, 1; Banneretli, 11; Milites, 102; Armigeri, 264; Sagittarii equites, 384; Sagittarii pedites, 69; Capillarii, 1; *Chirurgii*, 1; Vexillarii, 5; Vinarii, 25; Peditis, 480; Clamatores, 1; Total, 1370. It was brought under the notice of Parliament, subsequently to the siege, that several inexperienced boys had been armed and arrayed, instead of the gallant and competent persons." (Vaillantez et sufficientz gentz.) The army which Edward III. led to victory at Crecy was composed of English, Welsh, and Irish, numbering, exclusive of lords, 31,294 men (4,000 men-at-arms, 10,000 archers, Irish and Welsh foot.)

Every man-at arms in the kingdom *in good health* was summoned to attend personally, or send a substitute. The pay was according to social position, but was in addition to plunder and ransom. Money at this time was at least ten times its present value. Some of the items are curious. The daily pay of the Prince was £1; the Bishop of Durham, 6s. 8d.; thirteen earls, 6s. 8d. each; forty-four barons and baronets, 4s.; 1,046 knights, 2s.; 4,022 esquires, constables, captains, and leaders, 1s.; 5,104 vintenars and archers on horseback, 6d.; 335 paunceners and 15,480 foot-archers, 3d.; 314 masons, carpenters, smiths, tent-makers, armourers, gunners, and artillerymen at 12d., 10d., 6d., and 3d.; 4,474 Welsh foot at 4d.; the rest at 2d. The profession of the soldier was then by no means an unprofitable one; his daily pay of 6d. was in addition to the contingent allowance as regards (bounty), plunder, and ransom of prisoners—a lucrative attraction to the marauding corps of "Rascalles" who followed the army in its wake. The rapidity with which it was raised was the best proof of its popularity. The arrayors, when making the feudal mustering of the districts, were, by 16th Edward II. (1322), authorised to reject the incapable and make choice only of the most efficient. We can best understand the value of money when we find Cox telling us that in 1369 a cow could be bought for ten groats, or 3s. 4d., in Dublin, when the soldier was paid 2d., half of which sum went for his victuals. At this time the soldier only enlisted for short periods, living idle the rest of the year, often the rest of his life, one successful campaign in pay, plunder, and ransom of prisoners (one month's pay for a common soldier) was supposed to be a small fortune for a man. Chaucer—who served in the French War under Edward III., and was taken prisoner in the retreat towards Brittany, and pined away five or six years in a French prison, and who had heard the cries of "The lillies of France," and "St. George for Merrie England," had seen the long line of spears full level and bear upon the men of Artois and Picardy, the bowmen let fly their shafts of death, and the horsemen of Burgundy go rolling down before them, the squires kneeling by their dead masters, the solemn heralds counting the slain, and the monks holding the crucifix before the glaring eyes—thus paints the scene of conflict in his days:—

"East and west,
In go the spears into the level rest;
Sharp pricks the spur into the horse's side,
For these are warriors who can joust and ride.
Up spring the spears full twenty feet in height,
Out flash the swords that are so silver bright.
The helms they hew, and all to shivers shred;
Out bursts the blood with cruel gush of red;
With mighty maces bones are reft and burst,
He in the thickest of the throng is first."

Such was the battle-field of the fourteenth century. In his prologue to the "Canterbury Tales," he paints the good knight in his toils and dangers, with beside him his son, his squire of twenty summers, a strong and agile youth who had already acquitted himself well in Flanders, Artois and Picardy; the yeoman-attendant, a sturdy fellow, with close-cropped head, honest brown face, clad in his green coat and hood, with the sheaf of good arrows and peacocks' feathers in his belt, a mighty bow in his hand, and by his side his sword and rounded buckler, balanced by a gay dagger as sharp as a spear; a long horn hanging by a green baldrick, and on his broad chest shining a silver Saint Christopher. He does not forget the Doctor of Physic of the day—"fond of gold, and given to quote Æsculapius and Dioscorides.

Between 1312 and 1340, gunpowder had been invented. In 1347, cannon were first used by the English at Calais. The Moors were said to have used these weapons in their Spanish wars as early as 1312; they were also employed by the Turks in their siege of Constantinople, and in their many attacks on Malta. This invention of gunpowder, while it certainly tended to the saving of many lives in battle, yet must have produced much individual misery. Charms, prayers, incantations entered largely into the treatment of the new species of wounds presented to the view of the surgeons of the day, and the poisonous nature of the ingredients, which formed the gunpowder or the balls projected by it, were the principal subjects of their theoretical disquisitions. Wounds from arquebusades or hand-guns were first mentioned by Philip de Comines in his account of the siege of Morat in 1476. As a remedy, arquebusade-water was originally carefully prepared from a large number of aromatic herbs, a mild remedy in comparison to the tortures inflicted by boiling pitch, oil of elders scalding hot, or other specifics of the time.

In 1415, in the third year of his reign, Henry V. undertook the invasion of France with an army of 6,000 men-at-arms and 24,000 archers. Nicholas Colnet was appointed his field-surgeon for a year, under the condition that he was to carry with him three archers on horseback, and to accompany the King wherever he went. He was to have as pay *ten marks* every quarter, and twelve pennies a day as subsistence money; each of his archers had twenty marks a year and six pennies daily for subsistence. Thomas Morstede was appointed chief army-surgeon, with fifteen assistants, three of whom were to be archers, and the remaining twelve of his own profession—"Hommes de son métier." The indenture commenced, "Indentura cum chirurgico Regis et Retinentia sua." In a "Petitio Chirurgico Regis" from Morstede to the King, dated 26th May, 1415, he asks, in addition for pay for himself and his assistants to provide necessaries for the voyage, and a proper number of persons and carriages. The King granted him twelve persons and one chariot and "deux soniers." He also asked for Letters of Commission for the campaign under the Privy Seal. In addition to their regulated pay, Colnet and Morstede were permitted to receive prisoners and plunder; but if the latter amounted to twenty pounds sterling in value, a third part was to be given to the King. This account, given in Rymer's *Fœdera*, is among the earliest authenticated instances of the employment of regular army-surgeons with the English forces. In this campaign the mortality was very great. Epidemic dysentery prevailed from the incautious eating of fruit. Two thousand persons died, including many of the higher ranks; a great number besides were incapacitated from duty, so that at Honfleur the army was reduced to 10,000 men, opposed to 100,000. The indomitable courage of Henry, however, led his followers to victory at Agincourt. "Daily it rained and nightly it breezed; of fuel there was great scarcity, of floods plenty," wrote old Holinshed of the eve of this memorable battle.

Before undertaking his second expedition into France in 1417, when he succeeded in conquering the whole of Normandy, a Warrant (De sururgicis providendis, pro viagio Regis) was issued to Morstede and William Bradewardyn, to press as many surgeons and instrument-makers as they could find, either in London or elsewhere—a rather summary way of providing medical assistance for his troops, and showing that the chief surgeons had the power to command the presence of those of an inferior rank. Morstede was Sheriff of London in 1436, and surgeon to Henry IV., V., and VI.; and from his position of sergeant, or as it was sometimes called, knight-surgeon, was naturally selected to accompany the King in his campaigns. This curious warrant runs as follows:—
"Suatis quod assignavimus vos, conjunctim et divisim ad tot sururgicos, et artifices, pro certis instrumentis misteræ vestræ necessariis et compatentibus faciendis quot pro præsenti viagio nostro supra mare necessarii fuerint et opportuni, ubicumque invenire poterunt, tum infra civitatem nostrum Londoniæ, quam alibi, sine dilatione capiendum et providendum; et ideo vobis præcipumus quod cicca præmissa diligenter indendatis, et ea faciatis et exaquamini in forma prædicta." The arrangement then appears to have consisted in the employment of a chief-surgeon, having the inspection of the field-surgeons and their assistants; the duty of the latter being to drag the wounded from the heaps of slain, and convey them to the former for treatment. Forty marks a year was then the pay of an esquire.

The field-surgeons who then accompanied the English army were few in number, and destined more for the use of the commanders and principal officers, than for the service of the private soldiers, and as they were authorised by their commissions to receive prisoners and booty, and, like the knights, had to bring with them archers, it is not improbable that they occasionally entered into the spirit of the fray as combatants. The poorer soldier had to trust to a large extent to the assistance of his comrades, who in turn obtained some experience in dressing wounds, and demanded a day's pay as their *honorarium* for the assistance rendered. In the ninth year of Henry's reign, an attempt was made to put down the many unqualified persons who undertook to practise surgery, and by their ignorance brought the profession into disrepute. The Act of Parliament 9th Henry V., 1422, ran thus:—" No one shall use the mysterie of fysyk, unless he hath studied it in some university, and is at least a bachelor in that science." (Petyt's MSS). In the succeeding reign of Henry VI., a large number of qualified surgeons came over from France, and were in 1461-2 incorporated into the Company of Surgeons by Edward IV. Their first Master was William Legge, and the Wardens, Hugh Harte and Thomas Folliott. In a manuscript volume on vellum, dated 10th May, 1435, are now preserved the arms of the Company emblazoned, and underneath is written:—

"The year of our Lord MCCCCLXXXXII., at the goyng ovyr the see of our Sovryn Lord Kyng Harry VI. in to Fraunsse. Thes armys were geven on to the Crafte of Surgeons of London the VII yere of his reyng. In the time of Hewe Clapton, Mayr." No one was now allowed to practise without the lease of the Company, and none but persons who, after examination, were found able and sufficiently learned in the "mysterie of surgery." About this date, or a little before, were transcribed in the Black-Book of the Admiralty, the Laws of Oberon, in which mariners are directed to get one meal a day with wine, or two without, and where minute directions are given for the treatment of sick sailors.

The following petition to Henry VI. from an old soldier, one Thomas Hastell, who had been wounded at Harfleur, and who had served at Agincourt, gives a graphic picture of these stirring times in very quaint and pathetic language:—" Resurchette meekly your poor liegeman and humble orator, Thomas Hastell, that in consideration of his services, done to your noble progenitors, of full blessed memory, King Henry IV. and King Henry V., whom will God assail, being at the siege of Harfleur, then smitten with a springalt (espin-gold) through the head, losing his one eye and his cheek-bone broken. When at the battle of Agincourt, and after the taking of the carracks on the sea, then with a yad of iron his plates smitten asunder and sore hurt, maimed and wounded, by means whereof being sore feebled and debrusied, now fallen to great age and poverty, greatly indebted, and may not help himself, having not wherewith to be sustained nor relieved, but of men's gracious almasse, and being for his said services never yet recompensed nor rewarded, may it please your high and excellent grace, the promises tenderly considered of your beninge pity and grace to relieve and refresh your said poor orator, as it may please you with your most gracious almasse at the reverence of God, and in want of charity, and he shall devoutly pray for the souls of your said noble progenitors, and for your most noble and high estate."

From the Rolls of Parliament 4th Edward IV., A.D. 1464, in which "an annuity of iiii marks is given to John Sclatter for the loss of his hand at the battle of Wakefield, when under the command of the Duke of York, and his other hand so maimed that he could neither clothe nor feed himself," it would appear that the severely wounded on petition might obtain a gratuity or pension. The fifteenth century contained two events of vast import to surgery; the invention of printing about 1450, and the alleged importation of veneral disease from America, giving variola in exchange in 1493. In the beginning of the following century Vesalius gave birth to modern anatomy, illuminated by which science, surgery became an interesting object of pursuit to men of talents and education, and under their cultivation it has gradually been raised to an enlightened and liberal profession. Some of the most celebrated physicians still held high Church appointments. For example, in 1497 we read of Gaspar Torella, Bishop of St. Justa, and physician to Pope Alexander VI., employing mercury in small quantities, and vegetable remedies for the new disease which was already beginning to cause such havoc among the armies of the Continent. His plan for the extirpation of syphilis was anticipatory of the Contagious Diseases Acts of modern times, viz. :—to arrest all the infected females, place them under strict control, and cure them before allowing them to return to the town and their nefarious trade. In this century and for long afterwards, Montpellier was the leading school of medicine, partly because of the fostering care of the Pope, while resident at Avignon, and from the rich store of Arabian manuscripts the University had acquired, and which, before printing was invented, was in itself a sufficient claim to distinction. The Italian fleets at this time carried for attendance on the admiral a "Maestro di cirurgia," whose pay was "ten golden florins a month," while the Geonese galleys each armed with 210 men, carried a surgeon and a surgeon's mate as early as 1337.

A practice was now springing up in England by commuting military service for the acquirement of a money revenue, the King usually covenanting with influential persons to serve him with a specific number of followers in terms of indenture or contract. The money advanced was called "imprest money," to provide equipment and necessaries for the field. For expeditions beyond the frontiers of the kingdom likely to last longer than forty days, it was found necessary to pay the feudal troops or to engage bodies of mercenaries. Gradually the practice of employing hired troops grew, and in 1214 the Count of Flanders and Boulogne, the Duke of Brabant, the English and the Emperor Otho, gave battle with 150.000 men, of whom only 10,000 had been feudal cavalry. The mercenary bands which, under the titles of cotereaux and boutlers, hired themselves out to the highest bidder, and changed sides as often as suited their convenience or caprice took them, caused the greatest misery in the kingdoms which were the scenes of their operations. When out of employ, they plundered all sides for a livelihood. To put an end to this scourge, Charles VI. of France instituted *compagnies d'ordonnance*, i e., troops permanently or during the campaign under the orders of the King—the Free Lances acknowledging only the authority of their respective chiefs. Charles VII. issued an *ordonnance* for the raising of money to maintain fifteen of these companies, each of which was 600 strong. The example was not followed in England until after the battle of Bosworth in 1485, when a small band of fifty archers, under a captain, called yeoman of the guard, was raised by Henry VII. These were the first attempts at a standing army; but before this date in England a species of troops did garrison duty in fortified places, such as Calais, Tower of London, Portsmouth, Dover Castle, Berwick, Carlisle, and other small forts—they were chiefly mercenaries From 1445 may be dated the virtual downfal of the feudal system, and the inauguration of mercenary and permanent armies. At first these were, even in the greatest States, numerically very weak. In 1525 Francis I. fought the battle of Pavia with only 30,000 men; and in 1532 Charles V., menaced by 200,000 Turks, could, after the greatest efforts, collect but 70,000, including Italian and Spaniards. At the conclusion of a war it was the practice to disband some and reduce the strength of other corps. Henry IV. of France, from 1600 to 1609, had on the rolls of his army rather less than 10,000 men. Until the sixteenth century the military force in France was raised by conscription, each parish being ordered to furnish an archer, called *franc archer*, because exempt from taxes. In 1540 the plan of voluntary enlistment for money was substituted, each recruit receiving a bounty of from three to four livres (2s. 6d. to 3s. 4d.) People were then so poor that there was an ample number of volunteers. An officer who served in the army of Charles IX. (1560—1574) described the soldiers as being mostly the refuse of society, men with matted beards, who for their crimes had their shoulders branded, and their ears cut off. The infantry consisted of " boys, rascals and vagabonds, scoundrels ill-equipped and ill-looking, pilchers, plunderers and devourers of the people." Even in our then embryo standing armies criminals were sometimes pardoned on condition of serving the King abroad, given charters of pardon, and directed to repair to certain seaports to enter into the pay and service of the King. Under Louis XIII. the French army had reached at one time a total of 100,000 men; but to keep up the establishment the most arbitrary measures were adopted. For instance, all building operations were suspended in order to drive the masons into the ranks, and vagabonds were enlisted by force. The term "regiment," as signifying a body of troops composed of several companies, was first used in the reign of Charles IX. In the reign of Philip and Mary an Act, recognising the right of the Crown to levy men for service in war, and imposing a penalty on persons absenting themselves from musters, was passed by Parliament.

By an Act passed 32nd, Henry VIII., 1541, surgeons were "exempted from the bearing of armour, or to be put upon watches or inquests," and they were also allowed "Four persons condemned, adjudged, and put to death, by the due order of the King's laws of this realm, for anatomies." An important privilege to a scientific body who owed to Thomas Vicary, Sergeant-Surgeon to King Henry VIII., and chief-surgeon to Bartholomew's Hospital, the first anatomical work published in the English language. Another eminent surgeon of this period, Thomas Gale, served as principal medical officer of the Army of Henry VIII. at Montreal in 1554, and afterwards at St. Quintin, in 1557, under Philip, King Consort of England. In his works are found "numerous complaints of the intrusion of illiterate pretenders and empirics into the practice of medicine and surgery." On his return to England in 1562 he saw in St. Thomas's and in St. Bartholomew's Hospitals more than three hundred poor people, so diseased from the treatment of unlearned and ignorant quacks, that not more than one hundred and twenty of them could ever hope to be recovered. A number of such appeared to have followed the army to the Continent to prey upon the superstition and credulity of the soldier. He goes on to say, "When I was at the wars of Muttrel, in the days of that most famous prince, King Henry VIII., there was a great rabblement there that took upon them to be surgeons. . . This noble set did such great cures that they got themselves a perpetual name; for in two dressings they did commonly make their cures whole and sound *for ever*, so that they felt neither heat nor cold, nor manner of pain after. But when the Duke of Norfolk, who was then general, understood how the people did die, and that of small wounds, he sent for me and certain other surgeons. And we, according to our commandment, made search how these men came by their death—whether it were by the grievousness of their wounds, or by the lack of knowledge of the surgeons. And we, according to our commandment, made search through all the camp, and found many of the same good fellows, which took upon them the name of surgeons—not only the name, but the wages also. . . But in the end this worthy rabblement was committed to the Marshalsea, and threatened by the Duke's grace to be hanged for their worthy deeds, unless they would disclose what they were, and of what occupation; and in the end they did confess, as I have declared to you before." The King had always evinced a great interest in the study of medicine, and in the early part of his reign when a dismal pestilence broke out in the metropolis in 1528, spent a considerable time with his physician, Dr. Butts, in the preparation of various remedies, the receipt of one of which was made public for the benefit of England under the name of "the King's plaster." There were always two Royal physicians in attendance, of whom Dr. Butts was the second in rank. In one of his amorous letters to Anne Boleyn, to whom he sent his physician when she lay ill with the prevailing epidemic, he writes in terms of great affection of his medical attendant, who he tells her "he will love, if he can, more than ever," if he succeeds in preserving her from the dire disease from which she was then suffering. Painful and long intermittents were then one of the severest scourges in England, and continued so until improved cultivation and drainage, and the introduction of the Jesuits' bark into the Materia Medica, in the reign of Charles II. Some of the castles of those days do not appear to have been very pleasant abodes; De Marque tells us that after Richard's return from Ireland he found those in Wales so totally unfurnished that he had to sleep on straw during his sojourn in them. A farthing's worth of victuals was not to be found in any of them. "Certes, I cannot tell the misery of the King's train now at Carnarvon," writes the chronicler.

Francis I., Henry's gallant competitor in arms, ordered in France that all soldiers who were put "hors de service," should not only be exempt from the *tailles* and other charges, but should be enrolled to such small employments under the State as they could easily fulfil. In England, Queen Mary, in her will, dated 30th of March, 1588, ordered her executors to provide a house in London, with an income of 400 marks yearly "for the relief, succour and helpe of pore, impotent and aged soldiers, and chiefly those that be fallen into extreme poverte, having no pensyon or other pretense of lyvyng, or are become hurt or maymed in the warres of this realm or in any service for the defense and suerti of their prince and their countrey, or of the domynions thereunt belonging." These humane acts were of infinite value to the poor destitute and sick soldier of the day. The experience gained in the ever recurring wars of this period led to the rise of some very distinguished surgeons, among whom may be mentioned Jacques, Côme, Franco and above all Ambrose Paré. Paracelsus in his "Great Surgery," published in 1556 was far in advance of his cotemporaries when he condemned the complicated system in favour with many, and wrote "Warily must the surgeon take heed not to remove or interfere with Nature's balsam, but protect and defend it in its working and virtue. It is the nature of flesh to possess in itself no innate balsam which healeth wounds. Every limb has its own healing in itself; Nature has her own doctor in every limb; wherefore every chirurgeon should know, that it is not he, but Nature, who heals. What do wounds need? Nothing. Inasmuch as the flesh grows from within outwards, and not from without inwards; so the surgery of a wound is a mere defensive, to prevent Nature from suffering any accident from without, so that she may proceed unchecked in her operations." Such sound maxims, however, were little, if at all, regarded; and it has been reserved for our day to see their full adoption.

CHAPTER IV.

During the sixteenth century considerable progress had been made in medicine and surgery. Sir John Chambre and other surgeons received a fresh charter of incorporation from Henry VIII. in the handsome semi-clerical dress of the period; the cap and scarlet furred gown, embroidered with gold. Linacre, through the interest of Cardinal Wolsey, had obtained letters patent constituting a corporate body of regularly educated physicians in London. In the words of the Charter before this period " a great multitude of ignorant persons, of whom the greater part had no insight into the practice of physic, nor in any other kind of learning, boldly and accustomably took upon themselves great cures to the high displeasure of God, great injury of the faculty, and grievous hurt, damage, and destruction of the King's liege people." It is more than probable that many of these unqualified persons found their way into the lower ranks of the Army when they no doubt occupied a position commensurate with their merits. St. Thomas's Hospital had been founded in the reign of Edward VI., following upon that of St. Bartholomew's, commenced in the previous one. Gale, on his return from the French Wars, published his "Institution of a Chirurgeon," and a treatise on gunshot wounds, in which he repeated the opinion entertained by several continental writers, concerning the poisonous nature of gunpowder, and actual "ustion" produced by the ball. Ambrose Paré, the Surgeon and Councillor of Henry IV, "forced upward by no influence but that of his own genius and enterprise" made at nineteen his first great discovery, when he accidentally found how injurious it was to employ the actual cautery and boiling oil in gunshot wounds. His discovery of the ligature in amputation was the means of preventing much misery and the saving of innumerable lives. During a terrible outbreak of hospital gargrene he used a mixture of turpentine, aromatics and alcohol, a vast improvement upon the extraordinary concoction in vogue. Paré first joined the French armies at Turin in 1536, and followed them in all their operations down to the Battle of Moncontour in 1569. Like Gale, principal surgeon to Henry VIIIth's. army, he found many unqualified persons following in its train. He attributed his great discovery to the inspiration of Heaven, " for the good of mankind and honor of surgery." Paré was also the first to tie a band round the limb so as to command the bleeding during amputation. Before his time, the tape had been merely used to hold back the soft parts; perhaps no single discovery had had so happy and wide-spread an influence on the progress of military and civil surgery. His great work published in 1572 marked an era in the history of the science and was adopted throughout Europe. Maggius and Rota of Bologna, Leonardus Botallus of Lyons, de Vigo and others added their quota to the improvement of the treatment of the " Playes d'Arquebusades." Carcanus, Director of the Military Hospital at Milan, published an excellent work " De Vulneribus Capitis." Henry IV. established the first field-hospitals in France, at the Siege of Amiens in 1597—a boon so grateful to the soldiers, that, by way of pre-eminence they distinguished the military operations in which they were thus engaged, as " The Velvet Campaign." As we have already seen, humanity to the wounded had been a marked trait in the character of nearly all the French monarchs. Henry IV. also laid the first plan of an hospital for decayed and wounded soldiers, which the magnificence of Louis XIV, perfected into the present " Hôtel des Invalides." The original *ordonnance* is given in full in Count de Riencourt's "Militaires blessés et invalides." Another important improvement in the treatment of gunshot wounds was also originated by a military surgeon and cotemporary of Paré's at the Siege of Metz in 1553, by which the virtue of a more simple application was thoroughly established. We read that " Maitre Doublet, performed strange cures with simple white linen, and clean water from the fountains and wells; and everyone went to him, as if it were Maître Ambrose Paré himself—a man so celebrated, and considered the first of his day." In 1560, Gabriel Fallopius strongly recommended this simple element as " a fruitful source of success." He was followed and supported by other writers of eminence.

The establishment of the Army sent to St. Quintin in 1557, contains probably the first notice of medical officers being specially employed for the service of the Ordnance. The following were the rates of pay of the various officers—" master of the ordynance £1 6s. 8d. per diem, his lieutenant 13s. 4d., master of carriages 10s., French master 5s., a chaplain 1s., a clerk of the ordynance 2s., two clerks 2s., a surgeon 1s., bowers, fletchers, carpenters, smythes, guiders of ordynance, halberdgers, harquebusters come after at lower rates of pay." The staff and establishment of the lieutenant and captain-general of the wars of this period (1557), when the Duke of Somerset occupied the office, were " a secretary, another for the French tongue, two surgeons," &c., with a guard of halberdiers. The lieutenant-general was allowed one surgeon and a chaplain, &c. The high marischell, a master of the camp, chaplain, surgeon, &c. A General of horsemen had on his staff a lieutenant, chaplain, surgeon, four commissioners, a trumpeter, and fifteen halberdiers. The Captain-General of the Footmen, who commanded the infantry, was allowed as his staff a lieutenant, a sergeant-major (major), six wyfflers, a chaplain, surgeon. We have here the first attempt at the formation of a regular army medical staff. In the reign of Elizabeth officers of the same rank did not always command according to seniority, but were equal the one with the other, under single superior command. After the formation of a standing army officers of cavalry at first took rank according to date of commission; infantry, according to seniority of the corps to which they belonged. Recruiting chiefly depended on the captain of companies, each of whom recruited his own, which was in some measure his own property. When levied to its complete establishment, he was allowed the pay of two soldiers in time of peace, and of five in time of war to keep up its numbers, and to preserve its efficiency. The Commissions or Letters for lodging the men were granted by the Sovereign. The term regiment was introduced into our Service in this century. "A certain number of companies joined in one body under one head" (Sir James Turner). These regiments varied at first from six to twenty companies, a force equalling 3,000 men. Sometimes the companies numbered as many as 300 men. In the reign of Queen Elizabeth a surgeon was attached to each company of "one hundred footmen." The pay of these company surgeons was about equal to that of an ensign, viz., "five shillings by way of imprest, and two shillings to the full value thereof in good apparel of different kinds." These sums were paid "by the poll weekly," on Saturday. The captain received his full entertainment of 28s., the lieutenant 14s., the ensign 7s. In the army raised to repel the Armada the pay of the surgeon was 1s. 6d. daily. He ranked next after the chaplain or "clerk." This low rate of pay was largely supplemented in some instances by a "honorarium or donation of twopence a man per month," the origin not unlikely of the system of hospital stoppages of later years. For this honorarium the surgeon was bound to provide surgical instruments together with surgical remedies exclusive of medicines for the treatment of medical cases. Similar donations were given to the priests or chaplains of our infant Navy. The origin of this custom of stoppages from the pay of the soldier is very obscure, but it is recorded that in the reign of Edward I. Thomas de Brotherton, as Marshall of England, took from every merchant or suttler buying or selling in the army, from every prostitute, and from those who erected lodges or stalls, the sum of 4d. for every week or part of a week. That this custom prevailed as late as the reign of Henry VIII., is proved by a later manuscript (Cotton) in which is defined "what the mareshal shall have of every artificer." For instance "the mareshall should have of every merchant, armourer, taylor, barber, and every man that buyeth or selleth in the field, every Saturday in and for assigning them their places, four pence; and likewise he shall have of the said persons sojourning but two or three days in one place." This interesting document, quoted by Smart, throws much light on the economy of camps (*temp.* Henry VIII.) A MS. of Ralph Smith, quoted by Grose (*temp.* Elizabeth) contains the joint authentic notice of this stoppage as far as regards the surgeon, and shows that he wore a distinguishing "*baldricke*" over his shoulder as a protection for his vocation in the field, viz., " That every souldier, at the paye daye, doe give unto the surgeon 2*d.* as in time past hath been accustomed, to the augmention of his paye; in consideration whereof, the surgeon might readilie to employ his industrie uppon the soare and wounded soldiers, not intermedlinge with any other cures to them noysome. Such surgeons muste weare their *baldricke*, whereby they may be known in the tyme of slaughter ; it is their charter in the field."

Thomas Gale, the " trusty old soldier surgeon," died in 1572, the army which he accompanied to St. Quintin, in 1557, consisted of 1000 horse, and 4000 foot, 200 prisoners, a complement of officers, and train of artillery, to which were attached fifty-seven surgeons, two of whom belonged to the staff of the general, one to the lieutenant-general, one to the high marshall, one to the general of horsemen, one to the general of infantry, and one to the master of ordnance. The surgeon of horse received a daily pay of 2*s.*, of infantry 1*s.* There had been great difficulty in providing medical officers for this expedition, which Gale hoped would not again occur in consequence of the lately chartered company of surgeons. He writes to the Queen, " I have myself helpe to furnish out of London in one year seventy-two surgeons, who were good men, which served by sea and land, and were well able to serve, and all Englishmen. Now, there are not thirty-four of all the whole company of Englishmen, and yet the most part of them be in noblemen's service, so that if we should have need, I do not know where to find twelve sufficient men." From this we must conclude that the most efficient of the Royal surgeons were those furnished by the newly incorporated College of Surgeons of London.

While the regimental surgeons in those days received rates of pay equivalent to that accorded to the junior officers, the Royal physicians who still continued to hold the highest rank in the profession, were far more largely remunerated. In the list of an army sent to Ireland under Lord Deputy Mountjoy, in 1599, there was a great increase of pay, the Lord Deputy's " Doctor of Physic" receiving the same rate of pay as his chaplain—£5 a week—a considerable sum at this date. In these " warres in Ireland," during the reign of Elizabeth, the medical officers attached to the army saw much hard service. At the time there was only one apothecary in all Ireland, a Mr. Thomas Smyth of Dublin, to whom, in 1566, was granted a consideration to receive "the yearly sum of one day's pay of the Lord Deputy and the whole army in Ireland, and also twenty shillings of each sworn councillor, in order to encourage the said Smyth to continue in the discharge of his ministry in Ireland." In the previous reign, by an Act 3rd Henry VIII., an attempt was made to add to the efficiency of the fighting forces by excluding ineffective men." Every man being the King's subject not lame, decrepit or maimed, within the age of sixty, except spiritual men, Justices of the Peace and Barons of the Exchequer, being directed to use and exercise shooting at the longbow. At a subsequent period Markham recommended that "the strong, tall, and best persons be put to pikes; squared and broadest to carry muskests; least and nimblest to the harqueback," and in the general muster for training to arms in 1573, it was ordered that "all from 16 years and upwards *capable* of bearing arms" be enrolled. An attempt had also been made by Henry VIII., to assuage to some extent the savagery of war. By the 48th Article of his "Statutes and Ordinance of Warre," in action every soldier was directed to "bear a cross of St. George, sufficiently large upon the payne, that if he be wounded or slayne in the default thereof, he that so wounded or slayeth him shall bear no paine therefore." The red cross on the white ground thus appears to have protected the wearer in our army, when wounded, long anterior to the date of the Geneva Convention. That it was necessary, is shown by a remark of Patten's in 1548, that at the battle of Musselborough, a great slaughter of the gallant Scots took place, their poor appearance giving little hope of their ability to pay a ransom, showing that the ability to pay ransoms was still to a great extent the only protection to the unfortunate soldiers when poor and helpless on the battle-field during this troublous period of our history. By the 48th of Elizabeth power was given to the majority of the Justices of the Peace to charge every parish for a weekly relief of maimed soldiers and mariners, so that no parish paid weekly above tenpence nor under twopence.

In the reign of Elizabeth Irish kerns began to be more regularly imported for service with the English armies abroad. Fifteen hundred Irish formed part of the auxiliary forces despatched by the Queen to the Netherlands when the English soldiers suffered much from the want of clothes, an inconvenience not apparently felt by the Irish, for we are told by Motley that they habitually dispensed with clothing, an apron from the waist to the knee being their only protection; they were also described as the wildest beings, eating raw flesh. Saint Leger, the Lord Deputy, in a letter to Henry VIII., described the Irish Gallowglasses which he might command out of Ireland to France as "naked men with only their shirts and small coats, and many times when they come into the fight but bare naked saving their shirts to save their privities." These men were maintained in Ireland by *coyne* and *livery*, nearly equivalent to free quarters on the tenants of their lands. About this time the great body of the people in Ireland had no separate properties, the chief families had portions appropriated to their use in perpetuity. There were also lands appropriated to the selected chief, as also for the Tanist who was to succeed him. Other portions were also enjoyed hereditarily by the Brehons, bards and physicians of the tribe (Prendergast). Campion, an English Jesuit, who travelled in Ireland during Elizabeth's reign, speaks of young men, about to be physicians, " conning by rote the aphorisms of Hippocrates." The fighting kerns who entered into the King's pay in 1548, had been chiefly raised in Leinster and Meath. Then such naked foot soon showed that they were not to be despised. Henry VIII. had chiefly governed Ireland by a permanent force and small bodies of King's levies from England, raised chiefly in Cheshire and Lancashire, who were spoken of as " poore creatures that are more meete ffor the plou at home than ffor any servysse heare." Essex, on the other hand, wrote to the Queen that her Irish kerns had " better bodies, and more perfect use of their arms." Two years of hard usage, the damp climate, sickness, and general mismanagement, had so deteriorated the English levies in *morale* and *physique*, that in 1559 a considerable body of them were put to flight by inferior forces of the Irish. This so enraged Essex, that he cashiered the officers and decimated the private men. The wretched existence of the soldiers serving in Ireland was then extreme. The usual hardships of his condition were aggravated by disease—dysentery, principally caused by scarcity and bad quality of his food, was a terrible scourge of the English forces serving there in the sixteenth century. Scarcely any grain was grown in the country, the troops had consequently to be supplied by biscuits from England, and, as contractors were no more honest at that time than they have proved themselves to be in modern days, the bread provided was of the most wretched quality. The natural dampness of the Irish climate was then much increased by the dense forests that covered the greater part of the island, rendering intermittent fevers as great a pest as dysentery. Moreover, from the dirtiness of the town, the plague broke out with great virulence in many places in 1574. The monasteries and abbeys, with the hospitals and houses of entertainment attached to them, had been suppressed, and the poor man's physicians, the monks, dispersed, to these evils were then added the almost complete dearth of medical assistance. A soldier of fortune writes to Lord Burghley from Drogheda, " I have my Lord, thank God, recovered my health, having no other physytyne nor ffrende to looke to but hym." The sick when unable to be carried to the nearest castles or towns were left behind to the tender mercy of the enemy, whose own wounded were chiefly tended in caves and other secret localities by the young physicians who followed the fortunes of their tribes in these conflicts with the English. In Boyle's retreat from Ballyshannon, after his defeat by O'Donnel, we find that "the women, their attendants, *their maimed people, their wounded,* and all the beasts of burden, were placed in front. The archers and musketeers protecting them from the predatory Irish " who generally decapitated the chiefs they had slain in battle, not considering them dead until they had cut off their heads." It was probably in this manner that the wounded and sick were often carried and protected during the many incursions from the English rule by the English generals, which were then of constant occurrence. " Provisions of drink, of beeves and biscuit," were supplied to the outlying garrisons under large escorts, but often for whole seasons the army lived to a great extent upon plunder, chiefly cattle, taken from the natives. The superior officers were almost invariably carried to the nearest towns when wounded. We sometimes read of men dying a year after the receipt of their wounds from mortification. Essex had more than 20,000 men with him in Ireland. From the following curious list we may form some idea of the food then supplied to the soldiers in garrison. In 1534 the Castle of Dublin was provisioned for a siege with " 20 tons of wine, 24 tons of beer, 2,000 dry ling, 16 hogsheads of beef," and various other articles. Towards the close of the century the money coined for the Army in Ireland contained only three parts of silver to nine of brass; this being extensively circulated, caused goods and provisions of all kinds to rise to double their former prices, producing impoverishment and much discontent. Tents were used in these campaigns. According to Morrison, in the forty-five years of war in Ireland during the reign of Elizabeth, at least 70,000 of the troops that came from England fell, and about 30,000 Anglo-Irish auxiliaries. A great many officers died of wounds or disease. In 1598 the public expenditure in the support of the Army and other charges had reached the large sum, for those days, of £299,000 and £50,000 for contingencies. The uniform of an officer in Elizabeth's time in Ireland, was a cassock of broad cloth with bags trimmed with silk lace, a doublet or waistcoat of canvas, with silk buttons, and lined with white linen; kersey stockings, shoes, breeches of broadcloth, with silver lace—all at the expense of the Crown. The surgeon wore a *baldrick* in addition. The soldier's cassock was of broadcloth, lined with cotton and trimmed with buttons and loops, canvas doublet linen lining, coloured hat-cap, breeches, holland shirts and bands; a Ruff coat was frequently worn as an outer coat, (Sir John Harrison Smyth). Great-coats or cloaks were introduced in this reign, and in the following century, during the great Civil wars " knapsackbags " were introduced—both great boons to the soldier. In the French wars of the fifteenth century the marches averaged about three leagues daily, no stragglers being left behind. Towards the close of Elizabeth's reign a regiment consisted of five companies of 500 men, each with its own colours, which were guarded by the halberdiers, the pikemen were on either flank of the halberdiers, then came the musketeers, archers, and on each extreme flank the arquebusiers to act as skirmishers. The English and Irish soldiers were in separate companies. The increase in the numerical units of the company added largely to the duty of the surgeon, who had ample opportunity of studying wounds inflicted by a great variety of weapons. Towards the close of the century the large towns and castles, where the greater portion of the troops were quartered, consisted chiefly of mixed garrisons of horse and foot, chiefly upon the borders facing Ulster; varying from 300 foot and a few horse, to 1000 foot and sixty horse. These various garrisons, under Lord-Deputy Mountjoy, who arrived in 1597, amounted to 10,000 men; besides these 10,000 men in garrison, there were 12,000 horse and foot appointed to act against O'Neil and O'Donnel in Ulster. With this large force must have been a considerable number of military surgeons, the company still remaining the unit of medical assistance. One-third of the Queen's armed force consisted of Irish kerns, gallowglasses and cavalry, who had been taken into the service by Sir John Perrott to save the heavy charges for the troops. Cox says, "Lord-Deputy Fitzwilliam took many Irish into the army, and improvidently sent others of these to the Low Countries, where they became excellent soldiers and returned stout rebels!" Moryson, who accompanied Lord-Deputy Mountjoy to Ireland and throughout the wars against Tyrone, gives an amusing account of his mode of life, " he breakfasted on a dry crust of bread, butter and sage in spring time, with a cup of beer flavored with sugar and nutmeg." He indulged in tobacco abundantly, to preserve good health in the bogs of Ireland, and for the relief of the " violent headaches which attacked him every three weeks like an ague." At the same time in England you could dine at the common table of an inn for 6d., at some places for 4d., after eating which we are informed that "if he pleased the traveller might *with credit* set a part away for next day's breakfast." Horses in travelling could be hired for 2s. the first day, and 1s. 6d. for each succeeding days. From these facts we may form some idea of the relative value of the pay granted to officers.

The next military surgeon of eminence whom we hear of is William Clowes, who had first served in the Navy, and became surgeon to St. Bartholomew's and Christ's Hospitals, and finally surgeon to the Queen. He and William Godarus, sergeant-surgeon to Elizabeth, were sent on application from the Earl of Leicester, General of the English Forces in the Low Countries, to take care of his wounded. Before this reign, kings did not contract to supply their armies with subsistence, the high rate of pay covering all, but in the economical reign of Elizabeth, the ration was given in part payment of the soldier's wages, and a Provient-Master-General, or head of this contract department, introduced. The nominal ration in the field was not a bad one, according to Turner, consisting of the following ingredients, viz., 2 lbs. of bread, 1 lb. of flesh, or 1 lb. of cheese, one pottle of wine, or two pottles of beer; but as a matter of fact it does not appear to have been supplied to the men, owing to the cupidity of the contractors who purveyed for the army.

So early as 1558, in Ireland, Perrott, the Lord Deputy, had been asked " whether it were better to give the souldiers (of the regular army) sterling pay and no victuals, or to continue victuals and the old rate of Irish pay." The Queen intimated that she " would no longer allow both victuals and increased pay." Standing forces existed in Ireland from this reign. Sir John Smith attributes to this system and the bad quality of the supplies, and the scarcity of provender also, as well as to " evil lodging," the thousands of deaths which occurred in Leicester's army in the Low Countries. Great numbers of these sick and starved soldiers were sent by the Earl of Leicester's orders by transports into Essex and Kent and other parts of England to recover their health, "of which Dore said great numbers of miserable and pitiful ghosts" (writes Sir John Smith) " or either shadows of men the Essex and Kentish carts and carters (that carried them) can testifie, of which scarce the fortieth man escaped with life." Leicester writes, in 1586, " They (the soldiers) perish for want of victuals and clothing in great numbers." Clowes, like his predecessor Gale, had to lament the number of empirical pretenders who took upon themselves the name of surgeon, to the great detriment of the army. He writes in 1596 (when holding the high appointment of surgeon to the Queen), in a work entitled " A Profitable and Necessary Book of Observation for all those that are Burned with the Flame of Gunpowder, and also for the Curing of Wounds made with Musket and Caliver, Shot, &c."—" It is most truly said there is no coine so current but hath in it some counterfeits, which make it suspicious; so it is there is no profession so good but hath also some counterfeits, which breed in it disgrace; and none so much, I suppose, as there bee in some these daies, that take upon them the honest title and name of travelling surgeons. . . . Therefore, friendly reader, let this be a warning unto thee, to take heed of these unclean birds, who do daily abuse many worthy persons, captaines, gentlemen, masters of ships, and merchants of good account, by reason of the shameless braggings and boastings of their great, divine, magnificent skills in physick and surgerie, wherewith they say they are adorned and exceed all others, under color hereof, by their fraud and subtle means; they have beene and daily are entertained to be principal surgeons of great ships of war, and charge of numbers of men . . . Truly many a brave souldier and mariner hath perished, and sometimes the generall and captaines themselves." These abuses did not appear to have been confined to England, for according to Clowes, Guillemein, surgeon to the French King, made a similar complaint in his country.

Another distinguished military surgeon was John Woodall, who accompanied the troops sent by Queen Elizabeth to the assistance of Henry IV. of France, under Lord Willoughby. He afterwards served in the navy in the East Indies, and became surgeon-general to the infant company of merchant adventurers, who were formed into "a body corporate and politic" by Royal Charter, 31st December, 1599, by which was laid the foundation of our great Empire in the East. Woodall, after having made many voyages, settled in London as surgeon to St. Bartholomew's in 1612, and it was at this time that he was selected by the East India Company to become their first surgeon-general, having the charge of appointing surgeons and mates to all their ships, and furnishing their chests with medicines, instruments, and necessaries. In 1626 he was appointed by the King first supervisor of the medical department of the Navy, and to his advocacy, from observation and experience, was due the introduction of lemon-juice for the prevention and cure of scurvy, and many improvements in military surgery. Shortly after the Queen's death he published his "Surgeon's Mate; or, Military and Domestique Surgery." His works contained many useful practical facts, and evinced considerable learning and great humanity, and his "Viaticum," published in 1628, gives some graphic sketches of the Service, immediately preceding the Commonwealth.

To the solicitation of a cotemporary of Woodall's, Dr. Boughton, who, from his medical services, stood high in favour with the Shah Jehan, the East India Company owed permission to form their first settlement on the Hooghley. The country thus owes to one of its surgeons the early foundation and favourable reception of the East India Company in Bengal, as did the Dutch to one of their medical officers the first suggestion of occupying our now flourishing colony at the Cape of Good Hope.

The English regiment despatched by James I. in 1620 to aid the Protestant Princes of Germany, 2,200 strong, commanded by Sir Horatio Vere, suffered great privation from the inclemency of winter; on one occasion they were obliged to burn a great many of their wagons for fuel, owing to the great violence of the frost. Four years later took place Count Mansfield's expedition to the United Netherlands, consisting of 12,000 foot and 200 horse, levied by press and formed into six regiments. In a few weeks subsequent to their arrival they were reduced to one-half from the effects of a contagious disease which broke out amongst them. Both expeditions were accompanied by a due proportion of medical officers. The low rate of pay still continued for the regimental ranks—ensign, 1s.; lieutenant, 2s.; captain, 4s. daily. Living was, however, about six times cheaper than at present; but in the original estimate for the army of 25,000 foot, 5,000 horse, and twenty pieces of artillery, which it was proposed should be sent to the Palatinate in 1620, there had been a liberal complement of medical officers, but no allowance of provision whatever for medicines or an hospital, although there was a minute detail of almost every other necessary store.

It was proposed that there should be "in the General's trayne two physicians, at 6s. 8d. per diem each; two apothecaries, at 3s. 4d.; and two surgeons, each at 6s. 8d.

"Every regiment of foot consisted of twelve companies of one hundred and fifty men each, and had one chief-surgeon at 4s. per diem (pay of a captain), and another surgeon to each company at 1s. per diem (pay of an ensign.)

"Among the general officers of horse is one chief-surgeon at 4s. a day.

"To every troop, which was to consist of one hundred men, one surgeon, his daily pay 2s. 6d. (slightly in excess of the pay of a lieutenant of infantry.)

"To the ordnance and pioneers one surgeon at 2s. per diem, and two under-surgeons at 6d. a day each."

These last were probably unqualified assistants, or servants to the surgeon, as they were then sometimes called.

In the "Art of Warre," by the Lord of Praissac, published in 1639, nineteen years later, under the head of the "Chirurgeon," we are told that "In everie companie there must be a chirurgeon, to attend which are sick, to dress the wounds of such as are hurt (being as an assistant to the chirurgeon of the regiment), having proper remedies to stanch the blood, to hinder inflammation, and to assuage the pain." About this date (*temp.* Charles I.) the establishment of a cavalry regiment was very similar to that of the present time, viz., lieutenant-colonel, sergeant-major (major); to each troop a captain (pay of 8s. per diem), lieutenant (5s.), cornet (4s.), a chirurgeon (2s. 6d), three corporals, two trumpeters, one quartermaster, and eighty horsemen.

In 1629, Germany and the Low Countries were the resort of those young Englishmen whose taste, or the state of whose fortunes drove them to the profession of arms, as well as of those whose activity languished in their own country, which was at peace with Europe, and not yet embroiled by its own liberties. It then appeared to have been the custom for these young officers to enlist with the rank of ensign in the army. Monk, afterwards Duke of Albemarle, appears to have been one of those who did so, according to his biographer, Wortley.

In Essex's Army in Ireland in 1598, the troop consisted of fifty privates; each company the usual complement of officers, a chirurgeon, two sergeants, one drummer, and ninety-four men. The necessity for company-surgeons at this date was self-evident.

In the great majority of instances the company was an independent command acting separately, often on detached duty, where no medical assistance was obtainable, and only just commencing to assemble together under one head in the form of a regiment, which in the English Service originated in the sixteenth century.

The Pay List of the Army of Charles I., despatched against the Scots in 1639, contains the following items:—Lord-General's train, two chaplains and two physicians at 6s. 8d. each, two apothecaries at 3s. 4d. each, two chirurgeons at 4s. each.. The pay of a major in the Train (artillery) was 6s.; "gentlemen" attached, 4s. The surgeon had a servant or assistant under him at 1s. per diem. Lord Conway describes the men composing this unfortunate expedition in the following terms:—"They were the meanest sort about London, ignorant of their duties." No wonder that they were defeated at Newburn.

The sweating sickness, a legacy left from the wars of York and Lancaster, having first developed itself in Richmond's army, which had been collected from abroad, over-fatigued by long marches in a very damp season, and probably ill-equipped with rations, had by this time altogether disappeared. During the "warres in Ireland," extending over the reigns of James I. and Charles I., the officers and men, including the medical officers, had undergone great hardships. An amusing incident illustrative of this occurred when the "arch rebel Tyrone," as he was called, was received with favour by James I. We are informed that the officers of Elizabeth's army who had "laboured after that knave's destruction," and "eaten horseflesh in Munster in toiling to quell him," were chagrined to see him "well liked and smiling in peace at those who did hazard their lives for his destruction." Spenser, in his "Faerie Queen," revels in the idea of making campaigns against the Irish kern or spearmen in winter, "when the aire is sharpe and bitter to blow through his naked sides and legges." At the conclusion of each of the great civil wars in that country, from the time of the Tudors to the reign of Charles I., large numbers of Irish soldiers took foreign service, and added to the glory of continental armies. The humane laws which now mitigate the horrors of war had not been established, and it was a common thing to put to the sword the garrison, and even the inhabitants of the places which had been taken by storm. Tents were usually carried, and sometimes before surrendering, the garrisons bargained for quarter. The slain were generally plundered and stripped; sometimes heads were cut off as trophies as late as the wars of 1641-53, curious particulars of which are given by an officer of Sir John Clothworthy's regiment who served in these campaigns. In 1643 the Scottish army suffered much, losing many men during the winter from cold, the Irish having cut off their supplies. The veteran troops employed against O'Neil in the northern campaign, owing to their being unaccustomed to the wet as well as the food

E

of Ireland, were little capable of bearing up against the perpetual harassing to which they had been exposed. Strafford's highly disciplined army was a thorn in the side of the Parliamentarians, who, to prevent any portion of it coming to the King's assistance in England, passed an Act that all troops coming from Ireland to fight under the Royal Banner, "should be denied quarter, and that all such taken should be hanged." Strafford did much to repress the license of the soldiery. Afterwards, at the siege of Clonmel, Cromwell, who had landed in Ireland in 1649 with 8,000 foot and 4,000 horse, lost many men from sickness. He wrote to Lord Brayhill that "he was in a miserable condition before Clonmel, where his army was suffering from the bloody flux, and that they had several repulses from the brave garrison."

When Monk went to Ireland, the greater part of his expeditions were confined to forages, of which the march was the worst danger for his exhausted soldiers, left by the Parliament without clothes and without shoes. Many, in consequence of this, remained by the roadside, unable to proceed. Yet so great was the popularity of the commander, it was said that "there was not a soldier ever so sick or so ill-shod, who would not make an effort to follow him." This exemplified a well-known trait among soldiers, who are always more disposed to obey when they have in a manner appropriated a commander to themselves, and when in their chief they recognise a comrade. Monk "took charge himself of the soldiers' food, did his best to provide them with quarters, watched over them in difficulties, and even had, when necessary, his remedies and prescriptions." (Wortley.) The conquered lands were given by the Privy Council to the commanders of corps *in custodium*, who set their soldiers to work them, and thus induced habits of industry destined to render their condition more tolerable, and maintained obedience and gaiety among the men. Monk relied upon detached and large depots of forage and biscuit, cold meat in abundance, short marches terminating at mid-day, light baggage, tobacco, temperance, and constant vigilance and care for the success of his expeditions. His soldiers sometimes took with them, when penetrating mountain fortresses, provisions for six days.

The superior officers, in these campaigns, when wounded, were generally carried on a horse litter. O'Neil, the commander of the Confederate Irish, was so carried at the head of his army; but it is evident that many of the wounded were received and tended by civilians. For instance, it is related that the Viscountess Thurles, at the breaking out of the war of 1641, had given her powerful protection in her town and castle of Thurles to many English who fled to her friendly shelter, and that when the neighbouring garrison of Archestown was yielded to the Irish forces, the commander and others of his company, "who were wounded and much spent out and weakened," were visited by the Countess, after which she brought his whole company to her house, where they were entertained for many weeks, after which term she sent them to the English garrison of Doneraile, "well *cured* and refreshed with supplies of money and provisions." (Prendergast.) On the surrender of Galway to Ludlow in 1652, all the Irish were directed to quit the town except the "sick and bed-rid." During the operations against the Irish Confederates the soldiers subsisted chiefly on meal and fresh beef, plundered from either side. At Limerick, Luton and many of his men died of the plague. Kilkenny, gallantly defended by Sir William Butler, was at last obliged to surrender, because the garrison had become "so weak for want of rest," and being also "reduced by wounds and disease." Clothworthy's officer makes a very pertinent remark as the result of his experience in these wars when he says, "A raw general and green soldiers are not for taking of towns, or to defend them manly against the storms of old soldiers."

There is some evidence on record that the Cromwellian forces in Ireland were indifferently supplied with medical assistance. The Parliamentarians had an apothecary-general in Dublin whose bills for medicines are extant, and during the transplantation of the Irish, the apothecaries of the towns were exempted on condition of making themselves useful to the new-comers (officers and soldiers). On the 12th September, 1656, we find an application to the Commissioners for the Affairs of Ireland in behalf of a Dr. Anthony Mulshanoque, " whose good affection to the English by his faithful advice and assistance in his profession was proved at the trial of the qualification of the ancient natures of book, by the certificate of Sir William Fenton and Major-General Jephson, and several other persons of quality, who prayed for his dispensation from transplantation, desiring that his residence amongst them might be permitted, being *destitute of physicians of ability.*" The request was granted by the Commissioners. This great scarcity of physicians in Ireland is also proved by a letter of Sir George Carew, President of Munster, who, when ill, and in want of medical attendance, wrote to the Queen from Cork, 29th September, 1602, " Ireland is destitute of learned men of English birth, and with Irish physicians, *knowing the good will they have for me,* if they were learned, I dare not venture !" A somewhat dubious compliment.

A Dr. Richard Madden, of Waterford, was also dispensed from transplantation upon the certificate of Colonel Leigh and other officers there in 1654. Very probably there were many similar petitions and dispensations. Subsequently, when the Commonwealth Parliament in 1653 passed an Act, guaranteeing £1,550,000 worth of land in Ireland to be divided amongst the officers and soldiers for their arrears of pay, the officers of the army had such confidence in the Parliamentary Physician-General in Ireland,

Sir William Petty, a graduate of the University of Oxford, that they requested he might be appointed to make accurate maps of the forfeited lands previous to their distribution. The Articles were signed in the Castle of Dublin, 11th December, 1654. The regiments and companies were almost set down upon the lands which they had conquered without much picking or choosing. The first work of the survey was carried on by foot soldiers, instructed by Sir William Petty, and selected by him as "hardy men, to whom such hardships as to wade through bogs and water, climb rocks, bad fare and lodging were familiar." Cromwell's army in Ireland then consisted of some 35,000 men, among them his regiment of Life Guards, the Train, regiments of horse, dragoons, of foot, and loose companies commanded by majors or captains. The regiments had been raised by the different colonels to whom they belonged. Upon this survey of a medical officer of the Irish army, a considerable portion of the land in Ireland is now held, and the surgeons of the different regiments benefited largely in some instances by the Parliamentary grant. Previous to the outbreak of the Civil War, a large contingent of Irish soldiers had been sent to the Low Countries. Writing in 1615, the Prince of Orange described them as "fine soldiers." "There lives," he went on to say, "not a people more hardy, active, and who in their way will endure the miseries of warre or famine, watching, heat, cold, wet, travel, and the like, so naturally and with such facility and courage as they do."

When Charles I. resolved to prosecute the war both with France and Spain with vigour, it became necessary to reorganize to some extent the surgical corporation of London, in order to provide an adequate number of medical officers for the expedition. To the Corporation of Surgeons was assigned the office of providing these last for the service of the State, and the important office of inspecting the provision of medicines, &c., to meet the wants of the men. An Order in Council, signed 10th July, 1626, recognised the duty of the State of providing medicines for the treatment of internal diseases, the surgical remedies being paid for by the men out of the stoppage of twopence per month still given to the surgeons according to ancient custom. The Company were in effect at this time Director-Generals of the Army and Navy. Woodall, who was the guiding spirit of the Company in these affairs, in order to induce young surgeons to enter into the Service, presented to them the following advantages, a most interesting record of the state of the Service in his day :—

"I acquaint the younger sort of surgeons, my brethren, with these especial favours which it then (1626) pleased our most gracious King Charles to bestow upon our Corporation in particular, above and beyond his ever blessed ancestors, for the good of his souldiers and seamen, and our encouragements, thereby to animate and inable us the more heartily to serve him. And namely :—

" First. His Highness was graciously pleased to augment each surgeon and surgeon's mate in H.M.'s service by sea and land to above a third penny from former custome, namely, from nineteen shillings foure pence a moneth to 30s. to surgeons, and 20s. to mates . . . And nevertheless all the surgeons in His Highnesse's service have, as formerly, by the head of all men that are in pay in any of his ships or land service two pence of each man by the moneth. And for the surgeons in his land service he alloweth to the surgeon-major of the whole campe 5s. a day (equal to about 25s, of our present money); and for his two mates or servants 4s. a day. Also His Majestie allowed to each surgeon 2s. 6d. the day, which is £3 15s. the moneth, and to each mate £3 a moneth, and moreover alloweth and gave to each surgeon appointed to 250 men a surgery chest of £17 valew, free of account : and moreover His Majestie alloweth to the surgeon-major a store-chest or a magazeen chest of £48 valew, for a supply to furnish upon all wants and occasions. And His Highness was yet further well pleased to give authority unto the Masters and Governors of our Society for to have the making, compounding, fitting and ordering of all the medicines, as well physicall as chirurgicall, together with all other provisious belonging unto the surgeon's chests."

" And further His Highnesse has referred to the ancient Masters and Governors of our Society, the pressing of all surgeons and surgeons' mates or servants to surgeons ; with also the taking up of any instrument chests, or ready made medicines in His Highnesse's name for his service, if occasion be not otherwise."

" These favours and privileges our Corporation have received from His Highnesse, together with a new Charter, wherein he hath likewise beene graciously pleased to confirme all our privileges for the better subsistence of our said Corporation in future times; as also we have never been desired, as formerly, to have moneys imprested beforehand for the providing a chest with surgery instruments and salves."

" In regard whereof, and for that surgeons should with the better courage be instigated faithfully to performe his duties, I have presumed, in this preface, to explain His Highnesse's former favours, as aforesaid, whereby our younger brethren from age to age may better keepe it in remembrance."

The foregoing regulations were in the form of an Order of the then Lords of the King's Most Honorable Privy Council. The Charter alluded to by Woodall provided for the election of ten examiners to ascertain the fitness of all candidates for admission into the Company. Apprentices were to be acquainted with the Latin language, and a lecture on surgery was to be read once a week or otherwise. The Bishop of London, or Dean of St. Paul's, and their examiners were still allowed to retain their power of examining all practitioners in surgery, a privilege continued until 18 Geo. II., 1745, when John Ranby was Master and Governor and principal Sergeant-Surgeon to the King. The arbitrary power of impressment given to the Company was that of forcing the members or freemen of their corporation who had undergone the ordinary examinations to qualify them to practise in London, to serve with the Army. The following mandate issued by the King to the Company in 1628, on the eve of the unfortunate expedition to Rochelle, will serve as an example of the manner in which his Majesty's Army was sometimes furnished with medical officers:—

"After our hearty congratulations, whereas there is present use for a convenient number of chirurgeons for the 4000 land souldiers that are to be sent with his Majesty's fleet, now preparing for the relief of Rochelle; these shall be to will and require you, the Master and Wardens of the Company of Chirurgeons forthwith to impress and take up, for the service aforesaid, sixteen able and efficient chirurgeons, and that you take special care, that they be such in particular, as are best experienced in the cure of wounds made by gun-shot, and likewise that their chests be sufficiently furnished with all necessary provisions requisite for the said employment, and that you charge them upon their allegience, as they will answer the contrary at their perils, to repair to Portsmouth by the 10th of July, to go along with such commanders in whose company they shall be appointed to serve. And you are further, by virtue hereof, to require and charge all mayors, sheriffs, justices of the peace, bailiffs, constables, headboroughs, and all other His Majesty's officers and loving subjects, to be anxious and assisting with you in the full and due execution of this our letter, whereof neither you nor they may fail of your perils, and this shall be your warrant.—Dated at Whitehall, this last day of June, 1628,—Your loving friend."

This Order is signed by several of the Lords of the Council. This power given to the Company by charter of improvement, and which was frequently confirmed by the judges, was not usually exercised except upon the order of the King as above signed by the Lords of the Council. The last entry of the kind in the records of the Company refers to the reign of William and Mary. From the journals of the House of Commons, October 12, 1644, it would appear that the Parliament endeavoured to make the medical service voluntary rather than compulsory. "Ordered that it be referred to the Masters and Wardens of the Apothecaries and Surgeons, to make choice of able and fit men for surgeons to be sent to My Lord General's Army; and if such as be chosen and appointed by them shall refuse to go, that they repair to the Committee of the Militia; and that they give orders to the pressing of them for the said service." None of these orders refer to the higher rank of physicians, who were graduates in medicine of one of the several

Universities. They are referred to in the following ordinance of the House, dated 1st of July, 1643. "Ordered that Dr. Paul de Laune, and Dr. Nathalean Chamberlaine, Physicians, be forthwith sent to the Army for the service of the Army; and this House doth declare that whatever physicians or surgeons shall be employed by the House, shall have the same allowances as others formerly have had. And the two surgeons now to be employed shall have their chests furnished with medicines, each of them to the value of twenty pounds." The Committee of Safety were further ordered to give warrants for the pay and provisions of these persons, and the Masters and Wardens of the Apothecaries were ordered to view the chests "that they bee good." After the defeat of the Parliamentarians near Newbury, September, 1643, a correspondent of the "Mercurius Anglicus," alludes to these chests and adduces as " a further evident argument of the victory His Majesty's Army obtained over the Rebels, that they were forced to leave behind them heavy carriages, with many barrels of Whiskey and Pistoll Bullets and *very many chirurgeon's chests full of medicaments.*" The writer goes on to say that His Majesty gave a strict command for " the cure of the wounded by His own warrant to the Maior of Newbury, a copy whereof we have here transcribed."

" Our will and command is that you forthwith send into the townes and villages adjacent, and bring hence all the sicke and hurt souldiers of the Earl of Essex's army, and though they be Rebels and deserve the punishment of Treators yet out of our tender compassion upon them as being Our subjects Our will and pleasure is that you carefully provide for their recovery as well as for those of our Own Armay, and then to send them to Oxford. Given, &c. " To the Maior of Newbury and the officers thereof."

After the second battle of Newbury and the King's retreat, his wounded were left behind at Donnington Castle, and captured by the Parliamentarians, who it is to be hoped acted with equal humanity. From an ordinance of the Parliament, dated 23rd March, 1642, we find the pay of the Commonwealth medical officers to have been as follows, " For the Scot's army two physicians at 5s., two surgeons at 4s., four mates at 2s., and two apothecaries at 2s. 6d. a-day." The title of surgeon's mate appears to have been derived originally from the Navy; mates, now sub-lieutenents, being only abolished within the last few years. Many of the army surgeons of the Commonwealth served subsequently in the Navy, as De Laune, who was physician to the fleet that captured Jamaica.

Richard Wiseman was one of the most noted surgeons who followed the royal cause during these wars. As a reward for his services and fidelity he was appointed sergeant-surgeon to Charles II. One of his eight chirurgical treatises published in 1676, treats expressly on gunshot wounds, derived from his experience as a military and naval surgeon. Wiseman was the first to advocate the advantage of primary amputation immediately after the receipt of the injury, and the possibility of preserving the wounded limbs. Munro, another surgeon of eminence, during his expedition with McKay's Scots regiment, raised in 1626, gives a graphic description of the deadly effects of artillery, then only coming into general use, and the appaling effect of the wounds inflicted, and the consternation it occasioned among the troops. Brown, afterwards "Chirurgeon in Ordinary" to Charles II., who had served in the Dutch War of 1665, when he was severely wounded, was also a contributor to the literature of his speciality at this period. The illustrious Harvey had been present with the King at Oxford in his capacity of a physician, and Dr. Edward Verney, the King's Standard-bearer, was killed at Edge-hill. Some of the King's garrisons appear to have been well supplied with provisions. For example, at the surrender of Newcastle to the Scots army in 1640, in the King's magazine was found "good store of biskett and cheese" (Baillie). The provisions of Nottingham Castle for a siege consisted of the following articles, 1150lbs. of butter, as much cheese, eleven quarters of bread-corn, seven beeves, 214 flitches of bacon, 560 fishes, and fifteen hogsheads of beer. The garrison numbered 400 men. When the Armada was in sight two reigns previously, Leicester went to Walsingham for "bear and befe" for the maintenance of his garrisons. From these facts we can form a good idea of the soldier's ration during the Civil wars. The Cavaliers were on arrival billeted by their quartermasters on the inhabitants of the towns occupied by them. The Royal Army consisted chiefly of regiments raised by the nobility, who espoused the cause of the King, the Parliamentary forces were chiefly stipendiary troops who were at first invariably defeated, because, as Cromwell put it to Hampden, "Your troops are most of them old, decayed serving men and tapsters, and such kind of fellows; the King's forces are composed of gentlemen's younger sons, and persons of good quality; and do you think the mean spirits of such base and low fellows as ours will ever be able to encounter gentlemen who have honour and courage and resolution in them. You must get men who have the fear of God before them, and some conscience of what they do—men of a spirit that are likely to go as far as gentlemen will go, or else I am sure you will be beaten as you have hitherto been in every encounter." On this principle Cromwell had acted, he began with a troop of horse, enlisting the sons of farmers and freeholders, and incorporating among them all the most zealous fanatics he could find. He augmented the troop to a regiment, and thus formed that "unconquered and unconquerable soldiery who for discipline and self-government was unrivalled," as evidenced at Marston, Naseby, Dunbar, and Worcester. The Royalist armies were soon obliged not to exercise much delicacy and recruit from the roystering brigands who poured into England at the first trumpet blast of the war (Fairfax Memorials). The brilliant but imperfect successes which the meteoric genius of Prince Rupert effected was invariably followed by the serious slaughter of his followers, while Fairfax understood the art of achieving important measures with trifling losses, sparing the effusion of blood when he could, frequently entering into treaties when the broken condition of the Royalists, pent up in small towns and reduced to the last extremity, rendered them an easy prey to his arms. The Parliamentarians were often put to severe straits for want of adequate medical assistance. For example, during the attack on Nottingham Castle by the Cavaliers, the commandant complains among other things that "not so much as a surgeon was amongst them," and relates how "one weak old man was shot the first day, who, for want of a surgeon, bled to death before they could carry him to the Governor's wife, who at that time supplied the want as well as she could," and on another occasion we are told that the Governor's wife having some "excellent balsams and plaisters in her closet, with the assistance of a gentleman who had some skill, dressed all their wounds, whereof some were dangerous (being all shots) with such good success, that they were all well cured in convenient time."

During these unfortunate wars we often read of soldiers dying of "fevers little less than a plague" (typhus); many also died on their return from the attacks, being found dead in the woods and towns they passed through. The wounded were sometimes stript naked, others crept into their tenants' houses and had their wounds bound up; while on the other hand the private charity of the officers went often to assist the sick, wounded, and necessitous soldiers.

The Parliamentarians lived at free quarters in the Royalist towns, and in return, when allowed to surrender on conditions, were "pillaged to their shirts," many captains being sent "quite naked away." Some of the Commonwealth regiments in later years were described as "good, stout fighting men." Sometimes, as after the attack on Reading by the Earl of Essex in 1643, they were promised their pay and a gratuity to spare the place from plunder, but ineffectually. Afterwards a great mortality occurred amongst them from the "infected air of the town," so much so that Essex was forced to retire and quarter his sick and weak army about Kingston and other towns near London. The Parliamentary troops generally wore grey coats. According to Macaulay, Monk's Parliamentary troops were the first red-coats in the British Army. Both sides, however, appear to have worn green, blue, and red indifferently. The first regiments ordered by the Parliament to Ireland to operate against the confederate forces had amongst them many "boon companions, old blades, stout men and well-nerved," who were much discontented on finding no beer or cheese, a food they lived on to a large extent in England. According to one of their Articles of War they were forbidden to have any "amours" with Irish girls on the pain of being flogged, a remedy found not in the end to be in the least deterrent. Shortly before, the only English forces quartered there consisted of 300 foot and 900 horse, billeted in small parties all over the country and far from the capital, raised by the energy of Strafford to a well-disciplined army of 8,000 men for the King.

During sieges straw was generally supplied to the trenches. At the siege of Newark the Parliamentary Army lay most of the winter in the fields about the town. Many captains and soldiers suffered a good deal, the higher officers only had tents. When performing any active exercise, the men were obliged to put off their suits of musket-proof armour worn over their buff coats, owing to the great heat generated. At the siege of Carlisle the King's troops were so reduced that they were obliged to eat horse-flesh before yielding. Thus war repeats itself in every century.

Baillie, referring to the Scotch Contingent, wrote to the Parliament that "upon tuck of drum men would be got together, if it were believed, which is verily the truth, that every soldier will get meat his full, much more than at home, and for the present some money monthly, and if God bless, not a little fair rewards." This contingent numbered 18,000 foot, 2,000 horse, and 500 dragoons, and was, I presume, supplied by a due quota of medical officers. The extract is interesting, as showing the manner and facility for recruiting in those days, and the inducements to join the ranks.

Dr. Wilson was physician to King Charles I. during the war, and accompanied him a prisoner to Hampton Court, where he shared his captivity. Towards the end of this reign regiments were first designated. On the Continent they were reduced in strength to 1,000 men by Gustavus Adolphus, one of whose greatest improvements was the reduction in the heavy weights then carried by the soldier. Armour having become penetrable by the heavy bullets then in use, was gradually being discarded by the infantry, who were reduced to two classes—*musketeers*, armed with matchlock-muskets, swords and daggers, and *pikemen* with pikes fourteen to eighteen feet long. Gunpowder was made up in cartridges and carried in pouches instead of in a bandolier across the shoulder. Each regiment was formed into two wings of musketeers and a centre of pikemen, who guarded the three colours still retained. Four of such regiments formed a brigade.

The following passage in Schiller's "Wallenstein's Camp," gives a very good and amusing idea of the mercenary of this period, his life and discipline:—

First Jäger.—"How we were harassed and plagued by that teazing Gustavus of Sweden! He turned his camp into a church, had prayers night and morning, both at *reveille* and tattoo; and were we at times rather jolly he would himself preach to us from his saddle. A lass, too, was never tolerated unless when taken to church. No, I could stand it no longer, so I cut my stick."

He now takes service with Tilly when he tells us, " We had drink, play and lass in abundance, and faith the fare was not to be despised, for Tilly understood how to command. Strict towards himself, he was indulgent to the soldier, and, provided the needful did not come out of his own chest, his saying was ' live and let live.' But fortune was not constant to him. After the Leipzig calamity, things sped out badly. The ancient respect for us was gone, so I left for the Saxons, thinking I would have better luck with them. It went badly here however. Discipline was severe, we could not behave like an enemy ; had the imperial fortress given to us to guard, numberless ceremonies and compliments to pay ; carried on the war as if in a joke ; so having little heart for all this, and finding scant honour to be earned, I got out of all patience, and should certainly have been obliged to take refuge at my desk once more, had I not found an enrolment going on for Wallenstein."

Corporal.—" Well, and how long do you think of staying with us ?"

First Jäger.—" You joke ; I shall not dream of bolting while things go well !"

The musketeer with his unwieldly weapon was comparatively defenceless when it was fired. Sir J. Smythe remarked of this class of soldier, " it doth behove musquethers to be strong and puissant body, without sickness, aches or other impediments." In addition to the heavy weights (which had been reduced by Gustavus Adolphus) his energies had been taxed by an amount of training to which the modern manual and platoon was nothing. His drill regulations contained *forty* postures, viz., five standing, three marching, eighteen charging, and fourteen discharging. Muskets had been first used in Italy in 1530, but owing to the powder being weak, the time they took to load (quarter of an hour) and the uncertainty of their action were thought greatly inferior to arrows. Artillery was also so inefficient in the field at first that its use was confined almost exclusively to sieges. Red hot balls, first used at the siege of Dantzig in 1575, and bomb-shells against Vakterdone on the Rhine in 1588, and bayonets first recorded in the Memoirs of Puységur in 1647, were among the principal changes in military weapons during the sixteenth and first half of the seventeenth century, which had their influence on Military Surgery. On the Continent, the Swiss and Spanish infantry (the former exclusively pikemen, and the latter armed with a sword and shield) were in the highest estimate as soldiers.

During Charles the First's Civil Wars, a resolution passed through Parliament, March 6, 1643, empowering the raising of parochial funds for the relief of disabled soldiers, and the widows and fatherless children of the slain persons. It is curious to observe that in this same century the Buccaneers of the Spanish Main had made a law for recompensing their wounded. This fact is related by Raveneau de Lussan, who tells us that on the 7th of May, 1688, at Cheriquito, they came to an arrangement with their wounded, giving those who were crippled for life 1,000 pieces of eight, and the others whose hurts were of less consequence, 600.

On the 1st of January, 1660, Monk's Army in a brilliant front passed the Tweed. The soldiers sunk up to their knees in snow, never "trod upon plain earth" between Edinburgh and London so great was the frost. They arrived at York on the 11th of January, and set out again on the 16th, 4,000 infantry and 1,800 horse. While in Scotland, the soldiers had been dispersed in distant quarters, in wild and dreary garrisons. They were well paid, well disciplined, inured to toil, to fatigue, and to the rigours of a Scottish climate. These forces, when in Scotland in 1654, were described by Baillie as "very stout resolute men as ever took the field, and most of them old soldiers." They arrived at Nottingham on the 19th, where they stayed two days. On the 1st of February reached London by Gray's Inn Lane, exhausted with privations and their toilsome march, but liked by the people because they were "modest, orderly and peaceable, paid with punctuality, and gave no cause for disturbance or alarm." They were shortly afterwards reviewed on Blackheath by the King, who owed to their commander the restoration of his Crown, and we are told that the "frozen mien of the aged soldiers and officers indicated mere obedience and no enthusiasm." Their disbanding was shortly afterwards voted by Parliament. This was accomplished on Tower Hill, where was dispersed into civil life those iron hearts of the Commonwealth, and with them the medical officers who had shared their varying fortunes at Edgehill, Reading, Lansdown, Gloucester, Marston Moor, and to the King, fatal field of Nazeby. The fall of the Commonwealth marks a distinct epoch in Military Medical history. Company surgeons were soon to disappear, and a complete change to take place in the Constitution of the medical service which was again to serve under the Crown. To the reign of Charles I. or his immediate predecessors, we owe the introduction of the rank of physician-general, originating with the Irish army, surgeon-general with the company of adventurers to India, regimental-surgeon, surgeon's mate, derived from the Navy, and the Directorate of the Corporation of Surgeons in London, who for many years were chiefly concerned in educating and raising surgeons for the Royal Army. The few physicians employed came from Oxford or the Continental Universities. One of these, Dr. Thomas Skinner, accompanied Monk as principal physician during his memorable march from Scotland, of which in his journal he has left us many interesting particulars.

CHAPTER V.

Shortly after the accession of Charles II., the soldiers of the late Parliamentary Army, numbering in the three kingdoms some 60,000 men, were disbanded with their Medical Staff. Monk's regiment (now the Coldstream Guards) and a corps of cavalry (the present Life Guards) being alone retained by Royal Ordinance. A few independent companies of infantry were also established under the title of " Guards and Garrisons." The Cavaliers at Dunkirk were withdrawn to England to become the Grenadier Foot Guards, and from the Medical officers attached to this small force arose anew the present Corps of Royal Surgeons, who from this period became, if possible, more intimately united to the Army. The Medical officers at this time wore the picturesque scarlet uniform of their respective regiments. Each of the three troops of Life Guards (numbering from 150 to 200 privates, for the most part gentlemen who had fought during the Civil wars) had a "chirurgeon," the last link connecting the medical officers of companies of former reigns with the regimental surgeons of the standing Army, which, up to the year 1680, consisted of only four regiments, viz.: 1st "Royal Scots," 2nd, or "Queens," 3rd, or "Old Buffs," and 4th "King's Own," in addition to the Guards; forming in all some 5,000 men, embodied by the authority of the Crown only, and paid out of the Civil List. Two of these regiments had been levied by the Earl of Peterborough to garrison Tangiers, when for twenty years, the new Medical Staff of the Army had, for the first time, an opportunity of exercising their art in relieving the sufferings of their comrades, wounded in the many encounters with the Moors. This service was of the most arduous description. Dysentery and fever carrying off large numbers of the officers and men.

According to Sir James Turner, the duties of a soldier at this period were:—

1. To give exact and perfect obedience to all lawful enactments of superiors.

2. *To endure the fatigue, travel, and discommodation of war, whether it be in marching, or working of trenches, approaches and sieges, hunger, thirst, and cold, with an exemplary patience.*

3. In time of battle, skirmish or assault, to either overcome or die.

Turner noticed early some points in practical military hygiene in commenting on the want of cloaks as a means of protection against the vicissitudes of weather, and of some means by which the soldier could carry his scanty kit on the march.

In this reign, Louis XIV. in France, anticipated us a long way by founding Military Hospitals in all the fortified towns of his dominions and conquests, which were much attended to by succeeding monarchs. These were all new modelled in 1747, and schools of military surgery and medicines constituted at those of Brest, Toulon, Metz, Strasbourg and Lille.

On the first formation of regiments subsequent to the Restoration, the " Field and Staff officers " were shown in the Army List at the head of the corps as follows :—

"*Field-Officers and Staff.*"
Colonel as *colonel* . . . 12s. 0d. per diem and troop.
Major as *major* . . . . 5s. 6d. ,, ,,
Chaplain . . . . . 6s. 8d. ,,
Chirurgeon (4s. and one horse to carry his chest 2s.) . . . 6s. 0d. ,,

The above extract refers to the Regiment of Horse Guards in 1661. The mates holding their appointment by warrant from the colonel did not appear in the Army List until commissioned as assistant-surgeons. In 1670 war was declared against Holland, and during its continuance in 1672, we find 'an order from the King directing the Company of Surgeons of London to provide "twenty chirurgeons and twenty chirurgeon's mates," for service in the Army.

In 1674 peace was made with the Republic, upon the conclusion of which six chirurgeons and six chirurgeon's mates accompanied their corps to the continent where they were for a time placed upon the Dutch Establishment. It was not at all uncommon at this date for large contingents of British troops to serve in foreign armies. In 1630, a few years before, the Scotch troops in Sweden amounted to no less than 12,000 men and 800 officers, each regiment being 1,000 strong. The composition of these regiments may be inferred from the following list of payments given to the different ranks, and quoted by Lehming in his " payment of the Scots' Brigade," and from which it will be seen that each regiment was provided with no less than four surgeons. The colonel received in the shape of "serie and posse monies," nine dollars, valued at 4s. each per head. " To every colonel and lieutenant-colonel per month 184 rix dollars ; adjutant, sixty-one ; quartermaster, thirty ; trenchers, each eighteen ; *to four surgeons*, each twelve ; clerk of the regiment, thirty; clerk of the council of war, eighteen ; stock knights, each three ; *secondly*-captain, sixty-one ; lieutenant, thirty; ancient of ensign, ten ; sergeant, nine ; fuhrer (a sort of assistant-ensign), seven ; drums and pipers, each, four ; six corporals, each six ; common soldier, each, three and a-half dollars." There was also a provost or hangman, attached to the staff of each regiment. The staff (including the surgeons) are here shown as taking priority of the other officers. This record is interesting, as showing the exact position of medical officers at this date in foreign levies, where they appeared to have occupied a rank somewhere between the ancient or ensign and lieutenant.

Shortly after the Restoration, the condition of the soldiers in

England appears to have been a most pitiable one. Writing in 1664, from Sandwich Castle, Kent, where he was imprisoned. Colonel Hutchinson described his domicile, one of the King's garrisons as "a lamentable old ruined place, almost a mile distant from the town, the rooms all out of repair, not weather-proof, with no kind of accommodation, either for lodging or diet, or any convenience of life, half-a-dozen soldiers, and a poor lieutenant and his wife and children, two or three cannoniers, and a few guns almost dismounted upon rotten carriages," representing the garrison and armament. On the colonel's arrival, a company of foot soldiers from Dover were sent to help to guard the place. He describes them as "pitiful weak fellows, half-starved, and eaten up with vermin, whom the Governor of Dover cheated of half their pay, and the other half they spent in drink. They had no beds, but a nasty court of guard where a sutler lived, within a partition made of boards, with his wife and family." What a contrast to the present day!

According to the same writer, many of the physicians who had "belonged to the Army" during the Civil wars, had settled in different towns in private practice.

During the reign of Charles II., the sister kingdom, Ireland, with its then local army, had enjoyed several years of peace. The army living without action produced in about twenty years many old soldiers, who in the quaint language of the time "having honestly served the King from the time of their youth, and being arrived at old age, which rendered them incapable of further service, they could not properly be continued any longer in the same; and they by their constant service therein having neglected all other ways of procuring a livelihood by arts or trades, must of necessity starve, if dismist." To obviate this unfortunate necessity, His Majesty directed James, Duke of Ormonde, then Lord-Lieutenant of Ireland, by Letters Patent, dated 27th of October, 1679, to cause to be erected for the maintenance of these aged and disabled soldiers, the present Royal Hospital at Kilmainham, near Dublin, to be afterwards maintained by a deduction of sixpence in the pound out of all the pay that afterwards should "grow due by Our Establishment to Our Military List." The small standing army in Ireland consisted of about 7,000 men, and from the muster rolls returned by the Commissaries of such men as were not fit to continue longer in the Army, it was found that the number so returned did not amount to 300, being less than a twentieth part of the Army, and that "if the twentieth part of the said Army were purged or driven out, that number would die away, or be reduced to nothing, before the like number in the Army, in time of peace, should become fit for the hospital. For admitting that out of every ten old men in the hospital, one in the year should die, consequently out of 300 would die thirty; it follows that the whole number dies off every ten years, which would for ever keep the Army free from disabled men." This is one of the earliest records giving any definite idea as to the rate of mortality and invaliding among the soldiers of the Irish Army, who were evidently enlisted for life. Upon the completion of the hospital, two medical officers, a physician and a surgeon were appointed to it.

From the letters of the Earl of Orrery to the Duke of Ormonde, we can form some idea of the condition of the soldiers in Ireland a little before. Writing from Munster he says, "Your Grace's letter mentions five hundred recruits, which are to be distributed to the Army. I humbly beg your Grace, when they are sent to the several companies, care may be taken for some pay for them, else they will all perish. For they are mustered for three months, and probably receive no assignments for a month after the three months they are mustered for, and then not their money for two months after, so that coming over without money, and being likely to stay six months before they receive any, their condition will be sad. I had the greatest difficulty to get the officers and towns to trust the first recruits for diet, and I am afraid their faith will not stretch to a second part to the same tune. Colonel St. Leger was here with me yesterday, to let me know the people where he is garrisoned will not give them one day's credit more. I have sent for the magistrates to try if I can prevail; and, rather than the men shall starve, I will be myself bound for their diet . . ." " These recruits will not work to augment their livelihood; the old soldiers help out what they want in pay by their daily labour." These letters were written in 1664.

In 1684 the 2nd Queen's, and remaining 2,300 troops were withdrawn from Tangiers with their Medical Staff, after twenty-two years' occupation, during which interval the loss in officers and men were immense. The garrison at the period of its evacuation consisted of four troops of horse, five companies of Foot Guards, sixteen companies of Dumbarton's or the 1st Royals, sixteen companies of Trelawny's or 4th Foot, one company of miners and four independent companies.

About this time Markham made a curious remark. He says, " during this long siege of Buda by Spinola, it was observed that the married soldiers fared better, looked more vigorously, and were able to do more duty than the bachelors."

Upon the accession of James II., in 1685, the medical officers of the 5th and 6th Regiments, which had been formed in Holland returned with their corps to England, and eleven chirurgeons, and the same number of chirurgeon's mates were added to the establishment of the regular army between 1685-88, on the formation of the 7th to the 17th Regiments. They first saw active service during Monmouth's unfortunate rebellion. One of these new regiments, the 17th or " Richards," was raised, embodied, armed and clothed in London three weeks' after the colonel received the letter of service for its formation, and I may remark in passing that it was then by no means uncommon for medical officers to hold double commissions, purchasing their commissions as ensigns, and obtaining 2s. 6d. a day staff pay for the extra or hospital duty, a system, as we will see subsequently, continued for a very long period. As they advanced in their combatant rank they left the hospital duties for the then superior attractions of the more military position.

The staffs of the regiment are still continued at the head of the regimental list, the only difference being the additions of an adjutant and quartermaster, who were then junior to the surgeon. The rank accorded may be inferred, and the rate of pay seen from the following pay list of Cornwall's (afterwards the 9th) Regiment in 1786, the year following the accession of James II.:—

	£	s.	d.	
" 1 Colonel *as* Colonel	0	12	0	per diem.
1 Lieut.-Colonel *as* Lieut.-Colonel	0	7	0	,,
1 Major *as* Major	0	6	8	,,
1 Chirurgeon 4s., 1 chirurgeon's mate 2s. 6d.	0	6	6	,,
1 Adjutant	0	4	0	,,
1 Quartermaster or marshall	0	4	0	,,
Total for Staff	2	5	2	

Colonel's Company.

	£	s.	d.	
" 1 Colonel *as* Captain	0	8	0	per diem.
1 Lieutenant	0	4	0	,,
1 Ensign	0	3	0	,,
2 Sergeants at 1s. 6d. each	0	3	0	,,
3 Corporals at 10d. each	0	3	0	,,
1 Drummer	0	1	0	,,
50 Private men at 8d. each	1	13	4	,,
Total Colonel's company	2	15	4	
Nine Companies at same rate	24	18	0	
Total per day	29	18	6	

Per annum £10,922 12s. 6d.

In the previous year, 1685, a Regulation was issued granting the "King's Bounty" to soldiers for the loss of an eye or limb, or total loss of the use of a limb, when "*certified by the surgeon-general,*" who at this date appears to have occupied the chief position in the Army Medical Service; the Directorate of the Company of Surgeons of London being, however, still supreme. The amount of bounty was one year's pay, so that the principal medical officer of the Royal Army at this time occupied a not unresponsible position in the service of the State. The rate of out pensions at this period varied from 5d. to a private soldier to 1s. 6d. to a corporal of Light Horse.

According to the War Office records it will be found that ten marks, amounting to £6 13s. 4d. was paid to each of four soldiers in the 2nd Queen's, wounded at the battle of Sedgemore, fought in 1685. During this reign a marine, called the admiral's regiment, was raised and clothed in yellow, and it was not uncommon for regiments of the regular army to be drafted on board the fleet for temporary service. It was not, however, the custom to have them accompanied by their medical staff, who were retained for general duties on shore. Some years later, viz., in 1698, no less than six regiments of regulars were placed for this purpose (to act as marines) on the establishment of the Navy.

Following the success of the Revolution in 1688, and accession of William III. to the Crown of England, and within a year, nine regiments (18th to 27th), with their medical officers were added to the establishment. A number of foreign surgeons accompanied the King's Dutch Guards to England, and the medical officers who remained faithful to the Royal cause retired with Sarsfield's troops to Ireland, where they were shortly to meet their *confrères* on the opposite side as enemies. In March, 1689, the fallen king landed at Kinsale with a considerable body of French troops, who were provided with a large medical staff in addition to the regimental surgeons. In August of the same year Schomberg, William's favourite general, landed in Ireland with 10,000 men, and almost immediately commenced active military operations. In the interval, a Mutiny Bill was brought in to make effectual provisions for regulating the discipline of the Army, the Crown reserving to itself the right to make articles of war for the better government of the forces; medical officers, among others, came within its provisions.

James' first essay was at the siege of Londonderry, when the women of the town "did good service, carrying ammunition, match, bread and drink to the men." On the retreat of the Irish, Mackenzie relates that they "carried away on their backs many of their dead and mortally wounded to shelter themselves the better from the storm of shot." During the continuance of the siege, the heat of the weather (it being summer time) increased so much that disease and mortality among a population closely cooped up within the walls, led to the death of no less than fifteen officers in one day. On the 17th of June the Inniskilliners captured 300 of the enemy on conditions that "the common soldiers were to have their lives spared, but to be stripped of their red coats." A curious episode at one of the first actions (Newtown-Butler) when the Inniskilliners, 2,500 strong, attacked 6000 of the Irish, the loss of the latter numbered no less than " 3,000;

2,000 slain, 500 drowned, 500 prisoners, 20 killed, 40 or 50 ill-wounded."

Schomberg's troops were of a most mixed composition. Twenty-three of the regiments were raised in England for service in Ireland, and completed within the short space of six weeks. To these were joined two battalions of Dutch, four of French Protestant refugees, to be joined in Ireland by the newly-raised Inniskilliners, some regiments from Scotland, and a body of 6,000 Danes. On no former or subsequent occasion were medical officers of so many nationalities assembled together for service in that part of the kingdom. Schomberg, then eighty years of age, on the 7th of September reached Dundalk from Carrickfergus, and established his camp in a low and damp ground about a mile north of the town. Many of his newly-raised levies died on the road from disease and the hardships they were compelled to endure; his camp was soon crowded with sick. The unhealthy situation of the camp, the change of diet and climate had affected adversely the soldiers, who deprived of their ordinary comforts, stinted in their food, ill-clothed, badly lodged, and exposed to every inclemency of the weather, were soon attacked with fevers, and fluxes. We are informed by historians that they had "surgeons well furnished against all the accidents of active war, but totally unprovided with the medicines necessary for the diseases generated by the causes just alluded to, and that disease spread to such an alarming degree that the camp at Dundalk seemed like a vast hospital. Some troops from Londonderry arrived at this juncture, to make matters worse by importing the contagion of an infected town into the camp." (Wright.)

The Irish Army, under King James, was encamped on the adjacent heights in a position which combined safety with comparative impunity. We are told that whenever the latter appeared the ardour of the English troops was excited in an instant, and that "even the sick rose and assumed their arms with alacrity." When at length the General gave orders to erect huts against the inclemency of the weather, the troops had scarcely the courage or will to carry them into execution, and when their sick companions were taken from the tents to hospital, those who remained complained of their removal for they had used them for pillows, so indifferent had they become to suffering. The Dutch suffered least, because more used to a moist climate, and because, being veteran troops, they had a larger acquaintance with hardships, and had early erected huts for themselves. The Irish finding it impossible to draw the English from their entrenchments, sat down to watch them, and then soon began to be visited by the same disasters until November, when the rains became so intolerable, both armies were obliged to quit their camps and retire to better quarters. The Irish being masters of the country to the south, had sent away their sick gradually and in small parties. As the huts and tents of the English camp were removed, it presented the appearance of a vast hospital, and the army appeared to consist only of those who were sick and those who were necessarily attendant upon them. Waggons were not sufficiently numerous to carry the former, and many were seen struggling along the way supported by their companions. Many were left behind for want of carriages, and others refused to be moved, the remainder were carried by sea. Schomberg, himself moved by compassion, ordered the superior officers to attend like corporals and sergeants upon the waggons and hospitals, and the old and veteran commander shivering with ague, stood exposed amid rain and cold on the bridge of Dundalk for hours together, thanking the sick for their services as the long line of waggons passed in sight of the army. Numbers died on the road, and it was computed that of 15,000 men who had at different times entered the English camp, not less than 8,000 perished through hardship and disease; and it was said that the loss of the Irish on that inactive campaign was not much less. It was stated that Schomberg's misfortunes arose from the neglect of a person named Schales, who held the office of purveyor to the Army, and who left it in want of artillery, carriages, horses, provisions, and even of medicines.

During these campaigns in Ireland the sick and wounded suffered many hardships. At the siege of Limerick they had no houses to shelter them, and when the siege was raised, they were conveyed to Carrick and Clonmel. In the town many of the wounded prisoners remained undressed. Story gives the following as the losses of the English Army, from the landing of the Duke of Schomberg to the termination of the war. "Officers killed 140, soldiers killed in the field 2,037, murdered by Rapparees 800, English and foreign officers who died during the three campaigns 320, soldiers who died since the landing in Ireland 7,000. In the two last campaigns few died except recruits, and such as died of their wounds.

The pay of the Irish soldiers was only 1d. a day, in addition to which two pairs of *brogues* and a pair of breeches and stockings were supplied to him. Frequently not having any pay at all, they lived at discretion, seizing the inhabitants' cattle, butter, wood, linen, and every other commodity, regardless of the orders and protests of bishops and nobles. Their losses in killed amounted to 617 officers and 12,676 soldiers.

In 1690, it was evident that a number of French surgeons were attached to James II.'s regiments, for twenty-four of these officers arrived with Lieutenant-General St. Ruth at Limerick on the 1st June, "for the use of the Irish Army." From a perusal of James II.'s Army List, it will be seen that each of his regiments had a "chirurgeon" attached to them.

In 1691, a party of the 5th Foot from Mountmelick attacked

two of these regiments, numbering about 400 men each, whilst marching through the woods at Castleduff, killing 150 of the Irish, and capturing one major, five captains, nine lieutenants, two ensigns, one adjutant, *one surgeon,* six sergeants, seventeen corporals, three drummers, and eighty-two private men. From the following list it will be seen King James's Army was provided by superintending medical officers of very high rank, who were included among the general and field officers of his staff.

" Account of the General and Field Officers of King James's Army, Muster Rolls, 2nd June, 1690. (D'Alton.)

Duke of Tyrconnel	Captain-General
„ Berwick	Lieut.-General
Richard Hamilton	„ „
Count Langau	General of the French
Monsieur Lery	Lieut.-General
Dominick Sheldon	Lieut.-General of the Horse
Patrick Sarsfield	Major-General
Monsieur Boiseleau	„ „
Anthony Hamilton	„ „
—— Walings	„ „
Thomas Maxwell	Brigadier
John Hamilton	„
Will Dorrington	„
Solomon Slater	Muster-Master-General
Richard Fitzgerald	Comptroller of the Musters
Sir Richard Nagle	Secretary at War
Sir Henry Bone	Receiver-General
Sir Michael Creagh	Paymaster-General
Felix O'Neil	Auditor-General
Dr. Archibald	Physician to the State
Patrick Archibald	Chirurgeon-General

On his arrival in Dublin, William III. was joined by the Physician-General to the Army, Dr., afterwards Sir Patrick Dun, who proceeded with him to the south of Ireland in the capacity of his principal medical officer, and was present at some scenes of historical interest. He was afterwards with the army designed for the capture of Waterford, accompanying General Douglas's forces to Golden Bridge, near Clonmel. He writes from Waterford, 16th September, 1690, to King, " Dr. Le Can is coming from the hospital near Dublin to relieve me. I hope to be with you in a few days after his arrival; he cometh by sea to Waterford." He goes on to say, " I praye you doe me the favour to send your servant to look after a stable for a night for five horses till I get time to send them to grass . . . The Army is near Golden Bridge, but many are gone into winter's quarters. We have a garrison still at Castle Clonmel, within four miles of Limerick." The hospital he alludes to was situated in James Street, and was one of the earliest general military hospitals established in Ireland. A century later it was in so dilapidated a condition as to render necessary the construction of the present Royal Military Infirmary in the Park.

Sir Patrick Dun was appointed, in 1676, "Physician to the State, and to my Lord-Lieutenant." In 1681, when only thirty-four years of age, he became President of the King and Queen's College of Physicians, and in 1688, Physician-General to the Army, at 10s. a day. He was knighted iu 1696, and was four times (three for Mullingar) elected to the Irish House of Commons. In 1725 the office of State Physician became separated from that of Physician-General. On his death, in 1713, nearly all his property, including his library, reverted, on his wife's death, to endow two professorships in a school of physic, and to provide a hall for the College of Physicians. In 1800, the School of Physic Act passed—almost the last Act of the Irish Parliament—which led to the erection of Sir Patrick Dun's Hospital, commenced in 1803, and completed, by the aid of Parliamentary grants, in 1816, and where at the present time soldiers' wives are trained to become army midwives. From the following entry from the Archives of the College of Physicians, it would appear that the President was held in high esteem. The entry bears date 1677.

"It.—Payd Mr. Boldey, of ye Castle Tavern, for a treate given Dr. Dun upon his address to ye College of Physicians, agt. Lewis, the summe of 10s. 6d."

This sum was, of course, then many times its present value. In an ancient book of the College of Physicians, beginning January 21st, 1672, is found the following very curious extract relating to the dissection of a body:—

It. to ye souldiers who kept ye body . . 4s. 6d.
It. for ye coffin for ye body . . . . 4s. 6d.
It. to ye souldiers who watched . . . 9s. 0d.
It. for ye said souldiers in drink . . . 3s. 0d.

An employment for soldiers few would have suspected.

Sir Thomas Molyneux, born 1661, succeeded Sir Patrick Dun as Physician-General to the Army in Ireland. He was created a baronet of that kingdom, 4th July, 1730. He bought Castle Dillon, near Armagh, and was the ancester of the Molyneux's of that county. In the Cathedral is a monument to his memory. He was the first medical baronet of Ireland, and, like Sir Patrick Dun, a very eminent physician. He was Regius Professor of Physic, Member for the Borough of Ratoath in the Irish Parliament in 1695, and a F.R.S.

The great surgeon in Ireland at the end of the seventeenth century was Thomas Proby, "Chirurgeon General to the Army of the winning side, and an ancestor of the Earl of Carysfort." With Molyneux he published several interesting works relating to his profession. Dean Swift called Proby "a person universally esteemed," and castigated with his bitter satire the then Lord-

Lieutenant (Wharton) for dispossessing him of a house, and part of the Phœnix Park, where now stands the King's Military Infirmary. Proby was also one of the trustees of Stephen's Hospital, and in virtue of his office as "Chirurgeon-General," examiner for the diploma in surgery in Ireland.

The following curious prescription of Sir Patrick Dun's, written in camp in 1691 for General de Ginkle, remains on record:—

"℞ Chester ale, claret, potted chicken and geese. This is the physic I advise you to take. I hope it will not be nauseous or disagreeable to the stomach. A little to be taken on a march."

The office of Apothecary-General to the forces in Ireland ceased during the Commonwealth, although for many years continued in England. That this resulted from the action of Sir William Petty is evident from the following extract relating to his first arrival in the Sister Isle:—

"The said doctor had not been landed two months, but, observing the vast and needless expense of medicaments, and how the Apothecary-General of the Army and his *three assistants* did not spend their time to the best advantage, did forthwith, to the content of all persons concerned, with the State's bare disbursement of about £120, save them five hundred pounds per annum of their former charge, and furnished the army, hospitals, garrisons, headquarters, &c., with medicaments, without the least noise or trouble, reducing that affair to a state of plainness, which was before held a mystery, and the vexation of such as laboured to administer it well." (Downs' Survey.)

From a surgeon of one of James II.'s Irish regiments, the ex-Lord Chancellor of Ireland traces his descent.

At this period the proportion of medical officers to a regiment appears to have remained the same irrespective of its strength, for we find that when the English regiments in the service of France were withdrawn, the Royal Scots, then coming for the first time on the Establishment, consisted of one lieutenant-colonel, one major, eighteen captains, one captain-lieutenant, forty-one lieutenants, twenty-one ensigns, one adjutant, one quartermaster or marshal, and only one chirurgeon and one chirurgeon's mate. The strength of the regiment numbered fifty privates per company, or 1,000 non-commissioned officers and men. Shortly afterwards a second chirurgeon's mate was added to the strength of the corps.

The 13th Foot afforded, in 1691, a very good example, showing the effect of campaigning in Ireland upon an individual regiment. From being employed at the siege of Cork and elsewhere during inclement weather, it suffered so much that out of an official strength of 678 rank and file, no less than 216 were sick in hospital and billets, so that the medical officers must have had in many instances very arduous duties to perform. The first siege of Limerick had been raised and the troops sent into winter quarters, owing to fatigue and excessive rains having so impaired the health of the troops that it was necessary to afford them a relief from the laborious services in which they had been engaged.

This unhappy war terminated at the surrender of Limerick to De Ginkle. One of the clauses of that oft-quoted treaty ran thus :—"The General will cause provision and medicine to be furnished to the sick and wounded officers, troopers, dragoons, and soldiers of the Irish Army who could not pass into France at the first embarkment, and after they are cured, will order them ships to pass into France if they are willing to go." Nineteen thousand men and a large proportion of surgeons of this army sailed for France to form the nucleus of that splendid brigade whose brilliant actions are recorded in the pages of history. Half a century later (1748) Lord Clare laid down the following regulation for its recruitment. The recruiting officers were to enlist "none but handsome men, not under five feet two inches (French measure) in height, well-limbed, and at most not over thirty-five years of age. They shall be examined by the surgeon-major of the hospital that they have no concealed defects or infirmities. The recruiting officer shall avoid as much as possible the enrolment of men who are actually sailors." The men were enlisted by bounty and brought over from Dover and Ireland to Calais and Boulogne. The term of service was six years, and the pay of each soldier four sols six farthings per diem.

On the conclusion of the general peace of Ryswick in 1697, the standing army in England was reduced to 7,000 men. A corresponding reduction took place in the medical staff, the reduced officers coming for the first time on the half-pay establishment. Shortly before this the Company of Surgeons of London had, as we have already seen, exercised for the last time the powers given to them in the reign of Charles I., of enforcing the attendance of the members of their College for the service of the Crown. In the following reign a large silver bowl, weighing 160 oz., was presented to them, "in acknowledgment of the services of the Company in examining the surgeons for the Army and the Navy." The purchase of the freedom of a surgeon at this time was ten guineas, and for taking up the Livery of the Company (which conferred several important privileges) £31, with five shillings "to the poor box."

From the following certificate relative to the appointment of a "chirurgeon's mate" to attend a party of the Royal Regiment of Horse Guards designed for foreign service in 1678 (War Office Records), it would appear that the regimental surgeons did, on order, provide medical assistance for divisions of their corps *en route* to head-quarters, and who could not be accompanied by the regimental assistants.

"I doe most humbly certify, that in consideration of a party designed for Flanders out of His Majesty's Regiment of Horse

Guards, to be commanded by Major Sir Francis Compton, upon the first forces that were sent thither, Mr. Sackville Whittle, Chirurgeon to the said Regiment of Horse, had order to provide an able chirurgeon to attend that party as his mate, and did contract and agree with an able chirurgeon pursuant thereto, on the 14th of March last past, from which day the said mate is by contract to enter His Majesty's pay, any provision being made by the late Establishment for the said mate only, to commence from the 1st May inst., the said chirurgeon will hereby fall short of pay due to him by the said contract, from the said 14th day of March inclusive to the said 1st May, being forty-eight days, which, according to His Majesty's Establishment, will amount to eight pounds eight shillings.

"Given under my hand the 31st day of May, 1678.

"JOHN KNIGHT."

Queen Anne had scarcely ascended the throne in 1702, when commenced the war of the Spanish Succession, which only terminated at the Peace of Utrecht in 1713. During this interval the genius of Marlborough marked a distinct epoch in military history, rendered conspicuous by the brilliant victories of Blenheim, Ramillies, Oudenarde, and Malplaquet. In these wars, England, with a population of 10,000,000, had only, at the highest point of the ten years' sanguinary conflict (1702-12), 40,000 men under arms, while France, with 20,000,000, had at least 200,000. Louis XIVth's Army was raised by voluntary enlistment, the Militia alone being raised by conscription. He was the first to introduce a uniform in the Army. Before his time the soldiers merely wore a *banderole* over their steel breastplates and ordinary dresses. This was a great and symptomatic improvement; it at once introduced an *esprit de corps* and a sense of responsibility. He first made the troops march with a measured step, and caused large bodies of men to march with the precision of a single company.

In 1703, the year after the commencement of the war, the number of British native troops in the Low Countries was only 20,000, raised in 1704 by extraordinary exertions to 30,000. A Bill was brought into Parliament for the purpose of recruiting the Army by forced conscription of men from each parish, but was rejected as unconstitutional. In the same session, however, an Act passed, empowering Justices of the Peace to *impress*, for land service, such men as were not entitled to vote for Members of Parliament, or who had no lawful calling or mode of subsistence, but no one was to be impressed under five feet five inches in height. Under this Act a number of vagrants and delinquents disgraced the profession of arms by their presence. The means by which regiments were recruited to their full complement were most disreputable. Drinking and other bad practices were rife, and Defoe, writing at the time upon the difficulty of getting men, says :—

"It is poverty that makes men soldiers, and drives crowds into the armies; and the difficulty to get Englishmen to enlist is because they live in plenty and ease; and he that earns 20s. a week at an easy, steady employment, must be drunk, or mad, when he lists for a soldier to be knocked on the head for 3s. 6d. a week. But if there was no work to be had—if the poor wanted employment, if they had not bread to eat, nor knew how to earn it, thousands of young fellows would fly to the pike and musket, and choose to die like men in the face of the enemy rather than lie at home, starve, or perish in poverty and distress."

Such causes have always had a marked influence upon voluntary recruitment. Towards the close of the war, famine and misery drove crowds of recruits to the French camp. Louis XIV. is reported to have said, "Hunger would compel his subjects to follow the bread-waggons." When the Allied Army advanced into French Flanders, the towns had all the marks of poverty. There was not a soul to be seen in the villages, the peasants flying as the Allies advanced, carrying everything they had with them, which left our forces, according to Hare, Marlborough's chaplain, "in want of everything, and made both officers and soldiers pass their time ill enough." "I will only add," he goes on to say, "that the Scots think an army in their own Highlands would shift better." In the march from Treves in 1705, the troops encountered unusual hardships. An eye-witness observed, "After we had quitted Juliers, you never saw so wretched a country. The soil barren, mountainous, fruitful in nothing but in iron, and the air strangely cold, as if it had been in the midst of winter." Active operations were usually commenced in the spring, and the only compensation the troops had was the wintering in pleasant quarters among the Dutch peasantry.

In 1702 commenced the custom of deducting annually one day's pay for the Hospital, and several of the Articles of War promulgated during the Queen's reign had reference to the sick. In the Articles of War for the forces beyond the sea, it was ordained as follows:—"1. All plunder taken before the enemy is entirely beaten, is forfeited for the use of the sick and maimed soldiers. 2. One-tenth part of the spoil is to be laid apart towards the relief of the sick and maimed." Few soldiers in this reign got their discharge except in case of age, infirmity, disability by wounds, lingering diseases, &c.

Marlborough's humanity to the wounded, alike of the enemy's army and his own, and his courtesy to the vanquished, was the theme of universal admiration. His uniform attention to the comforts of the men won the hearts of his soldiers. He discouraged to the utmost degree all intemperance and licentiousness, and constantly laboured to impress upon them a sense of moral duty and superior superintendence. Divine service was regularly performed in all his camps, both morning and evening; previous to a battle prayers were read at the head of every regiment, and after a victory was a solemn thanksgiving. "By these means," says a contemporary biographer, "his camp resembled a quiet, well-governed city." By such measures he turned the waifs and strays of humanity sent to him as recruits into brave and successful warriors.

Waggons laden with bread as well as herds of cattle followed the troops, and upon these they chiefly subsisted. The order of battle was in general in extended line in front of the tents, behind which were placed the surgeons awaiting the arrival of the wounded. Marlborough took a great personal interest in the latter, with whom he was in constant communication. After the memorable victory of Blenheim, he wrote to Godolphin (17th August, 1704), "Ever since the battle I have been so employed about our own wounded men and prisoners, that I have not had one hour's quiet." Previous to this action, after the chaplains had performed Divine service at the head of each regiment, he had, with his usual humanity, pointed out to the surgeons the proper posts for the care of his wounded. After the battle the French withdrew theirs from beyond Hochstadt, where they had been carried during the heat of the engagement. After this great battle, 7,500 Confederate wounded were thrown upon the hands of the medical officers, and the enemy, in their retreat, carried with them upwards of 7,000, near 1,000 of whom were wounded officers. They were obliged to burn many of their waggons in order to make use of the horses for *brancards*, in which the wounded officers were more easily conveyed. Such were the incumbrances which fell to the lot of a defeated commander before the sick and wounded were neutralized in war, and the difficulty was so great at times that important military movements could not be even attempted. As an example may be quoted the objection of the Dutch Deputies to the passage of the Ische, owing "to the difficulty of establishing hospitals or forwarding convoys of bread."

After some of these battles in the Netherlands the scenes depicted were most affecting. After Oudenard (fought almost without artillery, owing to the rapidity of the previous march), an eye-witness tells us, "With the return of day appeared a scene of the most distressing nature, which gave scope to the humanity of the British General. Among several thousand corpses lay a prodigious number of wounded of different nations, enveloped in carnage and surrounded by the wreck of war. By his orders the utmost exertion was instantly made to collect the survivors, and to bestow on all, without distinction, the care and relief which circumstances would permit." After the battle of Malplaquet, fought by troops on both sides harassed by fatigue and want of rest, and during the progress of which no quarter was given on either side, 12,706 wounded fell to the share of the surgeons of the Allies. The troops of Marlborough and Eugène numbered 129 battalions, 252 squadrons, and 101 pieces of artillery, in all 93,000 men. During the action numbers of wounded Dutch were seen returning from the hands of the surgeons to resume their stations in the ranks, so desperate was the engagement. On its termination, Marlborough was almost distracted by the numerous appeals made by officers of different nations in the Army to give orders for relieving the wounded and disposing of the sick. Many French officers and soldiers crept into the neighbouring houses and woods, wounded and in a miserable condition for want of surgical assistance. Marlborough ordered them every possible relief. Two days were taken to remove the wounded and bury the dead. The total allied loss numbered one in five of those engaged. It was the last great battle fought during the War of the Succession. Mons was so unhealthy while this eventful drama of war was being enacted, that Villars called it "the hospital of his Army."

At this time a general assault was followed by the giving of no quarter, so that garrisons frequently surrendered to avoid this, or of becoming prisoners of war. In 1709, Marlborough expressed the highest opinion of the valour and discipline of his Prussian auxiliaries, and when it was proposed to raise six new Portuguese regiments, stated that it would be a great and useless expense. "If half of this money," he writes to Godolphin, " had been employed in hiring of old troops, that might have been of use. The Portuguese are beaten too often in this war to do anything that may be vigorous;" and from one of his letters to the Duchess when in camp at Louvain, in which he says, " The kindness of the troops to me had transported me, for I had none in the last action but such as were with me last year," appeared to favour the presence of matured rather than youthful soldiers. Marlborough's campaigns are also to be remembered for two marches of historical interest. His celebrated march commencing 19th May, 1704, and ending in the crowning victory of Blenheim on the 13th August; and the march of the Prince of Hesse, rarely equalled for rapidity of execution. The first was commenced upon the breaking up of winter quarters, the troops returning in the autumn, during which they covered 1,176 miles. (Millner.) Sixteen thousand English soldiers were included among those composing the Allied Army. Marlborough moved at the first dawn, and completed his march before the heat became oppressive, and passed the remainder of the day in repose, or in preparing for the succeeding day's march. " We generally began our march," wrote one of the officers, "about three in the morning, proceeded about four or four and a-half leagues (fourteen to sixteen miles) each day, and reached our ground about nine. As we marched through the countries of our allies, commissaries were appointed to furnish us with all manner of necessaries for man and horse; these were brought to the ground before we arrived, and the soldiers had nothing to do but to pitch their tents, boil their kettles, and lie down to rest. Surely never was such a march carried on with more regularity and with less fatigue to man and horse." (Parker's Memoirs.) Sometimes he halted a day to refresh his cavalry, who were much fatigued by the constant marching. At one of the reviews of the troops the Elector was much struck with their cleanly and neat appearance. He said to Marlborough, "These gentlemen seem to be all dressed for a ball." From Mentz the General-in-Chief wrote to Godolphin, "Notwithstanding the continued marching, the men are extremely pleased with their expedition." The inhabitants were paid regularly for everything, and the troops consequently obtained an ample supply of provisions. Previous to the commencement of the march, Marlborough had directed commanding officers of regiments to make an early provision of stores and other necessaries, so that no hygienic measure contributing to its successful termination was neglected. Later on he was joined by two battalions of Prussian infantry. He writes concerning them that he was "highly gratified to observe that their recent fatigue had not affected their gallant air and healthy appearance." On the completion of the campaign, the horse marched back to Holland, and the infantry and sick sailed down the Rhine in boats to Nimeguen.

In the Prince of Hesse's march from the camp of Orchies to join Marlborough at a later period of the war, he traversed, notwithstanding violent storms and inundated roads, fifteen leagues or fifty-two and a-half English miles in fifty-six hours, only exceeded in the Peninsula by Mackenzie's brigade, which joined Wellington after the battle of Talavera, having marched, according to Napier, sixty-two English miles in twenty-six hours.

In 1711, an expedition was fitted out to proceed up the St. Lawrence. During a violent gale many of the transports were wrecked. Several officers of the Medical Staff were among those who perished on this occasion.

While these campaigns were being fought out in the Low Countries, the Medical Staff of the Army was for the occasion largely increased, but of individual officers little mention is made. In 1795, Radcliffe, one of the most celebrated physicians of his day, attended Lord Albemarle at Namur when he resided in camp for some time. He was also with William III. in the same capacity, and received for his service the large fee of £1,700, and the offer of a baronetcy, which he declined. Dr. Greenfield served in action under Lord Portland in 1705, and on arriving at the city of Grave, was appointed by the States of Holland "Physician-in-Chief" to the garrison of that castle (1705). "Every year of my life," wrote Radcliffe, "has convinced me more and more of the value of the education of the scholar and the gentleman to the physician." An opinion few will dispute.

In Spain, Lord Peterborough, with a small force of 5,000 men, landed at Barcelona, on the evacuation of which the French commander, the Marquis de Tessé, left behind his sick and wounded, committing them to the "humanity of the English General." Dr. Friend, who afterwards published an account of the expedition, and served with the Army during the years 1707 and 1708, was one of the principal physicians. Upon the departure of Lord Peterborough for England, the command devolved on the Earl of Galway, who, being joined by a party of Portuguese, encountered the Army of Philip at Almanza. The allied forces having marched many miles along the rugged district of Murcia under a hot sun, arrived, fatigued with toil and faint from excessive heat, in presence of their more numerous opponents about noon on the 25th April, and were unfortunately defeated. In this battle eighty-seven British officers were killed and 284 wounded; ninety-two were made prisoners. Three regimental staff officers were killed and nine wounded, including among them several medical officers. Those who survived were made prisoners of war. The Medical Staff also shared in the abortive attempt on Toulon, when the sick and wounded were embarked on board the fleet to facilitate the retreat of the Army; and in the rapid march to Scotland in anticipation of the landing of a French force in the interest of the Pretender. The French, who started from Dunkirk on this occasion, and returned from the coast of Scotland without landing, lost upwards of 4,000 men within a month from hardship and sickness alone. During several of these forced marches the British regiments lost many men from fatigue.

While these events were being enacted on the Continent, the Medical Staff of the Army in Ireland was reduced to small dimensions. In 1708, there was in that kingdom only six battalions of infantry, three regiments of cavalry, and three regiments of dragoons in charge of the physician and chirurgeon-general and twenty-four regimental medical officers (twelve surgeons and twelve surgeons' mates), the greater part of whom were disbanded in 1715 on motives of economy. The Queen died August 1st, 1714, a year after the Treaty of Utrecht. During her reign of thirteen years, nine regimental surgeons and their assistants were added to the permanent establishment of the infantry, and the former gazetted to the 28th and 39th Regiments inclusive. In the commencement of her reign, private soldiers were first styled "centinels," and a regiment usually embarked for foreign service with its chaplain, one officer who combined the office of adjutant and quartermaster, a surgeon and surgeon's mate, which last designation had replaced at this period the older one of "chirurgeon."

The peaceful reign of George I., 1714—1727, was only broken by the Jacobite rising of 1715; the surgeons and surgeons' mates of the 40th and 41st Regiments were alone added to the permanent establishment of the Army.

One of the earliest measures of his successor was the concession to our *confrères* of the Royal Navy of the privilege of half-pay when not employed afloat. By an Order in Council, dated 20th March, 1729, an allowance of half-pay was granted to the first forty surgeons on the list; one moiety at 2s. 6d., the others at 2s., on the condition of their being ready at all times to go afloat. Twenty years later ten more surgeons were brought within the half-pay list, increased in 1779 to 125. When the revolutionary war broke out, in order to give further encouragement to surgeons to enter the Navy, the scale of pay was raised to 4s. per diem each for the first twenty-five and 3s. 6d. for the next hundred surgeons. The pay given to subordinate officers of the Army and Navy was miserable in the extreme, resulting in practices to supplement it, so graphically pictured in the works of contemporary writers, which officers of the present day would blush to own to.

About 1760, surgeons in all rates of sloops-of-war only received £5 a month, together with the old pecuniary mulcts or regards in the shape of a stoppage of 2d. a month for each man of the complement. The first mate received £2 10s., the second £2., the third, fourth and fifth only £1 10s. a month each.

Whilst our own Army was reduced to its lowest peace establishment, recruiting for foreign services was carried on so extensively after the accession of George I. (especially in Ireland), that the utmost rigour failed to suppress it. In Ireland, many of the recruits were driven to enlist by the distress to which the Irish population was reduced. Some went to Spain, others to France. A curious ballad of the day (1721) gives in doggerel verse their reasons for doing so :—

"Nor never came it in our mind;
To seek for work we were inclined,
Because that we could get none here,
We fain would travel far and near."

In 1726, Archbishop Boulton, writing to the Lords Justices, laments the loss of such "lusty young fellows." In that year only eleven battalions of foot were serving in Ireland. "It is a curious fact, that the Irish carried from their native shores almost all their good qualities, and left behind them almost all their bad ones. With national facility they adapted themselves to the regular discipline of their new masters without losing any of their ancient impulsiveness. They became orderly and obedient in camp, cool and collected in the face of the enemy, and still unrivalled for a headlong charge at the most desperate odds. Several victories of the French were rendered more brilliant by their courage and spirit, and several defeats were rendered less disastrous by the same cause."

From calculations and researches made at the French War

Office by the Abbé Geoghehan, it was ascertained that from the arrival of the Irish troops in France in 1691 up to 1745, the year of the battle of Fontenoy, more than 450,000 Irishmen died in the service of that country. The " Gendarmerie Ecossais " were not less distinguished. The old Scottish corps in the King's service most nobly and rigidly transmitted to their aged parents in their far-distant homes the savings of their poor pay and prize-money gained by their blood in the Havannah and American wars. " Many poor fellows almost starved themselves for this purpose." An equally honourable trait is mentioned of the Irish soldier at the siege of Savannah, when Count d'Estaing madly proposed to take the fortress by a *coup de main*. Count Dillon proposed a reward of one hundred guineas to the first grenadier who would plant a fascine in the fosse, which was swept by the whole fire of the garrison. His purse was proferred in vain, not a soldier would advance. Dillon upbraided them with their cowardice, when the sergeant-major said, " Monsieur, had you not held out a sum of money as an incentive, your grenadiers would one and all have rushed to the assault." Count Dillon, " returning his purse to his pocket, cried ' Forward !' Out of 194 who composed the company, 104 left their bodies in the breach." The study of such traits as these is of the first importance to commanders of armies.

In the fourth year of this reign (1718), His Majesty's land forces consisted of the following :—one captain-general (Duke of Marlborough), four generals, twelve lieutenant-generals, twelve major-generals, twenty-nine brigadier-generals ; four troops of Horse Guards, two troops of Grenadier Guards, one regiment of Horse Guards, seven regiments of Horse, twenty regiments of Dragoons, three regiments of Foot Guards, forty-six regiments of foot. (Chamberlayne.)

These regiments were seldom moved from place to place. To this force was attached eighty-three surgeons and seventy-seven surgeons' mates. The total Medical Staff of the Army at this date not exceeding 170 officers.

In the commencement of the reign (1716) had been established at Woolwich the nucleus of the future Royal Regiment of Artillery in the shape of two companies of gunners.

In 1718, " The officers of His Majesty's Ordnance consisted of a master-general, a lieutenant-general, one master-gunner of Great Britain to exercise scholars to shoot in great ordnance, three master-gunners' mates, and sixty gunners ; one chief bombardier, twelve bombardiers ; one chief petardier, four petardiers ; one comptroller of the fireworks, one chief fire-worker, three fire-workers, one yeoman of the tents and toyles, one wagon-master, two proof-masters, one purveyor of hoys and vessels, two captains of the train of artillery, salary £60 each ; two lieutenants, salary £50 each ; two other lieutenants, salary £40 each. In 1727, the strength of the corps was raised to five companies, under a colonel and lieutenant-colonel, when a surgeon and surgeon's mate were for the first time attached to the Ordnance Department, under which latter denomination were included, in 1718, "three engineers, two engineers to travel in foreign parts to perfect themselves in the art of fortification." (Chamberlayne.)

Previous to the formation of this small regiment of Artillery, Thomas Binning, in a small work entitled "Light to the Art of Gunnery," published in 1689, laid down the following qualifications for a good gunner—interesting as a memento of the seventeenth century.

" 1st. That he feareth God more than his enemy.
" 2nd. That he be educated and expert in his profession.
" 3rd. That he be constant, and not given to change.
" 4th. That he be faithful, true, and honest."

During the reign of George II., the 42nd to the 70th Regiments were added to the permanent establishment of the Army, and fifteen second battalions, necessitating a corresponding increase in the medical staff. The regimental staff was then arranged in the following order, viz., chaplain, surgeon, adjutant, quartermaster.

In 1737 war broke out between England and Spain resulting in the capture of Portobello by Admiral Vernon. Four regiments of marines were raised at New York three years afterwards for service in the American seas, because as natives of the climate, they were supposed better calculated for the service for which they were destined than Europeans. They wore camlet coats, brown linen waistcoats, and canvass trousers, and in the following year (1741) a body of 1,000 negroes was enlisted at Jamaica for the attack on Cuba, with a view to sustain the peculiar duties of fatigue, naturally expected to arise on this service. The troops composing the expedition were landed, but nothing being attempted towards affecting a conquest; sickness, the never failing result of inactivity in those climes, began its ravages, and led to the evacuation of the island. Out of 2,654 officers and men 566 were on the sick list. In the same year occurred the attack on Carthagena, but the time for active operations faded away, the soldiers passed their nights in the open air for want of tents and tools; their health was seriously impaired, and they rapidly decreased in numbers from the effects of hard duties and climate. After the failure of the attack on the castle, violent periodical rains commenced, deluging the country with water and drenching the men with rain. After they returned on board the fleet, numbers died of local distempers. During these two abortive attempts the duties performed by the medical staff were of the most arduous description, and numbers succumbed to the effect of climate and disease. At this period the West Indies was considered "a charnal house for Europeans."

Dr. Dalrymple, who was one of the physicians to the Army at Carthagena, is stated to have rescued many of the most desperate cases of remittent fever, by wrapping the patients in blankets wetted with warm decoctions, which threw them into a profuse perspiration, and so carried off the disease, thus anticipating a mode of treatment, advocated as something modern in the nineteenth century.

About this time the peace of the continent was disturbed by a contest for the Imperial throne between the rival claimants, Maria Theresa and the Elector of Bavaria. Engaging on the side of the former, an army of 16,000 men was sent to the Low Countries under Lord Stair, increased shortly afterwards by an equal number of Hanoverians. This army was encamped at Hoetch, on the River Maine, and on June 9, 1743, was joined by the King and his son, the Duke of Cumberland. Opposed to them was a French force of 60,000 men under the Duke de Noailles. The King was attended by John Ranby, his prime sergeant-surgeon, the last occasion on which the knight-surgeon of the Sovereign was present with the troops in action. In the previous year Sir John Pringle was physician to the Military Hospital in Flanders, and was shortly afterwards appointed "physician-general to the British Forces beyond the seas." Dr. Francis Home, afterwards Professor of Materia Medica in the University of Edinburgh, served also during this and subsequent campaigns in Flanders. All of them have left most interesting records of their observations during this war.

On his return to England Ranby published his work on gunshot wounds, containing the result of his observations while he had the honour of attending the King to the wars in Germany. "This work," he writes, "was penned in a camp, and was intended to recommend plentiful bleeding very early, in the treatment of gun-shot wounds; to advise likewise the application of light easy dressings to them, and particularly to introduce the signal use of the bark." Some ten years previously (1732) Zamorier contended that there were few wounds which could not be healed by the application of common water, more promptly and satisfactorily than by any other means. Ranby confirmed the practice advocated by Wiseman during the Civil Wars, of immediate or primary amputations when such operations became necessary in the field. To quote the words of Wiseman, "In the heat of fight, whether it be at sea or land, the chirurgeon ought to consider at the first dressing what possibility there is of preserving the wounded member; and accordingly if there is no hopes of saving it, to make his amputation at that instant whilst the patient is free from fever, &c." So late as 1762, Bilquer, surgeon-general of the Prussian Army, would not suffer amputations to be performed, trusting to the weary processes of nature unassisted to complete a cure, forgetting the maxim of the celebrated French military surgeon Le Dran, "That when amputation is necessary in a case of gun-shot wound, it should be done as soon as possible after the injury, or the state of the patient would permit."

Previous to the battle and victory of Dettingen, the army had been much in want of provisions, the soldiers having been for some time on half rations. These circumstances added much to the suffering of the wounded, and anxiety of the medical staff. Sir John Pringle's works contain the most interesting account of this campaign. During the progress of hostilities, the medical arrangements were chiefly regimental, supplemented by the addition of temporary general hospitals, one of which was established at Ghent. As was the custom, the sick in garrison were committed to the care of their respective regimental medical officers. A battalion completed to its full complement then consisted of 813 officers, non-commissioned officers and men. The only document required from the surgeon was a weekly return of sick to the commanding officer. This included all accidents unfitting a soldier for the performance of his duty. With some few exceptions, the highest return of sick did not exceed seventy for a battalion, forty for a regiment of dragoons, excluding epidemics. The surgeons attached to the corps appear to have had little experience in the cure of diseases incidental to a moist and malarious climate. This was given by Pringle as the reason why fevers were less successfully treated at first in the corps hospitals than was afterwards the case. The General Hospital at Ghent contained about 600 of the sick and wounded collected from the surrounding garrisons. Other hospitals were opened subsequently, one at Feikenheim, after the battle of Dettingen, which received no less than 1,500 sick, besides the wounded after the battle, the greater part ill of dysentery, arising from exposure immediately after the action. We are told that in a short time the air of this establishment became so vitiated that the disease spread to the other patients, apothecaries, nurses and attendants, as well as to most of the inhabitants of the village—those who were unavoidably detained in the camp hospitals, alone escaping. The system then in practice during the war was to treat the milder cases in the regimental or field-hospitals, sending the more seriously sick, and the greater part of the wounded to the general hospitals in the rear. The regimental surgeons received an allowance of medicines and all other necessaries at the public expense. In each of the garrisons was a physician, to whom the surgeons were directed to apply occasionally for assistance. Immediately after a battle a general hospital was opened for the reception of the wounded, as at Ath, after Fontenoy, when some 600 wounded were received. On the outbreak of hostilities, a convention was entered into between the Earl of Stair, commanding the Anglo-Hanoverian forces in the Netherlands, and the humane Duke de Noailles, to alleviate the suffering of the sick and wounded, arising from the necessity of their being constantly shifted for greater security. In this convention it was agreed that the hospitals on both sides should be considered "sanctuaries for the sick," and be mutually protected; which agreement was strictly observed on both sides during the campaign of 1743. When the troops returned to England, in the rapid advance on Carlisle in pursuit of Prince Charles-Edward, the sick who fell ill *en route*, were left in the towns on the road to the care of the civil surgeons and apothecaries, by whom, Sir John Pringle states, they were well-treated. At the time the regimental surgeons had orders to provide quarters for their men as they were taken ill, with liberty to send to the general hospital such a proportion of the worst cases as might be necessary to lessen their labour, and at the same time avoid crowding the houses used as temporary hospitals. By this dispersion of the sick, and the preservation of pure air in the wards, it was hoped that contagion might be isolated, if not altogether prevented. Cleanliness was also strictly enforced.

The number of physicians appointed to the general hospitals in Flanders appears at this time to have been altogether too few; one occasionally having the nominal treatment of no less than 700 cases at a time. In consequence of such inadequate medical assistance, their practice was so little successful that at the most moderate computation, one in ten of their patients died. The hospitals, formed during the campaigns in the Low Countries, 1743-48, were of two kinds, viz.: the flying hospital attending the camps at some convenient distance in the rear, and the stationary hospitals fixed in one place, generally the large towns. Owing to the fact that the convalescents were scarcely ever (after having suffered from a severe disease) able to return to their duty during the same campaign, it was arranged that they should be employed in the several garrisons, in preference to service in the field.

The causes which influence the health of armies are admirably pictured by Sir John Pringle. In these wars, intermittent and remittent fevers were of common occurrence amongst the troops, and justly attributed to a residence in a flat marshy country; winds blowing over the oozy beaches of the western Scheldt; inundation of the land leading to putrid and insalutary vapours during the autumn and summer; evaporation of ground water near to but not appearing on the surface; stagnation of the air and consequent imperfect ventilation in low-lying situations; over plantation; impurity of the water in common use. The intensity of the diseases lessening in proportion to the coolness of the season, and the height and dryness of the grounds. Dysentery and scurvy were also common diseases, both attributed to similar causes, aggravated by the use of salted meats. It was remarked that the higher classes of the people who lived in "dry houses, apartments raised above the ground, and moderate exercise without labour in the sun, or in the evening damps, took a just quantity of fermented liquors, and victuals of good nourishment," proved to be " least liable to diseases of the marshes."

In the beginning of June, 1742, the British troops had begun to embark for Flanders, in all about 16,000 horse and foot. The head-quarters were at Ghent. The officers continued healthy, but in the summer and autumn many of the privates sickened, especially those who were quartered in the lower part of the town, mostly on the ground-floor of damp, empty houses, so damp that they could scarcely keep their shoes and belts from moulding. In July one battalion of the Guards had 140 sick in hospital, only two of the patients coming from the companies quartered in a higher and dry situation on the hill. On the mere change to higher and better quarters the sickness suddenly abated—a remarkable instance of the mal-effects of a defective site. It was remarked that wherever the barracks were damp, without drains, and in low situations, even on high ground, as at Oudenard, the highest division of Flanders, the men unusually suffered in proportion, and many of the remittents degenerated into fatal continued fevers or dysenteries; with the frosts of November malarial affections were replaced by bronchial disorders and rheumatism, intermittents ceased appearing, unless upon catching a chill or as relapses in such as had been ill during the autumn. Owing to the want of an adequate inspection previous to embarkation, a few cases of undetected psora communicated the disease to several of the men. In the course of the campaign, typhus, the never failing accompaniment of foul air, overcrowding and defective diet appeared in the hospitals.

The first flying-hospital was opened at Nied, a village in the neighbourhood of the camp at Hoechst, on the banks of the Main, which the troops reached in the beginning of May, having broken up their winter quarters in the commencement of February, 1743; all the sick and weak, to the number of 600, being collected from all the garrisons, and transferred to the general hospital at Ghent. In three weeks this flying-hospital received about 250 sick. When the number was 220, the diseases were classed as follows:—

Pleurisies and pneumonias	71
Rheumatic pains with fever	51
Inflammatory fevers	25
Intermittents	30
Hard coughs with fever	9
Old coughs and consumption	7
Fluxes and other affections	27
Total	220

Such were the diseases of the camps on the outbreak of the war for the imperial throne, which, according to the Physician-General of the English Forces, " with little variation was the first state of the camp diseases."

On the 22nd of June the enemy marched to Aschaffenburg, where 500 sick were left, so that in five weeks the proportion of sick to the whole was about 1 in 29 ; sickness usually decreasing by the motion of the troops and evacuation of the weakest to hospital. On the 27th was fought the battle of Dettingen, on the night following which the men lay on the field of battle without tents, exposed to a heavy rain. In the space of eight days about 500 were seized with dysentery, and in a few weeks nearly half the men were either ill or had recovered from it. On the 25th of October the troops began to return to the Netherlands, leaving about 3,000 sick in Germany, suffering chiefly from typhus and dysentery. The proportion of men left in the hospitals at the end of the campaign, to those who came safe into garrison, was about three to twelve (Pringle). Several of those who returned in apparent health to Flanders, were during the winter, while in good quarters, attacked with remittent fever, the seeds of which had been sown during active military operations. The necessity for warm and dry barracks, with a sufficient allowance of fuel in winter quarters, was much insisted upon (Sir John Pringle).

On the breaking up of the hospitals at Tournay, Ghent and Brussels in 1744, about 1,500 sick were evacuated, the seventeenth part of all that took the field in that year. Not more than 300 died in hospital. The mildness of the season, the dry encampment, the frequent exercise given to the troops by foraging parties, and the early retreat into winter quarters, all concurred to preserve the health of the army. After the battle of Fontenoy, fought on the 11th of May, 1745, 600 wounded were received into the hospital at Ath, the rest, to the amount of 1,200, being carried off by the French. When the campaign ended, there were in hospital at Antwerp, Brussels, and Mons only 1,000 sick, a small number considering that there had been in Flanders, besides the cavalry, twenty-nine battalions, some of which had never been in the field before. From the beginning to the end of the campaign, exclusive of those who were killed in battle, or died of their wounds, the deaths did not exceed 200.

Sir John Pringle accompanied the Royal Army on the march to Scotland, in 1745, when he alludes to the advantages to the soldiers of a present of flannel under-waistcoats made by the Quakers. Typhus fever was imported into this force from the continent, intensified by overcrowding ; it became so contagious that most of the nurses and medical attendants in the hospitals were seized with it. This necessitated the leaving behind of a considerable number of sick with the effect of reducing much of the effective fighting strength of the battalions. The continual remitting fever " dignified with many symptoms of cold" could also be traced in the troops that came over from Flanders till the frosts of December put an end to it. After the battle of Culloden two malt-barns at Inverness received the wounded; in all 270. Several had cuts of the broad-sword " till then," writes Sir John Pringle, "uncommon wounds in our hospitals." They were, however, easily healed, "as the openings were large in proportion to the depth." From the middle of February, when the Army crossed the Forth, to the end of the campaign, there had been in hospital upwards of 3,000 men, including the wounded, of which number about 300 died chiefly from typhus.

At the end of the campaign in Flanders, in 1747, above 4,000 remained in the hospitals, exclusive of the wounded, somewhat more than a fifth-part of the whole number. In 1748 Sir John Pringle returned to the Continent, and went through the campaign of that year. One regiment of the Greys, cantoned at Veicht, a village surrounded with marshy meadow, after remaining five weeks in this situation returned 150 sick, after two months' increased to 260, above half the regiment; and at the end of the campaign they had in all but thirty men who had never been ill. Throughout all the cantonments, the officers who had good beds, dry rooms, and a better diet, were remarkably less sickly than the common soldiers.

In the middle of November peace was concluded, the troops were removed to England, and a large number of the sick were received into the general hospital opened at Ipswich, to the number of 400, chiefly suffering from contagious typhus. A great number of these cases were brought over in the "*hospital-ships*" already in use for the reception of the sick. " At first the mortality was considerable; but by the largeness of the wards, and by billeting in the town as soon as each convalescent recovered (thereby removing him from new contagion, and gaining more room for those who were still sick) the air was daily purified, and the distemper abated sooner than could have been expected. The hospital then broke up, after it had continued about three months' in England." Sir John Pringle insisted upon two rules, the wisdom of which is now generally acknowledged, viz., that the more fresh air there was let into hospitals the less danger there would be of breeding distempers, and that the corps hospitals should be scattered, and the sick dispersed as much as possible; hence his orders to the medical officers not to send the sick in such numbers to the general hospitals as would vitiate the air, but to treat the slighter cases in camp, and the remainder in field-hospitals, directions peculiarly applicable to the slow and tiresome mode of warfare then in vogue. After his return to England, Sir John Pringle continued to superintend the medical concerns of the Army for some years, after which he retired from the Service with the honour of a baronetcy, and the appointment of Physician in ordinary to the King. His " Observations on the Diseases of the

Army" went through several editions, and may be read with interest and profit even at this distant date, as being the result of actual observation and service with soldiers. He was almost the first of the military physicians who had attempted to systematise the hygiene and diseases of military life.

The general peace signed at Aix-la-Chapelle, October 7, 1748, ended for a time the active military career of a large number of medical officers, who carried into civil life the great and varied experience and knowledge of their profession gained in foreign wars.

CHAPTER VI.

In 1716 Sir Hans Sloane was created First Medical Baronet by George I., and appointed Physician-General to the Forces. He had served in Jamaica on the staff of the Duke of Buckingham, and in 1719 became President of the College of Physicians and Physician to the King. He succeeded Sir Isaac Newton as President of the Royal Society. In 1747 a warrant of George II. created him Apothecary-General, "perpetual furnisher, with remainder to his heirs, of all the medicines necessary for the general services of the land forces of Great Britain." A few years before George Cleghorn, surgeon of Brigadier-General Offarrell's regiment, had written on the diseases of Minorca, dedicating his work to "The Society of Surgeons of his Majesty's Navy." In Flanders, in 1748, Middleton, Surgeon to the Forces, had introduced the system of properly-equipped hospitals, when the patients were provided with separate beds, clean linen, and trained nurses, under the supervision of clerks and hospital storekeepers, one of the greatest improvements of the day. Barracks were only erected for the first time in England in 1739, but were low and ill-ventilated buildings, generating disease and sweeping off men like a perpetual pestilence (Brocklesby). In the Impress Act of 1745, rupture was first officially assigned as a disqualifying disability, at which date no medical opinion was apparently required as to the qualification of recruits.

A goat-skin bag, or knapsack, for carrying surplus clothing, was now supplied to the soldier, who was armed with a musket, bayonet, and sword, which latter weapon ceased to be carried in the reign of George II., when light companies were first added to regiments of the line — very material improvements in the direction of lightening the weights, while at the same time rendering more effective the weapons of the soldier. Shortly afterwards (1751) the standards, colours, and clothing of the army were, for the first, regulated, without altering the uniforms worn by medical officers, which was that of the corps to which they belonged.

The Medical officers of the 39th Foot (which proceeded from Ireland to the East Indies in 1754) were the first surgeons of the British Medical staff who saw service in Bengal. They were early engaged at the battle of Plassey, fought in 1757. While marching to meet the enemy, the troops underwent incessant hardships, owing to the continued rains, which compelled them to occupy the houses of the native towns and villages through which they passed during that brilliant campaign, which ended by adding to the British Empire a magnificent province.

In 1755 war broke out again between France and Great Britain, eventually involving the whole of Europe, and enduring for seven years. The English army was immediately raised from twenty to thirty-five thousand men, involving a corresponding addition to its medical staff. Immediately upon the outbreak of hostilities a Bill passed through Parliament for the more easy recruitment of His Majesty's forces, very similar to the Act of 1745, which ordained that "none but able-bodied men, free from rupture and every other distemper and impunity that may render them unfit for duty, not under seventeen or above forty, of a minimum height of five feet four inches, should be attested, the final approval resting with the field-officer of the regiment to which assigned." They were entitled to their discharge after three years' service.

In the commencement of 1756, the Duke of Cumberland, then Commander-in-Chief, directed Viscount Barrington, the Secretary of War, to establish an Hospital Board for the medical service of the army then intended to take the field. The Board was to consist of the physicians belonging to the hospitals, the Surgeon-General, and the principal surgeon and purveyor to the hospitals, who were conjointly to digest certain rules for the regulation of all hospital matters. This Board agreed that the physicians were to examine, and at all times to superintend and control, a sufficient number of hospital mates, the surgeons nominating the surgical mates. After some time a special commission was issued, as "Inspector of the Regimental Infirmaries," to the principal hospital surgeon, who in effect did the greater part of the business of the Hospital Board—collecting, admitting, and nominating all surgeons, also mates, medical as well as surgical. In this way the Hospital Board fell into disuse, commissions being granted to such surgeons as had interest enough to obtain them.

In 1758 Oliver Goldsmith, who had obtained from the East India Company a nomination to one of their factories on the Coast of Coromandel as surgeon's mate, probably fortunately for his fame as an author, failed in the examination at the College of Surgeons, as evidenced by the following extract from the Register: "At a Court of Examiners, held at the Theatre, 21st December, 1758—James Barwood, mate to an hospital—Oliver Goldsmith found not qualified for ditto." This most interesting note shows, in addition, that the hospital mates of the Company underwent a preliminary surgical examination before being admitted to the Service.

The attempt to raise men by ballot (substitutes being allowed) for the prosecution of the war was not very successful. Of 32,100 of the fixed number, only 17,436 appeared; on the second occasion, in 1760, only 24,093, nearly all substitutes. In Ireland, on the outbreak of the general war in 1756, the following officers are shown as serving on the staff of the army in that kingdom:—

Commander-in-Chief. . . .	General Viscount Molesworth.
Aide-de-Camp	Captain Christophilus Usher.
Lieut.-General and Governor of Duncairn	Earl of Rothes.
Aide-de-Camp.	Hon. Major W. Leslie.
Lieutenant-Generals	Sir J. Cope, Governor of Limerick.
,, ...	Henry Hawley.
,, ...	Lord Tyrawley.
,, ...	James St. Clair.
,, ...	Philip Bragg.
,, ...	Thomas Bligh.
Major-General.	J. Folliat, Governor of Ross Castle.
Quartermaster-General . . .	Colonel George Lord Forbes.
Deputy Quartermaster-General	Lieut.-Colonel Charles Burknall.
Adjutant-General.	Captain Robert Cunningham.
Physician-General.	Edward Barry, M.D.
Surgeon-General	John Nicholls.
Judge Advocate-General . .	Walter Hora.
Provost-Marshal	James Butler.

There were serving with the forces—twenty-one surgeons and the same number of surgeons' mates, attached to ten regiments of cavalry and eleven regiments of infantry, viz., 1st, 2nd, 3rd, and 4th Horse, 5th, 8th, 9th, 12th, 13th, and 14th Regiments of Dragoons, 1st, 2nd, 10th, 16th, 17th, 22nd, 27th, 28th, 29th, 43rd, and 46th Regiments of Foot, and the "Artillery Company of Ireland," consisting of five officers, three sergeants, three corporals, six bombardiers, two drummers, and 28 gunners. There were no Engineers in this command. In this year, the pay and subsistence of the Regiments of Foot were as below:—

Rank.	Daily Pay.		Subsistence.		Total Yearly.		
	s.	d.	s.	d.	£	s.	d.
Colonel and Captain . .	18	0	6	0	438	0	0
Lieut.-Colonel and Captain	13	0	4	0	310	5	0
Major and Captain . . .	11	6	3	6	273	15	0
Captain	7	6	2	6	182	10	0
Lieutenant	3	6	1	2	85	3	4
Ensign	3	0	0	8	66	18	4
Chaplain	5	0	1	8	121	13	4
Adjutant	3	0	1	0	73	0	0
Quartermaster	3	6	1	2	85	3	4
Surgeon	3	0	1	0	73	0	0
Surgeon's Mate	2	0	0	6	45	12	6
Sergeant	1	6	0	0	27	7	6
Corporal	0	8	0	4	18	5	0
Drummer	0	8	0	4	18	5	0
Private Man.	0	6	0	2	12	13	4

From these rates of pay were made deductions for poundage, the hospital agency, warrants, and arrears. The contingent account granted for the hospital expenses of each regiment annually was then limited to £30, but was amply covered by the stoppage of one day's pay from each officer, non-commissioned officer, and soldier in a regiment of infantry of 850 of all ranks, realising a sum of at least £60.

The Highlanders at this time were selected to proceed from North America to the West Indies, as their sobriety, abstemious habits, great activity and capability of bearing the vicissitudes of climate, was thought to render them well qualified for the service contemplated. In the expeditions against the Indians in 1765, they were conspicuous for their ability to undergo the extremes of heat and cold, with great toil and privation, after marching many miles through tracks in the wood, snow deep, without leaving a man behind. Only three men died of disease in this service in the summer and autumn of 1764, and only nineteen men were under the care of the regimental surgeon.

One of the earliest operations of the war was the attack on Minorca by the French. During its heroic defence many of the sick and wounded came out of hospital to assist in repelling the invaders at the last general assault of the citadel.

Canada was finally subdued in 1759. During the several actions round Quebec, it is on record that more than one medical officer fell a victim to the bullets of the enemy.

During these various affairs on both continents the medical staff of the army were actively engaged in succouring the wounded and ministering to the wants of the sick. They were represented at the battle of Minden, fought in 1759, and in the important actions, which wrested from Spain the Havannah and the Philippine Islands, and continued on active service until the Peace of Paris (concluded on the 10th February, 1763) put an end to the war for the moment. Garrison surgeons were immediately afterwards appointed to the new acquisitions of Minorca, Granada, St. Vincent, Dominica, Tobago, and the Senegal. Shortly before the close of military operations (1761), His Majesty's forces by sea and land consisted of the following, to which a large number of military surgeons were attached :—

	Strength of all ranks.
4 Troops of Horse and Horse Grenadier Guards	715
5 Regiments of Horse	1,556
3 Regiments of Dragoon Guards	1,540
21 Regiments of Dragoons	9,764
3 Regiments of Foot Guards	6,645
103 Regiments of Foot	110,218
1 Regiment of Artillery	3,103
1 Regiment of Irish Militia	456

	Strength of all ranks.
33 Regiments of Militia	22,972
Engineers	60
136 Companies of Marines	18,355
33 Companies of Independent Foot	3,734
23 Companies of Invalids	1,219
7 Royal Dock Regiments	5,000
Sailors	51,645
Hanoverians and Hessians	57,762
Militia and Independent Companies in North America	20,000
Total	322,754

(Captain Lloyd.)

The recruiting of this large force was attended with considerable difficulty. Concerning this, Colonel Dalrymple writes, in 1760:—" There are two ways of recruiting the British army, the first and most eligible by volunteers, the last and worst by press. By the first method numbers of good men are enrolled, but the army is greatly obliged to levity, accident, and the dexterity of recruiting-sergeants for them; by the second plan, the country gets rid of its banditti, and the ranks are filled up with the scum of every country—the refuse of mankind." So notorious had this evil become on the continent, that the Duc de Choiseul was obliged in 1764 to place under proper regulations the recruiting parties or crimps of the captains of companies in the French service. With a view of obtaining good recruits, Colonel Dalrymple proposed that an Act of Parliament should empower the lord-lieutenants of counties to raise the requisite number by ballot, and send them to the corps which bore the name of the county, limiting the period of service to five years for a foot soldier and seven years for a dragoon or trooper, thus anticipating to some extent the scheme for the localisation of regiments and the short service system of our day.

A war of such magnitude as that which had been concluded by the Peace of Paris could not have passed away without bringing to the front some of those able men and patient workers who have so often adorned the ranks of the medical staff of the British army. Brocklesby and Donald Munro were worthy successors of their predecessors in the medical service. One of the first results of the war was an advance in the wholly inadequate rate of pay of the regimental mate, which the love of adventure had drawn into the service. Brocklesby considered that the pay of the surgeon should be at least £250 per annum in time of peace. This was in the middle of the last century, when the purchasing price of money was infinitely greater than at the present time. According to him a regimental surgency was then, as were all other commissions, obtained by purchase, the usual price being £500, sometimes exceeded. He thought that the service should be recruited from " young gentlemen duly qualified, of a good education and liberal turn of mind, with £700 in their pocket to purchase their commission," by the adoption of which suggestion he was of opinion that many soldiers' lives would be saved, the practice being, in many instances, " for some great man to recommend some raw youth just emancipated from half of his apprenticeship," with a result not difficult to anticipate. Writing upon the relative prevalence of medical and surgical affections in a battalion, he relates the case of a regiment in the late war, which had been in two campaigns upon very hard service, and had sustained the severest shocks and losses of the tedious siege of Havannah, yet in seven years the surgeons had never met with more than 100 properly surgical cases in the regiment, though during that time 2,000 men had gone through the regimental books, including about 400 draughted out of it into different corps. On this account, he recommended that the examination of candidates for appointments should be transferred from the " Surgeon's Hall " to one of the censors of the College of Physicians, conjointly with a physician who knew the proper characteristics requisite in aspirants for the posts.

At this period, before a regiment came to its camping-ground, it was the custom to send the surgeons a day or two in advance, to obtain a good and convenient house for the sick. Sometimes this was so far distant, that great irregularities and much inconvenience resulted. Many of the hired buildings were wretched habitations. " Small houses, with low ceilings, no fire-places or ventilation, with damp walls, half-rotten boarded floors, which places were stuffed with from forty to eighty poor sick soldiers, all lying heel to head, so closely compressed together within them in stinking clothes, foul linen, &c., that it was enough to suffocate the patients, as well as others who were obliged to support them, the consequences being that· many simple diseases degenerated into spotted typhus from the bad infected air." Malignant sore throat was also in this way originated. What a contrast to the well-arranged and well-ordered military hospitals of the present day!

In 1758 a large number of sick, landed from the transports in the Isle of Wight, were placed in temporary deal sheds in the open streets, being thatched with straw, each capable of holding 120 patients. Notwithstanding the great cold and moisture to which the sick were exposed in these roughly got-up habitations, remarkably few died of the same disease, though treated with the same medicines and regimen than anywhere else. The convalescents recovered much sooner than in the warm huts and houses hired round Newport; the superiority of the temporary sheds being due to the ample current of pure air which circulated through them. In 1760 Brocklesby treated several sick of the 30th Regiment suffering from putrid or typhus fever, in wattle huts, with thatched roofs, on an elevated site, these huts being protected on the weather side by straw. Each hut had a brick chimney and fire-place, and accommodated forty sick. Only one or two of the admissions died, the pure, bracing air favouring their recovery. As additional precautions, the floors and walls were frequently scraped and cleaned. A similar plan was adopted at the camp at Winchester in 1761, when the daily returns of the Gloucester Militia only amounted to nearly one hundred sick. These hospital huts were completed and furnished at a small expense. Again in 1762 the sick were parcelled out into small field-hospitals, constructed upon a similar plan, with the best results. We see here anticipated in the English services the modern hut hospitals which are so generally adopted in modern wars, and so much in favour on the continent. At this time ten guineas or more were given for a militia recruit to replace those who died, many from preventible disease, hence the enormous saving to the country of the measures advocated by this able physician, who, in addition, recommended that in all expeditions a ship or two laden with lumber and boards should invariably attend the fleet, with a view to the formation of hut-camp-hospitals on shore. How many lives would have been saved had these simple but admirable suggestions been adopted in subsequent years, Brocklesby alludes *inter alia* to the losses sustained by the troops by ill-timed removals, and by the injudicious harassing of soldiers, sick in fever, from one hospital to another, sometimes distant 100 to 150 miles, the only means of transport being cumbrous open waggons, or open boats, too often without any requisite provision made for transporting them at all. One-third of those so removed perished.

The following regulations, highly commended by Brocklesby, were proposed and carried out by Mr. Robert Gordon, a military surgeon stationed at Winchester Camp in 1762, under the heading "Regulations for Hospital Management":—

1. A sergeant will be appointed to the hospital to preserve good order and regularity among the sick. He will provide all necessaries ordered by the surgeon, keep an account of the same open to the inspection of every officer, to see that nothing is brought out the hospital except by his order, especially strong liquor. Every night at tattoo he is to call a roll of the sick, lock the door, and be answerable that none stir out, but go to bed immediately.

2. The pay-sergeant of each company to pay into the hands of the hospital-sergeant every day the subsistence of his men, with all proper necessaries ordered by the surgeon. This account to be settled by the hospital-sergeant with the surgeon every week, and by the surgeon with the paymaster every month.

3. Two orderly men to be appointed by the surgeon, to assist in taking care of the sick at hospital, who are to take their orders from the surgeon or the sergeant of the hospital, which they are punctually to obey.

4. No man, on any pretence of illness, to be excused parade or any other duty, unless reported to the surgeon, and when reported the sergeant or corporal of his company is immediately to send him to hospital when taken ill; if unable to walk, he is to be carried.

5. After this order, every man found sick in his quarters, unless by leave of the surgeon, will be severely punished; any sergeant or corporal found remiss in sending men to hospital immediately, when taken ill, will be assigned or brought to court-martial, and degraded, for neglect.

6. Every man ordered to hospital to take with him his knapsack and necessaries, and deliver them to the hospital-sergeant, who is to take them in charge, and deliver them to the man when he recovers.

7. If any man in hospital is guilty of irregularity, or refuses to comply with orders of the hospital-physician or sergeant, or makes any disturbance, or shall misbehave himself to the sergeant or his superior officer of the hospital, he will be severely punished.

8. A sentry is to be posted at the hospital door during the morning, at the same time as at head-quarters, where instructions as to his duty will be put up at the door in writing, and read to the relieving sentry by the corporal of the guard at every mounting. Signed by the Colonel to enforce the necessary obedience.

The orders for the sentry were that no patient was to pass beyond his own guard without a ticket from the surgeon; that no strong liquors were to be brought out of hospital. He was to take care of the fire, and see that no mischief was done to the house, that no dirt was thrown near his post or anyone suffered to enter the hospital without cleaning or scraping his shoes, and he was to prevent too many people of the camp or heath from paying frequent or long visits to the hospital.

These suggestions are extremely interesting, as not only giving a general idea of the hospital administration of the day, but as being probably the first of their kind in our Service.

Brocklesby laid great stress—

1st. Of avoiding all manner of nastiness in every encampment.

2nd. To pay frequent attention to the shifting and covering in of all the privies in the rear as soon as, or before, ever they began to be offensive to those who are a few yards distant.

3rd. Always to keep as few possible sick in one room or under the same roof.

4th. To air and turn the straw on which the men lie in their tents twice or thrice a week in summer encampments.

5th. All buildings selected for military purposes to be as lofty and spacious as possible.

6th. The physician's power in a military or camp infirmary to be as peremptory as that of the commanding officer over all his corps out of that place.

7th. Simplicity as regards food, raiment, &c., to be the general object of military men in camps and on service.

8th. The physician to manifest, in all his management of the hospital, an inviolable attachment to method in all things; to fixed hours in dressing the wounded, visiting the sick, having their medicines prepared and proper medicated drinks, without which fixed method, whenever there were many sick, they would often suffer very much.

The chief diseases which soldiers suffered from in Brocklesby's day he tells us were—

1. Coughs, when neglected, establishing the foundation for various pulmonary and chronic complaints.

2. Acute rheumatism, arising from irregularities of soldiers on leaving their winter encampments.

3. Erysipelas as soon as the troops took the field in summertime.

4. Simple inflammatory fever at the same period.

5. Inflammatory sore throat.

6. True pleurisy in spring and autumn.

These were the vernal and inflammatory diseases of their author, who attributed their origin to "cold, obstructed perspiration, condensed solids, over-agitated and consequently vitiated fluids."

His autumnal affections were—

Autumnal bilious fever, followed by dysentery, from which disease upwards of 800 men and women fell ill after the return of the troops to the Isle of Wight, subsequent to the descent upon the coast of France in 1758.

The infectious diseases which he saw were—

1. Retechial or gaol fever. He remarks in passing, that "from the register kept of the mortality produced by fevers of various kinds in military life, it was shown that full eight times the number of men died of this cause of late than fell immediately by their wounds or in battle."

2. Small-pox, of which one in four of the soldiers attacked during the late war died.

3. The measles.

The chronic affections from which the men suffered were intermittents, and their sequels, jaundice and dropsy. Also vermes, psora, lues venerea, and gonorrhœa. Lastly, the scurvy, which affection was very prevalent amongst the French prisoners at Winchester and the British troops who had wintered at Quebec and those quartered at the Senegal in Western Africa.

In 1762, several men of the 3rd Regiment of Guards were infected with typhus when confined in the Savoy, where many newly-enlisted men were huddled together in great numbers in the course of the impressing service of the war. Mr. Fordyce, surgeon of the regiment, had pointed out without effect the impolicy of confining newly-enlisted men and deserters in such places.

Brocklesby's description of typhus is graphic and admirable, and in its treatment, as well as of all other putrescent diseases (as they were then called), nothing, in his opinion, was more conducive to the patient's recovery "than a continued attention to nurses, cleanliness, frequent shifting of foul linen, bedding, and invariably a free and almost uninterrupted current of fresh air, treating the patients in tents." He objected very strongly to the flock bedding then introduced into barracks and public repositories for the sick, as being liable to become infected with the putrid and contagious distempers of the sick. He preferred paliasses, " the contents of which could be frequently renewed by fresh supplies of wholesome straw."

He writes, farther on, "I find by the testimony of many sufferers, that ague-cake very often followed the double tertiaries and bilious fevers of the West Indies, especially of the Coast of Guinea, where the patients had been accustomed to drink of river waters that periodically inundated vast deserts of country, and exhaled their putrescent vapours by the action of the sun's intense heat, as at Senegal, Galam, &c., where our troops died like rotten sheep." According to Brocklesby, the quantities of Peruvian bark consumed by our soldiers, who perished at the Senegal in such numbers, was incredible, and the necessity for its use was so manifest to the private soldiers, "that mutiny amongst the troops was the alternative, if the surgeon would not undertake, at his own peril, that bark in sufficient quantities should be sent along with each detachment destined for Galam, Padore, and such unhealthy deserts in Africa." Mr. Mornington, then garrison surgeon at Goree, stated that "the price of bark in scarce times was at the rate of an ounce of gold-dust for the pound." Galam, where a detachment of British troops was stationed, was upwards of 900 miles from the mouth of the River Senegal. Of the party sent there, consisting of three captains, two lieutenants, one ensign, a surgeon's mate, three sergeants, three corporals, and fifty privates, the surgeon's mate alone survived (Boon).

The work concludes with a most interesting account of the Senegal by Mr. Boon, surgeon to the garrison for a period of three years, dated London, October 8th, 1763 — a lamentable picture of disease and death. The writer tells us that in the months of December, January, February, and March he had 400 patients "prodigiously ill of tertiary fevers, which were so obstinate, that he had been obliged to order bark to be taken almost as common food, and, indeed," he says, " had it not been for this medicine, we might not have had five men living on the island." From March to August, during which period the wind from the sea prevailed, there was little disease except scurvy and dysentery, which he attributed to the "badness of the water, salt provisions, and want of vegetables."

Goree had been taken from the French in 1758, but restored to them at the Peace of Paris, in 1763, in return for the Senegal, which was retained by us for several years, during which interval many medical officers of the regular army were quartered there. The nature of their duties may be surmised from the foregoing lamentable picture, almost the earliest record of the African service handed down to us. On the cession of the Forts to the Crown by the African company, a regiment to garrison them had been raised, and styled "A Corps of Foot serving in Africa." The regiment consisted of a lieutenant-colonel commandant, three captains, three lieutenants, three ensigns, and a regimental agent, but no regimental medical officer, the hospital and corps being in charge of "Garrison Surgeons," some of whose names appear in the older Army Lists. The succession of Colonels in this corps was as follows :—

Charles O'Hara . . 25th July, 1766.
John Clarke . . . 28th September, 1776.
Joseph Wall . . . 16th February, 1780.

It was disbanded in 1783, with two independent companies of Foot raised for service in Western Africa in 1781 and 1782, viz., Mackenzie's and Captain the Honourable Charles Cranstone's. Both of these companies had a captain, two lieutenants, and an ensign. The "Officers of the Hospital," as they were at this time called, then serving at the Senegal, were :—

Surgeon . . . . . John Boon.
    „   . . . . . William Bishop.
Apothecary . . . . Patrick Wemyss.

Brocklesby insisted upon the good effects of discipline and minute attention to the laws of health as essential to the welfare of an army. He drew up for General Draper, previous to his expedition against Manilla and the Phillipine Islands (at that time a two months' passage from Madras), the following excellent regulations for the preservation of the health of the soldiers embarked on board the transports :—

1. The ship's tonnage should be larger in summer than in winter, in hot climates than in colder. In a month's voyage, one and three-quarter tons for each man ; in long voyages, two to two and three-quarter tons.

2. Whilst troops are on board, the greatest cleanliness should be observed between decks, and these parts be continually well aired with ventilators or air sails.

3. All hammocks should be carried daily on deck, and in fine weather be exposed all day long, great care being taken to avoid wetting them; the ships should also be fumigated frequently, by placing a heated iron in pitch or tar.

4. No place between decks should be wetted after sunset.

5. The troops should be mustered on deck thrice daily in cold, four times in hot weather, for roll-calling, at stated intervals being compelled to remain there for an hour each time, carefully protected by awnings. During this hour they should be actively employed, which will keep them from the *misery of having nothing to do,* the cause of many distempers.

6. The quantity and quality of the salt meat should be looked to, and an allowance of fresh meat and vegetables be given to the troops when in port, and when the ship enters the hotter climate the ration should contain more of the vegetable element and subacid fruits, salt meat not being used more than once or twice a week, beef and pork alternately.

7. The greatest attention should be given to enforce sobriety and to avoid intemperance, the least excess in spirituous liquors being prohibited. Such excellent regulations are applicable in all time.

He next recommends the building of barracks and their general use, as it was impossible for the men of each company, scattered up and down the ale-houses of a great town, ever to be regularly messed together, or to make a private soldier always wholesome and cleanly; further, than at a stated hour, for momentary show. "The day of battle," he writes, " is once or twice in a long campaign, when men must be used as they are wanted, but an attention to the well-being of the men, and the preservation of their health, ought to be a constant, serious business, and an increasing care of their officers, as well as the physician." There were at this time only two barracks in existence in England, those at Chatham Lines and the one at Hilsea, constructed "upon an absurd and miserable plan, with low ceilings and without ventilators, and worse for the inhabitants than any tolerably clean King's ship. They were placed upon bad and humid sites, and built with saltwater bricks, ever attracting humidity, and, in addition, were undrained."

He animadverts strongly upon the want of system in the Military Hospital arrangements of his day, the "directors of which, especially upon the commencement of a war, acted too much always upon temporary shifts, and never had yet sufficiently preconcerted measures, so as to give the suffering soldier or the judicious officer content or satisfaction." . . . "It is well known," he tells us, " that numbers of brave men are annually lost in the hospitals for want of proper order and subordination among the physical officers, and that the most able and active men, except they have a military character, cannot prevent a total relaxation of that regularity which should be observed as well here as in the field among the soldiers and gentlemen of the profession." He goes on to say, "I see no just reason why each superior among physicians should not be constituted director of that hospital in which he resides, as he alone must be the most competent judge of all physical matters under himself on the spot, or why he should not be invested with a power from the Commander-in-Chief, or other sufficient authority, to establish a well-preconcerted plan for the hospital he has the care of"—a power now, happily for the interest of the Service, vested in the medical officers of the army.

Many military officers of distinction in that day endorsed everything that had been written by this most able physician. General Bland expressed an opinion that the preservation of the health of the men depended so much on attention to the necessaries and cleanliness of the men, and that "in those regiments where this method was duly observed, the men were generally healthful, but where it was neglected great numbers fell sick and died."

"La moindre négligence sur les hôpitaux peut causer un plus grand dommage au Roi et à l'Etat, que vingt batailles des plus sanglantes."—Guigard.

"Une armée sans bons hôpitaux périt aisément."—Mémoires de Feuquières.

Brocklesby's "Economical and Medical Observations" are based upon experiences extending between the years 1758—63, at which time the expense incurred for extras were allowed in the public accounts of the extra-ordinance of each year by the Secretary at War.

Mr. Sergeant Ranby was then in charge of Chelsea Hospital, which was described "as a perfect model of everything that is right for hospital management—cleanliness, order, and the treatment of sores and wounds—as he only had the merit of establishing." I have already referred to his opinion on such subjects. The small pittance then allowed as "medicine money" to each regiment was not nearly sufficient for the purpose. In General Hospitals greater latitude in this respect was allowed.

Mr. Adair was then Inspector of Regimental Infirmaries. Brocklesby was for a time Physician to the Military Hospital at Pimlico, and had as contemporaries Sir Clifton Wintringham, Sir John Pringle, Armstrong, and others.

Imperfect as our military medical system was at this time, it is evident from the remarks of Brocklesby that it was far in advance of that of our Continental neighbours. "The Germans," he says, "who speedily recruit their armies as they moulder away, take very little care of their Military Hospitals to this day" (1763), while the French, who were models of perfection in routine (a reputation they have preserved until now), nourished their sick whenever food was to be found near the army, clothed them, washed and kept them cleaner, yet lost, as did the Germans in their hospitals, a greater number of sick and wounded, "owing to the rude and barbarous practitioners" attached to the latter, and the ignorance of the physicians employed in the French Army. He pays a merited compliment to the French Military Surgeons, "who from their supreme knowledge of anatomy, were far superior to the British in this respect." A repetition of a very old story, that in the end (though probably at the onset the most expensive and difficult to obtain) officers well educated in their profession, to whatever line it may belong, are infinitely preferable, and in the long run the most economical, to the State.

Donald Munro, "Physician to His Majesty's Army and St. George's Hospital," gives us in his "Diseases of the British Military Hospitals in Germany, 1761—63, and Means of Preserving the Health of Soldiers" (a work dedicated to the King, "in consideration of His Majesty's consideration for every officer and soldier who suffered either by sickness or wounds in the late glorious war") some graphic pictures of our service in the field. One of his ancestors, John Munro, after serving an apprenticeship as surgeon with King William in Flanders, settled in Edinburgh in 1697. His only son became Professor of Anatomy in the University of Edinburgh in 1720, and in conjunction with Sir Andrew Balfour, who founded the College of Physicians in 1685, and his able coadjutors, Dr. Archibald Pitcairne and Sir Robert Tibbald, did much to establish the reputation of that School of Medicine which gave so many distinguished surgeons to the army in after years.

Cholera, inflammatory fever, inflammatory sore throat, pleurisy, inflammation of the lungs, catarrh, influenza, rheumasm, autumnal remittent fever, intermittent fever, jaundice, tertiary syphilis, paralytic complaints (from lying out at night in wet weather), incontinence of urine, epilepsy (from the severe duty of long marches in hot weather), small-pox, erysipelatous swellings, and the itch, were the diseases *par excellence* of these campaigns. The true scurvy was only seen at the hospital at Bremen, where it was confined altogether to the soldiers, "not one of the gentlemen belonging to the hospital, or to the commissariat, nor one of the military officers, or even the sergeants, being affected with it." Munro gave as a reason of its frequency among the soldiers, to the place being situated on a naturally very damp site, the men being quartered in very low, damp houses; no vegetables or greens were to be bought in the market; fresh meat and other fresh provisions were at so high a price that the men could not afford to buy them, but were obliged to live on salted meat and salted herrings during the winter, and what little money they had remaining they laid out in spirituous liquors, which were sold cheap."

The *full diet* in use in the hospitals during the war consisted of one pint of rice gruel, made with two ounces of rice, one spoonful of fine flour, a little common salt and fine sugar. This was given for breakfast. The dinner consisted of one pound of meat; the supper of the same ingredients as the breakfast; with a daily allowance of one pound of bread. As a drink, three pints of barley and rice water, to each pint of which were added two spoonfuls of brandy and a quarter of an ounce of sugar. Besides which, the physician might order an additional quantity of wine, brandy, or milk, or water gruel, or any other articles he thought proper for the sick.

In the autumn of 1760, a malignant fever and dysentery began to appear among the soldiers while the allied army remained encamped about Warburgh. During this time rain fell continuously, and the camp and neighbouring fields and villages were filled with the excrements of a numerous army and an infinite number of dead horses. Many of the dead, where the action had been fought on the 31st of July, were scarcely covered with earth. The sick crowded the hospitals, necessitating a speedy removal of the convalescents to relieve the overcrowding. The Guards, previous to their march into Hesse, left 132 sick in their regimental infirmaries, mostly ill of fever, which had become extremely malignant and infectious, owing to "the smallness and dirtiness of their hospitals." By the month of April all the sick of the British forces were evacuated to Osnaburg, and from there to Bremen. The French having taken the field with a numerous army, it was found impossible to protect the regimental infirmaries, " scattered up and down the country as they were." About 800 sick were at this time in the General Hospitals, the largest of which were at Bremen, Paderborn, Osnaburg, Bilifield, and Nutzungen. When a regiment removed from camp, these hospitals received the sick, but upon the army taking the field, the men who became subsequently non-effective from illness were treated in the regimental infirmaries, which must have been very cumbrous forms of field hospitals.

The physicians who served during the German campaign were Donald Munro, Sir Clifton Wintringham, Dr. Conyers, Dr. Musket, Dr. Brooke, Dr. Knox, Dr. John Armstrong, Dr. Robert Miller, and Dr. Turner. Mr. Cathcart was Director of Hospitals. During the three campaigns in Germany (1761-2-3), 25,000 successions of sick (according to Munro) passed through the regimental hospitals, and during the period most of the men in each camp must have been on the sick list, "many of them two, three, or four times." The regimental hospitals during the war consisted of a few tents placed in the rear of each corps, or some neighbouring house appropriated for the purpose, where the sick "were often obliged to remain one, two, three, and sometimes more weeks, before waggons could be got to transport them to the next General Hospital, which was commonly twelve or thirteen, and occasionally thirty or forty miles in the rear of the army."

During the retreat from the county of Hesse, the hospitals at Alsfeld and the medical officers attached were captured by the French, and a few wounded at Campen. In March, 1761, the monthly returns showed 309 casualties, only thirty of whom died in the General Hospitals. In the previous sudden advance, for want of waggons to transport them, many of the sick had been left "scattered up and down the country." Towards the end of 1760, Captain Douglass, 25th Regiment, a very good officer, was appointed "Military Inspector of the Hospitals" by the Marquis of Granby, chiefly with a view to taking charge of the convalescents as they were discharged from the infirmaries. He appears also to have had the custody of the hospital returns and papers relating to the hospitals.

On the 5th June, 1761, subsistence was paid to the inspector for 4,500 men discharged from the hospital, all of whom joined their regiments in perfect health at an important juncture, thus adding largely to the effective fighting strength.

In the following year a number of officers were sent down from the army to examine (along with the physicians and surgeons) all the men in hospital and convalescents who were judged to be unfit for service, either by age, disease, or wounds, in order that they might be sent home and recruits returned in their place. About 300 men were so invalided. Some 800 were killed in the great actions of the war; 500 died of their wounds only.

It was remarked during the German war that those regiments who kept their butchers in winter, and made stoppages of the men's pay, and obliged them to take a certain quantity of meat daily, were much more healthy than those who used no precaution of the kind.

At this time each regiment was accompanied by its surgeon and surgeon's mate, the former of which officers provided the hospital for the sick, as well as the medicines. To defray the expense of hiring a house for an hospital, Government allowed the surgeon the sum of £30 per annum, any surplus being applied for the purchase of wine for the sick, utensils for the hospitals, &c. Sixpence a day was supposed to be paid out of this munificent sum to a regimental nurse. Each private had to pay a penny a month, each non-commissioned officer three farthings, as medicine money, which, in an establishment of 646 rank and file, amounted to £80 9s. 6d. per annum, and in the peace establishment of 400 non-commissioned officers and men to less. According to Hamilton (who published his "Regimental Surgeon" a few years later), the surgeon received a commission signed by the Secretary of State for War, or, if abroad, by the commander-in-chief of the station, who had authority to grant it; the mate, his appointment by warrant from the colonel of the regiment into which he was about to enter. Medical officers who held double commissions were exempted from all combatant duty, such as "mounting guard, attending courts-martial, and such like." They ranked as staff officers. Regiments were then mostly quartered in billets, the head-quarters and mess-room in some public inn, in which it was customary for every guest, of whatever rank, to meet in the same room, surrounded with a crowd, drinking, smoking, and conversing promiscuously together. All officers under the rank of captain, with only their pay to support them, (according to Hamilton) suffered many and great inconveniences, being poorly accommodated by the innkeepers of the period, who looked with the greatest dislike upon the military, who were then a great tax upon them—the magistrates being frequently obliged to interfere in the officer's behalf.

At this period, and for many years afterwards, medicine and surgery were distinct professions in the army, but a physician or surgeon might hold a regimental appointment. The department was governed by a physician-general and surgeon-general in London, the general hospitals being principally under the supervision of the former, the regimental infirmaries under the latter. No system of regular inspection was carried out, nor any medical journals or statistical documents kept by the executive medical officers—a reform first suggested by Hamilton, as necessary to prevent unqualified persons undertaking the practice of the profession. The only attempt to treat disease scientifically was, as a rule, in the general hospitals, where many physicians of eminence were employed. In regimental hospitals at home the morning examination of the sick list consisted of little more "than in calling over the patients' names, the giving of some insignificant advice, or the ordering of something which the men were totally unable to procure from the small pittance of their subsistence" (Hamilton). Half-a-crown a week was allowed for the subsistence of the patients, which sum was put in the hands of the hospital sergeant, to be expended in the mess, or as the surgeon pointed out. The surgeon's mate performed the greater portion of the duty—the surgeons only paying occasional visits—and if particularly active in the discharge of his duties, never failed to get an admonition from head-quarters "to beware of expense in medicines," which had to be provided by the senior officer out of his annual allowance. Promotion to the rank of surgeon was very problematical, only occurring after a long time, or by some lucky chance. No inducements were, at this epoch, held out to men of regular education to induce them to enter the service or to continue in it—the mates, who then performed the duties of assistant-surgeons, not being required to pass his examination previous to admission—while in the sister service, then in advance of us, the candidates for appointment, after passing an examination at the "Surgeon's Hall," were sent to a physician appointed for the purpose, to be examined in medicine, a test which Brocklesby in 1764 (after the conclusion of the war) insisted upon, as necessary in the army, "as a requisite physical (medical) qualification for men who presume to superintend the lives and health of nine hundred soldiers," the complement of a regiment in the field.

The surgeon's appointment was then bought and sold like a military commission, as we have already seen, the surgeon-general —who was the ostensible or acting chief of the department—having no great power of patronage or gift. At the reconstruction of the department in 1783 the sale of medical commissions was officially suppressed, but, as we will see subsequently, was for a long period still carried on. The officer who obtained the appointment only required a certificate from a private medical teacher that he was qualified to practice surgery, a University degree or certificate from the Surgeons' Hall not being necessary. Can it be wondered that under such a system, the regimental service should have so degenerated as to merit the sarcasm of the celebrated John Hunter, who wrote in his essay on gunshot wounds that "it was hardly necessary for a man to be a surgeon to practice in the army." This opinion is confirmed by Hamilton, who relates an anecdote referring to a regimental mate, who had served seventeen years in that position, during eight of which he had sole care of his regiment, but on a vacancy occurring he was unable (at the Surgeons' Hall) to qualify for promotion, an examination of some sort having been in the meantime constituted. Brocklesby pointed out how necessary it was that military surgeons should be educated as physicians, quoting in proof of his assertion the then great preponderance of medical over surgical diseases during a campaign and in quarters. In some regiments it was the custom to allow the surgeon a professional *honorarium* of a guinea a year from each subaltern, two from each captain, three from each major, five from the lieutenant-colonel, and ten from the colonel, and for every soldier inoculated with the small-pox Government allowed a fee of a guinea. The steps of preferment for the regimental surgeon were few and far between—he could therefore hope for little advancement in his career. He had permission to sell his appointment when wishing to retire from the service, the only retirement (except upon reduction of establishment) he was entitled to. He consequently had no provision when superannuated and so infirm as to be no longer capable of performing his duty. The surgeons of Militia and Fencible corps then occupied a different position, as they all bore combatant commissions in addition to their medical ones. The surgeon-general, who was ostensible or acting chief of the department, having no great power of patronage or gift, was unable to reward in any way those officers of merit and distinction who served under him. When encamped, the surgeon was allowed forage for a horse, at the rate of £15 a year.

The gradations of rank were as follows:—Regimental mate, hospital mate, regimental surgeon, apothecary to a general hospital, surgeon to a hospital, surgeon-general. Surgeons to general hospitals were selected from the apothecaries and from the regimental surgeons indiscriminately. The first of these appointments was worth about £200 a year; a regimental surgeon's, including all allowances, not more than £100. The pay of the apothecary was 10s. per diem. Medicines were supplied from the public stores in time of war or on foreign service, and the surgeon was liable to be charged with the expense of medicines for the recruiting parties of his regiment in every part of the United Kingdom. These parties were selected from the "additionals," the name given to two of the companies which were always on the recruiting service, and were with the regiment either at home or abroad. They were attended by the civil surgeon of the town in which located.

The strength of a regiment in England was 764, in Ireland 270, or only twenty-seven men to the company. Encampments were very common in England (1789)—sixty-three regiments were under canvas. When several regiments were present, a physician was appointed to the camp and a general hospital established, with a staff of hospital mates, matrons, nurses, and attendants. The quartermaster selected the house for the hospital, and a contingent of £7 10s. a month was allowed to cover the expenses of sufficient accommodation. No system of orderly medical officer existed, and the surgeon was confined to the precincts of the camp. The usual number in the morning sick report of a regiment, 765 strong, one day with another, was a hundred. Of this number returned to the surgeon, we are told that not one-half required medical treatment of any kind whatever, owing to the mode of proceeding then in force, of putting all men unfit for duty, whether sick or not, in the surgeon's list, there being no other place to arrange them in the daily return to the commanding officer or War Office as receiving pay—a custom long obsolete. No more than one-half, or fifty, required to be visited daily, in weak regiments twenty-five. Hospital beds were double, and capable of accommodating two persons. The system of dieting men in hospital was introduced by John Bell, the surgeon to the 26th Regiment, previous to which reform the patients under treatment were obliged to subsist upon the ordinary ration of beef or salt pork, irrespective of the nature of their disease.

Hamilton piteously complains of the amount of pay granted to regimental mates, showing how inadequate it was in the following table:—

	£	s.	d.
Subsistence issued at 3s. per day	54	15	0
Poundage stopped by Government at the rate of 1s. per pound	3	3	10½
Chelsea Hospital, the day's full pay	0	3	6
Warrants and Contingencies, two day's pay	0	7	0
Agency, 2d. per pound	0	10	7½
	£59	0	0
Remains of 365 days, or one year's arrears, at 6d. per day	4	17	6
	£63	17	6

"Or he loses by his full pay, every year, no less than £4 5s. 6d., while the annual arrears or nett clearings, viz., £4 17s. 6d., are so irregularly paid, that they may be said likewise to be almost lost." In addition, the hospital mates were at this date entitled to no pension, and might be at last dismissed without anything to support them in their old age, unless fortunate enough to hold in addition a combatant commission. The surgeon, on the other hand, once appointed, if reduced, was entitled to his half-pay.

The physicians of the army, who were highly educated, and many of them distinguished graduates of the universities, were looked upon as the *élite* of the profession in the Service, and paid at a rate very much in advance of the regimental medical officers. They were few, indispensable, and could consequently command their own terms, fortunately for themselves. The surgeon-general paid a formal visit to each encampment and regimental hospital annually. Occasionally, during a war, surgeons were raised by the commander-in-chief to the rank of physician; which was considered "an unwarrantable encroachment on the rights of the regular physicians, or prerogative of the Universities." In the field, the nearest general hospital, which received all those ill of fever, fluxes, and other dangerous disorders, and those who were badly wounded or unfit to do duty with their regiment, was placed in the day of battle in some safe position in the rear. According to Munro, even in his time, when an army was in the field in face of the enemy, it was often obliged to march quickly, and sometimes made such long marches, that the regiments found it impossible to carry their sick and wounded with them; and as on such occasions the surgeons and their assistants were obliged to go with the regiments, to be near at hand in case of an action, it was found absolutely necessary to have proper hospitals in the rear of the army for the reception of the sick and wounded from the camps.

The hospitals commonly wanted for a large army acting on the Continent, Munro tells us, were:—

"1. One in the rear to follow their motions, so as to be always ready to receive the sick from camps, which are called the moveable flying hospitals.

"2. One, or more, at some distance in towns, to receive such of the sick as can be moved from the flying hospital, when they are obliged to go from one place to another, or when a greater number of sick is sent to them than they can easily take care of.

"Each of which hospitals should be provided with 'physicians, surgeons, mates, purveyors or commissaries, and others to attend and take care of the sick;' and be attended by waggons, provisions, and other necessaries, 'so as to be in no danger of wanting anything while the sick were on their journey.'" Munro also recommended "that a number of hospital marquees and a proper proportion of hospital mates should attend the army 'to be ready in case of an action.' These ought to be attached to the suite of the commanders of the different corps or brigades, and be quartered or encamped with them; and each surgeon should be provided with a waggon or some horses loaded with a proper chirurgical apparatus, as stimulants, bandages, lint, and other things necessary for taking care of the wounded. A small quantity of medicines, some wine, rice, portable soups, &c., and utensils for a small hospital, and two, three, or four hundred sets of bedding, should also be carried about with the army, in case of an action, for the use of the wounded, till they have time to receive assistance from the flying hospitals. Some sets of surgeon's instruments, bandages, lint and other dressing for recent wounds, and bedding should be carried on horseback, so as to be at hand when any of the surgeons were sent with detachments that were going upon an attack.

"It would be a right measure, in the beginning of every war, to settle by cartel that military hospitals on both sides should be considered as sanctuaries for the sick, and mutually protected. (Idem.)

This experienced and able officer thought that the direction of all military hospitals should be committed to the physicians who had immediate care of the hospitals, and that when an army was acting on the Continent, and a number of hospitals were located in different places, the physician who attended the commander-in-chief ought to be made the Physician-General and Director of Hospitals, with proper appointments, and that *all orders* at head-quarters ought to go immediately through this channel only, and that all orders should be punctually obeyed. That the purveying branches should be distinct from, but strictly under the orders of, the Medical Director of Hospitals, or physicians or surgeons in immediate charge of the smaller establishments; furnish the accounts for the inspection of the latter; and "never assume the name of director," which, we are informed, "they often did to mislead military officers."

In many instances during the continental expeditions of this period, surgical cases were treated in district hospitals under surgeons of experience, a practice Munro was in favour of, as also of the practice of arranging diseases and treating them in accordance with their natural selection rather than an artificial regimental division. He was fully alive to the evils of overcrowding and want of cleanliness, which gave such a bad odour to large hospitals, which under proper management and regulation of the sick, it has been oftentimes proved in practice they do not deserve. It will be seen from these few extracts that he anticipated by more than a century, many ideas believed to be of modern origin. His work is replete with practical suggestions for the preservation of the health of soldiers; which if they had been acted up to, would have been the means of saving thousands of lives to the State. The following extract from his work may be interesting to the younger medical officers of the present day.

Orders for the Mates in Germany 1761-2.

"1. All the gentlemen will attend at the apothecary's every morning at 8 a.m., to assist in making up the medicine for the day; afterwards will go round the hospitals with the physicians and surgeons.

"2. Every mate will have a book for writing the prescriptions of the physician, to be kept in the following order: Patient's name, regiment, day of admission, disease, prescription of physician, and after all, day of his discharge or death.

"3. Every mate will make up the physician's and surgeon's prescriptions for his own patients with proper directions; bleed his own patients; dress any slight ulcers they may have which do not require sending to the surgical hospital.

"4. Every mate will go round his patients in the evening; see everything well conducted; and report to the physician or apothecary anything extraordinary.

"5. Two mates will attend daily at the dispensary to receive the sick; place them properly; make up the medicines they immediately want; order each of them a bowl of water-gruel; and if anything extraordinary occurs send the orderly man to acquaint the physician or apothecary. Orderly mates will make up for officers or others all prescriptions sent to the dispensary throughout the day."

One of the mates lodged in the hospital. By Lord Granby's order "a pound of meat, roasted or boiled, for dinner, and a bottle of wine" was allowed to the orderly mates, so that "they might not absent themselves from their duty."

The apothecary in that day had custody of all the medicines; went round the hospital in the morning before the hour of the physician's visit; saw that the wards were kept in proper order; that the nurses and other servants had done their duty; examined into the state of the sick; saw that the provisions were good; made a faithful report of all these circumstances to the physician; and saw that the mates performed their duty. It was ordered that the apothecary should always be lodged near the hospital, "to assist in case of any accident happening, or if any such arose at the hospital."

A period of profound peace followed the Treaty of Paris, a lull between two great wars. The standing army had been more and more reduced, until in 1772 it numbered but 17,070 men, not including about half that number for the "Plantations," and there were only seventy regiments of the Line. The Army had no regular permanent head, and the dress of the ordinary British soldier was tight breeches, tail-coat, cocked-hat of the Nivernois pattern, with the inevitable pigtail. There were no sappers or miners, but in that year the foundation of that corps was laid by the establishment of the "Military Company of Artificers," for employment at Gibraltar. The artillery numbered about 170 officers in four battalions ; and the engineers not half that number. The Militia were only about 15,000 strong, and had only been once embodied since they had been re-organised about fifteen years before. The men could not pass into the ranks of the Regular Army, and the education of the latter may be somewhat estimated from the recorded fact, that in this year a cadet for the Ordnance corps was returned to his father, "in order that reading, writing, and the rule of three might be taught him before he came up for re-admission." In the Navy, seventy-four's had only lately come into fashion. In 1767, a system of honorary distinctions for long-continued good behaviour had been introduced into the 5th Regiment, which was found to stimulate the indifferent into good behaviour, thus having the best effects.

In "Review Order" it was laid down that "The staff officers are to be posted opposite to the interval between the grenadier company and the right of the battalion, dressing in the same line with the officers. The chaplain to the right, the quartermaster on the left, the surgeon on the left of the chaplain, the surgeon's mate on the left of the surgeon," showing that the latter, although not commissioned, or as yet shown in the Army List, enjoyed all the position and advantages of a regimental staff officer.

The troops of Horse Grenadiers have only chaplains and surgeons. The Cavalry, chaplains, surgeons and adjutants. The Infantry, quartermasters in addition. A corps of foot is serving in Africa and one in America, the latter allowed a surgeon. There are twenty-six independent companies of invalids; a regiment of invalids in Ireland of ten companies. There are twenty-three garrisons at home, seventeen abroad with their military governors and staff. George Millengen is garrison surgeon at Mobile. South Carolina has a garrison surgeon at £73 per annum, and two mates at 2s. 6d. a day each. Providence has a surgeon, and the Bermudas a surgeon's mate. A " Purveyor and Surgeon of the Hospitals," is shown on the staff of the " Governor-General of the West Indies (then an important command) Lord Macartney, K.B., at a salary of £273 15s., the same pay as given to the " Commissary-General of Stores and Provisions." The garrison surgeons receive £182 10s. per annum, the chaplains £121 13s. 4d. In order, after the garrisons, but before the Royal Regiment of Artillery, Corps of Engineers, and Marines are shown in a separate list.

Officers of the Hospitals for the Forces in North America.

Physicians—Michael Morris, Richard Veal, Charles Blagden, Robert Knox, Hugh Kennedy, John Mervin Nooth, *extraordinary.*

Surgeons.—Alexander Grant, George Field, Thompson Foster, Percival Cole, John Hayes, John Weir, Richard Hope, Jonathan Mallet.

Apothecaries—Michael Croker, George Brown, William Paine,

James Jameson, David Caldwell, Richard Mornington, Vincent Wood, Daniel Mandeville.
Purveyors—Jonathan Mallet, Dr. John Mervin Nooth, William Ban.
Chaplain—John Jones.

Garrison Surgeons.

Abraham Van Holst, Surgeon . . .	Annapolis Royal
Christopher Lethbridge, Surgeon's Mate .	St. John's
Adam Mabane, Surgeon	Quebec
Robert Cutherwood, Surgeon . . .	East Florida
John Lorimer, Surgeon	West Florida
George Millengen, Surgeon . . .	Mobile
William Douglas, Surgeon . . .	South Carolina
Edward Lancelles, Surgeon's Mate . .	Providence
Henry Howard, Surgeon's Mate . .	Providence
Francis Brown, Surgeon's Mate . .	Bermudas

Mediterranean.

	£	s.	d.
Gibraltar—Surgeon-Major Arthur Baines . .	182	10	0
,, Surgeon's Mate William Hunter . .	91	5	5
,, ,, Alexander Barnes . .	91	5	5
Minorca—Physician, Hon. Coote Molesworth			

The surgeon of the Royal Regiment of Artillery, James Irwin, is shown on the staff of the corps. His commission is dated 24th July, 1764. The Royal Regiment of Artillery in Ireland has also a surgeon, Arthur Winter, his commission dated 6th May, 1760, or twelve years before. The Engineers have not as yet been honoured with the word "Royal," and are shown with their civil and military titles; only a few years before (1757) had the latter been added to the former.

There were then serving in North America, under the command of General Sir William Howe, one regiment of dragoons and twenty-six regiments of infantry, in charge of twenty-seven surgeons and the same number of surgeons' mates.

Among the Staff Officers and Officers of the Hospitals on the Half Pay List, were :—

George Lawman, "Master-Surgeon of the Hospitals in the Low Countries," a quaint designation long since disappeared. Also John Cherrington, "Master-Surgeon of the late Garrison at Louisburgh ;" Richard Brocklesby, "Physician to the Hospitals in Great Britain ;" Philip Burlton, " Inspector-General and Chief Director of the Hospitals in Germany;" William Young, "Director-General of the Hospitals in Portugal;" John Bulger, "Physician to the Forces in Germany ;" John Hopkins, "Deputy-Director of the Hospitals at the Havannah ;" John Adair, "Director of the Hospitals at Martinique ;" George Corryer, "Purveyor of the Hospitals during the late Expedition to Guadaloupe ;" John

Napier, "Inspector-General and Chief Director of the Hospitals in North America;" John Boon, "Surgeon to the Forces," Senegal; Patrick Wemyss, "Apothecary to the Forces," Senegal; Edward Blithe, "Physician to the Forces," Belleisle; and for the first time in the Army but one, "Superannuated surgeon of a regiment, Wolston Bayley."

The 41st was then styled a regiment of invalids.

In 1775 broke out the unfortunate war which severed from our great Empire those "old Plantations" in America, which had been for so long among the most prized appanages of the Crown. The distance from the parent country, the delays occasioned by conveying soldiers and military stores across the Atlantic, the extensive woods and morasses, and the wild and savage character of the Indians, caused the war to be carried on with difficulty, and the military operations to be of the most fatiguing and hazardous nature.

In 1777, the English Army, under General Burgoyne, after enduring extraordinary hardships in marching through a country where the bridges were destroyed and the roads obstructed by fallen trees, was obliged to abandon its baggage, provisions, and *hospital*, with 300 sick, to the mercy of the colonists. In the affair at Pisquata, upwards of 200 Americans were left upon the hands of the British surgeons. At the siege of Boston, by Washington in the previous year, the slow but sure effects of the long blockade began to show themselves on the British troops. Provisions were scarce, no further supply was obtainable, and the men, previous to their embarkation for New York, were worn out by incessant toil. In North Carolina, Lord Cornwallis' army depended entirely for subsistence on the country through which it marched. The men were frequently two days without sustenance. We are told that "for five days the troops were supported on the Indian corn, collected as it stood in the fields, *five ears* being the allowance for two soldiers for twenty-four hours." There were no tents, the men bivouacked in the woods, under torrents of rain, while at every step the soldier sunk over his shoes in the mud. To expedite his movements in pursuit of the American General, he issued orders for the destruction of all superfluous baggage and spirits, which the men abandoned without a murmur. One or more rivers and creeks were forded daily, which were swollen by heavy rains. They marched generally all night. On coming up with the enemy, although much inferior in numbers (1,447 against 7,000), they at once attacked and signally defeated him.

During the investment of Boston in 1776, Washington's army numbered 21,800, encamped on the surrounding heights. The sick list amounted to no less than 2,700 (Sparks). On the evacuation of New York in September of the same year, his sick amounted to "one quarter of the whole army." The American Army was at this period mostly raw levies or Militia. In the previous month there were 3,668 sick out of 17,000 men present. This excessive sick-rate was attributed to the composition of his force (Militia suddenly called from their homes, unaccustomed to arms or exposure, or the hardships of a camp), the want of tents, and the season of the year. Dr. Cochran was Washington's surgeon-general, and a close and intimate friend. In the campaigns of 1776, the Americans took eleven British surgeons prisoners. The British forces in America in 1777 numbered 20,957; in 1778, 33,756; in 1779, 38,569; in 1780, 38,002; in 1781, 42,075; and in 1782, the last year of the war, 40,469, with a proportionate medical staff.

Our regimental hospitals there were " simple collections of sick men," huddled together with little order or arrangement, how they could and as they could. No comprehensive system existed. There was no attempt at classification, and no carefully-devised code of regulations respecting diet; hospital comforts were not dreamed of. No hospital clothing was provided by the State, and every sick man was expected to bring his own blanket. His choice of esculents was limited to salt beef or pork, which he might wash down with his ration of rum. Rush was the only author who published a medical work on the war and the diseases observed in the military hospitals; and the only important fact mentioned was the successful adoption of Ranby's plan of amputation in wounds of joints, and the superior fortitude with which the operations were borne immediately after a battle.

On the conclusion of a general peace in 1783, new regulations were printed for the Army, and some changes made in the organisation of the Medical Department. The surgeon of a regiment whose companies were fifty men or under, was allowed £70 a year, and in regiments of a greater complement, a proportionately larger sum in lieu of the peace money up to then stopped from the soldier, and which had been applied to the purchase of medicines. When a regiment was encamped, Government provided for the surgeon's use a medicine chest, and during active service an extra contingency of fifty pounds per annum was placed under the control of the officer commanding the corps, for the use of the regimental hospital, and the examination of recruits became a part of the duty of the medical officers.

Shortly before the general cessation of hostilities (1780), the strength of troops in Great Britain (exclusive of Artillery, Artificers, and Marines on shore) had been as below:—

In Camp.

Cavalry	Nil.
Regular Infantry	11,796
Militia	20,936
Total	32,732

In Quarters.

Cavalry	5,767
Regular Infantry	20,081
Militia	13,367
Total	39,155

Total, 71,887 of all ranks.

Twelve thousand men were on the Irish Establishment, and under the control of the House of Commons in that portion of the Kingdom. The soldier's daily pay was $6\frac{3}{4}d.$, and it was the usage of the Service for the men to obtain their necessaries through the quartermaster and sergeant at an exorbitant rate and of very inferior value. When billeted on inhabitants, they were wretchedly lodged. A man's common breakfast was a halfpenny roll and a halfpennyworth of Suffolk cheese, and hunger often compelled the unfortunate men to commit depredations, for which they were severely punished. It was related that at Perth an Irish regiment was under stoppages which only left them $3\frac{1}{2}d.$ a day. The pressgang was active in catching recruits, it being legal to seize "all *alleged* idle and disorderly persons, and persons convicted of smuggling." In Ireland, some corps had been raised under the pretence of serving as Militia, who were immediately placed under exercise, and shipped off for service in the West Indies; they were christened by their countrymen "the Green Linnets." The pay of an Irish labourer was then 6d. per diem. It was the custom at this time to form companies of all the invalids for garrison duty. In 1783, there were in Britain thirty-six of these companies, and in Ireland a regiment of invalids consisting of ten companies. The average rate of pay given to the garrison surgeons at home was £45 12s. 6d. per annum. On the staff of the Tower of London were the following officers:—

	£	s.	d.
Constable—Lieut.-Gen. Earl Cornwallis	1000	0	0
Lieutenant—Honble. Charles Vernon	700	0	0
Deputy-Lieutenant—John Gore	365	0	0
Town-Major—John Parr	182	10	0
Chaplain—Thomas Cooper	121	13	4
Gentleman-Porter—Sir Thomas Anson	88	6	8
Gentleman-Gaoler—David Bingham	70	0	0
Physician—Burgoyne Tomkins	182	10	0
Surgeon—Lewis Davis	45	12	6
Apothecary—Richard Jaques	100	0	0

In 1783, the number of the "Officers of the Hospitals" serving with the troops in North America and the West Indies was increased to ten physicians, twenty-one surgeons, fifteen apothecaries, four purveyors, and a chaplain, over whom was placed as "Superintendent-General," Doctor John Mervin Nooth, who in a former Army List was shown as one of the junior physicians *extraordinary* serving in the same command. There was then no separate list of Commissariat, Chaplains, or other Departments in the Army List.

The following Medical officers are shown as attached to the Royal Regiment of Artillery in Ireland:—

Surgeon—James Irwin		.	July 24, 1764
Surgeon's Mate—Dodo Ecken		.	Mar. 10, 1760
,,	,, Gustavus Irwin	.	Feb. 25, 1772
,,	,, James Henderson	.	Sept. 21, 1774
,,	,, McMillan Jameson	.	Feb. 10, 1778
,,	,, John Shale	.	Oct. 12, 1780
,,	,, Michael Morris	.	June 10, 1782

The first occasion on which regimental mates appear with their corps in the Army List. From the date of appointment, it will be seen that some of them had an extraordinarily long service.

In 1787, war had concluded. Each of the troops of Horse Guards and Horse Grenadier Guards had still their surgeons. The senior surgeon in the Cavalry was St. Leger Hinchley, 8th Royal Irish Regiment of Light Dragoons, whose commission dated as far back as the 8th May, 1764, twenty-three years before. He was serving with his regiment in 1793. The oldest surgeon in the Infantry was Hudson Lowe, of the 50th, his commission dating back to 1761. He was also still in the regiment in 1793, at which date he must have completed thirty-two years in the army. There were eight garrison surgeons, six "Surgeons to the Hospitals," drawing £172 17s. 6d. per annum, two garrison mates, one surgeon's mate, and one surgeon-major. The Artillery had a surgeon-general, James Irwin, and four surgeons serving under his orders, one to each of the four battalions. The following were the Medical officers of the Guard:—

Cavalry.

Valentine Jones, 12th April, 1781, First Troop of Horse Guards.

Richard Barker, 12th February, 1779, Second Troop of Horse Guards.

John Heavyside, 29th November, 1771, First Troop of Horse Grenadier Guards.

Joshua Jefferson, 5th October, 1775, Royal Regiment of Horse Guards.

Infantry of the Guard.

Thomas Keate, 2nd September, 1778, First Regiment of Foot Guards.

Francis Knight, 8th May, 1780, Coldstream Regiment of Foot Guards.

John Leslie, 16th June, 1779, Third Regiment of Foot Guards.

Establishment, 1787.

Cavalry of the Line and Guard Surgeons	31
Infantry of the Line and Guard Surgeons	75
Garrison Surgeons at Home	8
Garrison Mates	2
Surgeon-Major Abroad	1
Garrison Surgeons Abroad	11
Surgeon-General Royal Artillery	1
Surgeons Royal Artillery	4
Total on Full Pay	133

On Half Pay.

Surgeons of Disbanded and Reduced Regiments	59
Inspectors, Directors, Purveyors	19
Physicians	15
Surgeons	42
Apothecaries	26
Superannuated Surgeons	8
Surgeons on Irish Half Pay	9
Total on Half Pay	178

Effective List	133
Non-Effective List	178
Total	301

All the "Officers of the Hospitals" were on half pay, only the garrison surgeons and the surgeons to the hospitals abroad being retained on the effective list. The rates of half pay were as follows:—physicians, 10s.; surgeons, 5s.; apothecary, 5s.; regimental surgeons, 2s.

The various designations at this date in use were superintendent-general, director, inspector, physician, surgeon to the hospitals, surgeon-major, garrison surgeon, regimental surgeon, garrison, hospital, and regimental mate; apothecary, purveyor, and surgeon-general Royal Artillery. The higher titles only appear during war, when the staff-surgeons and physicians were selected from civil life on the spur of an expedition, and very rarely from the regimental surgeons.

In 1786, Mr. John Hunter was made deputy surgeon-general, and in 1791 appointed to the joint office of surgeon-general and inspector of regimental infirmaries, and in conjunction with the physician-general, Sir Clifton Wiltringham, held superintendence of the department. He had served as senior staff-surgeon at Bellisle in 1760, and in Portugal in 1763, when he was designated "Surgeon-General, Deputy-Purveyor, Inspector, and Director of General Hospitals." He was the first surgeon of the age in which he lived, and in 1794, published his " Treatise on the Blood, Inflammation, and Gun-shot Wounds," the materials for which were collected during his period of active service abroad in Belleisle and Portugal. Robert Jackson described him as "a man of an original mind and considerable discernment, but too little acquainted with military operations in the field to foresee everything that was likely to occur in military service, and provide on all occasions, from his own source of knowledge, the best means of remedy. He considered the cure of diseases, whether by manual operation, or the use of internal remedies, as the proper business of a medical man destined for the service of the army. He made a rule that no person should hold the rank of army-physician, who was not or had not been a staff-surgeon, regimental surgeon, or apothecary to the Forces—a rule abrogated after his death by his successors, who made service in the former ranks an absolute preclusive from the rank of physician to the army, which was in future to be confined to graduates of Oxford or Cambridge, members or licentiates of the College of Physicians of London." Mr. Hunter's constant advice to all aspirants to medical fame was this:— " Don't think, but try; be patient, be accurate." He ceased to hold office shortly before the peace of Amiens. On his death, the office of surgeon-general merged in a Board, formed by order of the King, issued through the Secretary of State for War in October, 1793, consisting of a physician-general, a surgeon-general, and an inspector of regimental infirmaries, who were invested with distinct but jarring powers. This Board continued to act until 1808, when it was dissolved, and new-modelled upon the basis of responsibility as a body, constituted of a Director-General and two Principal Inspectors. On the peace establishment of 1817, one of these latter officers ceased to be borne on the Return of the Staff of the Army.

Sir Lucas Pepys, the Physician-General who ranked first, was President of the College of Physicians. In virtue of his office, he was empowered to select and recommend physicians for service in the army. His labours here ended, for he neither allotted to them their duty, or superintended their official conduct. The hospital regulations, expressly stating that no one who had acted, or was acting as an army surgeon, could attain the better post and easier berth of physician to the forces, while the surgeon-general allotted the physician's duty, could delegate his superintending and controlling power to superior surgeons, apothecaries, hospital mates, or persons officially bearing the commission of purveyor. The officers to whom he delegated his controlling power, were then first termed " Principal Medical Officers of the Hospitals."

The Surgeon-General, Mr. Keate, who held a multiplicity of offices, was surgeon to the Queen, to H.R.H. the Prince of Wales, to Chelsea and York Hospital, Inspector of the National Cow-Pock Establishment, surgeon to St. George's Hospital, and in virtue of his office, Examiner at the College of Surgeons (the Royal Charter laying down that the sergeant-surgeon and surgeon-general should be of the Court of Examiners), selected and recommended the whole of the class of surgeons, whether staff-surgeons, surgeons of the Line, or surgeons' assistants. The staff-surgeon remained under the surgeon-general's jurisdiction during the whole of his aftercourse; for he was then supposed to act in general hospitals or under officers of the General Staff. The surgeon of the Line and his assistant were recommended by the Surgeon-General for appointment, but placed under the order of the Inspector-General (Mr. Knight), in virtue of his commission, extending to the control of regimental infirmaries; but he had no authority to recommend those who deserved well for promotion to the rank of surgeon. He was, however, furnished with a counterbalance of difficulties in being empowered to select and recommend apothecaries, purveyors, and hospital mates. Such was the composition of the Army Medical Board instituted in 1793. The inefficiency arising from such a heterogeneous combination, gave rise to the creation of a new class of officers, or order of inspectors, generally appointed from surgeons of the Line, as then best acquainted with military hospitals and the military duties necessary for the just conduct of the medical establishments in armies. The army physician thus became destined to remain in the position to which he was originally appointed, without, as heretofore, hope of further promotion.

The contingent account of £30 annually, granted for hospital expenses, and limited to that amount up to 1793, after that year became discretionary, and swelled to a great magnitude in the course of the subsequent year. This owed its origin to the sickness which prevailed on the Continent in the latter end of the year 1794, when the sufferings of the soldiers were great, and the mortality enormous. In consequence of this, regimental surgeons were authorised to supply the sick with wine, according to their discretion, drawing on their respective paymasters for the amount of the cost. This rule was introduced in Holland, and brought over to England with the army withdrawn from Continental service in 1793.

The general expenditure of the hospital was then under the control of the surgeon, who was responsible for the due appropriation of the fund allotted for its support, as well as the general conduct of the hospital, and the servants attached to it. On home service, it was the duty of the surgeon to provide every article of diet required for the sick at the market price, and of the best possible quality; the price being ascertained and verified by the commanding officer of the regiment, whose approving signature was necessary to authenticate the surgeon's accounts. As a matter of fact, the duty was performed by the hospital sergeant, under the orders of the surgeon. On foreign service, the more bulky articles of provisions were supplied by the Commissary; the especial duty of the surgeon being to see that they were of the best quality procurable, and to make an immediate report to his commanding officer if he should find them otherwise.

Previous to 1803, the stoppage from the soldier's pay on account of hospital subsistence was sixpence per diem; in that year new regulations were published, detailing the management of British regimental hospitals, annulling the discretional allowance for contingencies, and increasing the hospital stoppage to tenpence, which proved an advantage, as the large saving of money accruing to the soldier after a long confinement to hospital was spent in dissipation, and so served again to fill the hospital. The aggregate sum arising from these stoppages was then found, under ordinary circumstances and judicious management, fully adequate to the necessary hospital expenses. By some strange oversight, patients then treated in general hospitals were not subject to any hospital stoppage from their daily pay. This incongruity was subsequently remedied.

At this period the passage to India took about ten months, and the provisions supplied were exceedingly bad; lamentable results ensued. In 1782 the 72nd lost 247 men from scurvy and other diseases during the passage, and on arriving at Madras in April, was only able to muster 369 men fit for duty. The regiment embarked 975 rank and file in good health, a pertinent example of the mal-hygiene of the day. During our campaigns in that country at that date, considerable difficulty arose owing to the constant necessity present to commanders of protecting their hospitals. When marching against Tippoo in 1790, a strong garrison had to be left to protect the hospital establishment at Dinaporam, which unfortunately fell into the hands of the enemy—600 Europeans and 200 Sepoys capitulating on honourable terms, which were strictly observed to the honour of the conqueror. In 1778 commenced the romantic career of Robert Jackson, Inspector-General of army hospitals, an accomplished writer, an original thinker, and a distinguished man, who rose superior to the obsolete system which surrounded him on every side, and like some of his equally able successors became the best of all those who could not rise superior to their village politics and personal interests, of greater value in their eyes than the welfare of the soldier. His life is crowded with interesting illustrations of the medical service as it stood towards the close of the eighteenth century. New York was still in our hands when young Jackson arrived there in 1778 from Jamaica. The lines at Knightsbridge separating the British Forces from the Americans. Offering himself as a volunteer to the 71st, or Fraser's Highlanders, then quartered in MacGowan's Pass, he was at once accepted by the colonel (afterwards Sir Archibald Campbell) and came as eighteenth on the list of volunteers. Having been educated as a physician, the Colonel considerately gave him the temporary appointment of surgeon's mate, there being a vacancy for one of the officers in the regiment, thinking it would be more comfortable for him in the interim, than volunteer supernumerary, and as not proving a bar to advancement as a combatant officer should he continue to prefer it. In consequence of the increase of sickness in the regiment on its moving to Knightsbridge in July, division of labour took place between himself and the other surgeon's mate of the corps; he undertaking the hospital duties, and his colleague those of the camp. At this period these officers were appointed (as we have already seen) by the Colonel on the recommendation of the Surgeon-General. At the siege of York Town in Virginia, he was stationed in the most advanced redoubt, which a superior French force three times attempted to carry by storm, but were as often repulsed, although exceedingly ill, and exposed to the incessant cannonade of shot and shell from the enemy during the day and night. Sir Thomas Saumarez wrote, " Our gallant friend declared he was fully determined to remain with us to the last, in order to render every assistance in his power." His comrade in arms goes on to say " Dr. Jackson was ever greatly esteemed by all who had the good fortune of knowing his amiable qualities and very extraordinary talents." At the action of Cowpens he became a prisoner to the American General Morgan, in saving the life of the British Commander (afterwards General Tarleton) under circumstances which to-day would have earned for him over and over again the cross of honour. He remained with the wounded, and in default of dressings for them disrobed himself of his only shirt and tore it up into bandages, his noble conduct so greatly pleasing the American General, that when the British wounded could be exchanged he was sent back with them, no parole being required, nor exchange demanded. He returned to Europe in 1782, when thirty-two years of age. After travelling on the Continent on conclusion of peace with the French, he returned to Perth in 1784, when he rejoined his regiment, the 71st, just prior to its disbandment. He returned to Paris, studied at La Charité. In 1781 he submitted to the public the result of his experiences in Jamaica and America, a work which soon attracted deserved notice. In 1791 he was appointed surgeon to the Buffs by Mr. Hunter, and served in the Earl of Moira's expedition to the coast of France. He accompanied the regiment to Flanders in 1794, where he became personally acquainted with the Duke of York, afterwards Commander-in-Chief. The troops were in their retreat through Holland in a very sickly state; the sick were sent to hospitals whenever the army changed ground, and as it did so frequently the accumulation in the hospitals was great and the mortality enormous. Dr. Jackson, from his previous experience, was appointed Physician to the Forces, the Commander-in-Chief enforcing the appointment in opposition to the Medical Board, thus throwing open the Physician's rank again to the regimental surgeon and dissolving the monopoly of the College of Physicians. He joined the hospital as physician at Bremen. On the withdrawal of the infantry he was appointed by General Harcourt, head of the medical department, to superintend the embarkation of the sick, numbering nearly 500. On the death of Dr. Kennedy, Inspector of Hospitals on the Continent, Dr. Jackson was appointed his successor. When the troops were withdrawn, he returned to England and was ordered to Southampton to join the expedition, consisting of about 15,000 men, about to start under the command of Sir Ralph Abercrombie for the conquest of the French Carribean Islands, and for which Mr. Young was gazetted "Inspector-General of Hospitals." Dr. Jackson was appointed Assistant-Inspector and second to Mr. Weir, Senior Medical Officer to that part of the expedition destined for St. Domingo, which arrived at Cape St. Nicholas Mole, on the 1st of May, 1796. The colonels of colonial regiments had at that time a contract for the subsistence of their sick in hospital. The expense was enormous. By commuting the ration, fresh meat instead of salt meat, wine in place of rum ad *valorem*, with the power of changing with the commissary the species of provisions according to a fixed rate of value, he found the means of supplying every requisite subsistence, or extra refreshment which the sick required. The plan was approved and carried into effect with a saving to the public of not less than £80,000 per annum.

On the evacuation of Port au Prince by the British troops in 1798, Dr. Jackson and several of the medical officers returned to England after a short tour in the United States. After superintending with success the numerous hospitals of the troops returned from North Holland, he was appointed head of the Army Depot Hospital at Chatham, which he resigned in 1802, and entered upon the practice of his profession at Stockton-upon-Tees, where he wrote his "Remarks on the Constitution of the Medical Department of the Army." On General Simcoe being nominated Commander-in-Chief of the Forces in India in 1807, Dr. Jackson, who had served with him at St. Domingo, was offered the confidential post of military secretary which the sudden decease of his friend prevented him from accepting. When the army of reserve was formed at the commencement of the Peninsular War, he was appointed Inspector-General of Hospitals, in which rank he afterwards served in the West Indies. In 1815 he returned to England when sixty-five years of age. He died April 6, 1827, in his seventy-seventh year. Of his many works, none are more interesting than his "Formation, Discipline and Economy of Armies," of which Sir John Moore wrote his impression in the following terms:—
"My dear Jackson, I have perused your military book, with which I am much delighted. There are none of us, even the most experienced, who may not derive instruction from it; and I only regret that you, who possess a soldier's mind, had not been a soldier by profession."

Throughout all his works may be observed a prevailing anxiety for the health and well-being of the soldier, and everywhere he urges the necessity and importance of a constant reference on this subject to the experience and counsel of the best military surgeons, and became "the cardinal hinge of effect in armies." The health-history of the wars in Europe during the period of his active service were, according to him, "demonstration in proof of the important fact, that military life has been sacrificed in an enormous proportion to ignorance." The Royal Warrant of the 1st of January, 1806, fixing the rate of hospital stoppage at tenpence a-day, originated in the demonstration, so often furnished by Dr. Jackson, that the sum of money which feeds a soldier in barracks is sufficient to feed him and provide him with necessary comforts in hospital. The Medical Department occasioning, in such a case, an expense to the State beyond the salary of medical officers, medicines and lodgings. This must have effected an enormous saving at a time when peculation was rife in almost every branch of the public service. He declared that when medicine fixed its station amongst the sciences, it was more than probable that "it would owe its good fortune to the medical officers of armies, and more likely to the medical officers of the British army than to others." He urged the claim of the Medical Department of the Army to a share in military honors and distinctions on the fair ground that, "as the medical staff shares in the fatigues and dangers of war, in just return it is entitled to a share of advantages." In his remarks on the constitution of a medical staff, he considered that "the medical staff of the Army be sufficient for every form of duty which is likely to arise in time of war, but not more than sufficient, for superfluity here, as in other things, corrupts and vitiates the execution of duty." Two medical officers per 1000 men in most parts of Europe in time of peace and three in times of war, was from his experience the due proportion, but scarcely sufficient, in peace or war, in tropical or unhealthy climates. To the assistant-surgeons he assigns the duty of attending the regiment under actual fire on the field of battle, with a "mark of distinction, honorary or substantial," a staff-surgeon and three hospital assistants he proposed as the proper medical staff for a brigade of three regiments in addition to the then three regimental surgeons and six assistants. The staff-surgeon to have the power and means to open hospitals for the cure of diseases requiring longer time than could consist with the condition of regimental infirmaries, which he insisted in the field should be "establishments prepared at all times to be broken up at an hour's notice." For a division, a physician with a given number of hospital assistants, with power to establish hospitals for the reception of such sick and wounded as could not be properly accommodated in brigade hospitals or regimental infirmaries. The physician being senior medical officer of the division with full powers to direct every medical and surgical measure concerning the troops collected into a division. He also advocated the employment of "health officers," as an important part of an army, " as the health of the troops is a matter of the greatest importance to success in war ;" also that " no one be admitted into the class of assistant-surgeon who was not fit for the office, and that no one who was actually in the service should be moved from a lower to a higher rank, and more responsible duty, without some public evidence that he was competent in professional knowledge and writing in every respect for the promotion intended." He goes on to say, " if a medical officer be professionally skilful and morally correct, he is entitled, as he is eminently useful in his vocation, to a respectable place of rank in the military fabric. The medical officer claims to himself the rank of a gentleman, and the respect which is due to a man of science. Rank is everywhere the gift of power. If the officer of the medical staff were advanced in rank by a just and legitimate rule of gradation, the staff-surgeon would class with surgeons, the physicians with lieutenant-colonels, and the physician-in-chief with generals. The rank accorded to the medical officer does not injure, or even interfere with the military. Rank is of no intrinsic value to a man of science, but the opinion connected with rank makes an impression on the soldier, which aids materially in giving force to medical authority, and consequently to medical utility." Until the termination of the war in 1793 the rank of the Medical staff of the British Army was not distinctly defined. The assistant-surgeon entered a regiment with the rank of lieutenant, and the surgeon took rank with captains according to date of commission. In that year general hospitals were first formed in England, consequent upon the great increase of sickness following upon the expedition to Holland, at which time staff-surgeons were also introduced into the service, were entirely distinct from the regimental surgeons, and principally employed in the general hospitals. The sick returns of these establishments then comprehended nothing more than a list of general terms—"acute, chronic wounds, venereals, itch, convalescents with the gross number admitted, cured and buried in a given time. Shortly after the commencement of the present century, a regimental form of sick return was constructed of a better form and comprehending many points of useful notice ; the proportion of sick to strength being for the first time shown on the face of the return. It originated with the Irish Army Medical Board in 1795. On active service the regimental infirmaries received all manner of indispositions which did not promise to be of longer duration than ten days or a fortnight; such as slight fevers, flesh wounds on the upper parts of the body, &c., in fact all cases as might be transported in waggons without injury, when the necessity of changing a position occurred. The brigade hospital received such sick and wounded as could not expect to be well in a fortnight, or could not be moved with safety on every occasion of necessity, while the general hospital of the division was reserved for complicated diseases and wounds requiring special modes of treatment and medicated diet.

An assistant-surgeon attended close in rear of a battalion when it moved forward into action, in order to afford immediate assistance to the wounded, a necessity as pointed out by Jackson because " serving to give confidence to soldiers and even to officers apprehensive on the head of hemorrhage." Besides the presence of the surgeon with the Line while under fire, the quartermaster of the regiment, with the pioneers and band, furnished with light bearers, attended to remove the wounded instantly without the range of shot. A portion of the regimental and brigade staff furnished with the means of performing surgical operations, of dressing and refreshing the wounded, was usually present at some convenient spot out of the range of fire, or sheltered from it and rendered conspicuous by a flag or signal.

The gradation of rank and the amount of pay received by Medical officers in 1793, is shown in the following table. These were additional to the regimental establishments.

Brigade of three regiments in the field, 3000 strong:—

1 Inspector in Chief	£1	10	0 and 0	10	8	allowances.
2 Physicians	1	0	0 each 0	6	8	,,
3 Staff-Surgeons	0	10	0 ,, 0	3	6	,,
2 Apothecaries	0	10	0 ,, 0	3	6	,,
10 Hospital Mates	0	7	6 ,, 0	2	6	,,

To a division of five brigades or 15,000 men during war, or on foreign service, was allowed:—

1 Chief Inspector	£3	0	0 and 1	0	0	allowances.
2 Second Inspectors	2	0	0 each 0	13	4	,,
7 Physicians	1	0	0 ,, 0	6	8	,,
9 Staff-Surgeons	0	10	0 ,, 0	3	4	,,
5 Apothecaries	0	10	0 ,, 0	3	4	,,
20 Hospital Mates	0	7	6 ,, 0	2	6	,,

The total regimental pay and allowances of the brigade during home service, amounted to £2,190 per annum, the additional war or foreign service medical establishments, to £4,745. The regimental medical pay and allowances of a division were £11,093 6s. 8d. and £22,995 respectively.

In the West Indies, and at St. Domingo, Hospital Corps, wearing the traditional scarlet uniform of the Medical Staff, had been formed with adjutants and quartermasters and a corps of waggoners in Flanders, intended principally for the carriage of the sick and wounded. On 25th December, 1787, the regiment of invalids (41st Foot) had been reduced as an invalid regiment. In 1793 ninety-one "officers of the hospitals" were on half pay, including amongst them Thomas Hopkins, late Deputy-

Director to the Hospital at the Havannah, Sir Edward Grymes, Bart., surgeon's mate at St. Philip; Sir James Napier, Inspector-General of Regimental Infirmaries and late Chief-Director in North America; Alexander Grant, Field Inspector; John Jones, Chaplain to the Hospitals; John Cherington, Master-Surgeon, Louisburgh; Archibald Meares, Surgeon to the Brigade, &c. In 1799 there were on the establishment of the army thirty-eight regiments of cavalry, each with a surgeon and assistant surgeon; one regiment of mounted riflemen, three regiments of Guards, with seven surgeons and sixteen assistant-surgeons; ninety-two regiments of Foot; a New South Wales Corps, Queen's Rangers, York Hussars, Scotch Brigade, a regiment of Foot for the Island of Minorca, a Regiment of Foot, a French Regiment of Infantry, a Royal Garrison Battalion, twelve West India Regiments, three small recruiting corps, three Staff Corps of Infantry, three Company Levies, a Royal Waggon Train of eight companies, fifty-one independent companies of Invalids, and a corps of invalids in Ireland numbering five companies, requiring a large medical staff in the aggregate.

There were garrison surgeons at Berwick, Chelsea Hospital, Edinburgh, Gravesend, Tilbury, Hull, Fort George, Portsmouth, Sheerness, and the Tower of London. Gibraltar has a surgeon-major, extra surgeon and two hospital mates. In the West Indies, surgeons of hospitals are at Granada and St. Domingo, and surgeons at Tobago, Barbadoes, Antigua, St. Christopher, St. Lucia, Jamaica, Halifax, Island of Cape Breton, New Brunswick, Quebec, Upper Canada, Newfoundland. The seniors receiving £172 17s. 6d per annum, and the mates £60 10s. 1½d. The Royal Regiment of Artillery has still its surgeon-general and five surgeons, the senior has twenty years' service in the army. There are five assistant-surgeons. One Royal Regiment of Artillery of twenty companies is quartered in Ireland; a corps of Royal Engineers and a corps of artificers and drivers is attached to the Royal Irish Artillery. Such was the composition of the Army and its Medical Staff at the close of the last century. We find in the Gazettes of the period hospital mates being appointed assistant-surgeons of regiments; assistant-surgeons transferred from one regiment to another, and gentlemen appointed assistant-surgeons, and officers of the same rank of a few months standing gazetted surgeons of regiments. Some gentlemen are appointed at once to the latter rank. Service as hospital mates does not as yet count; only when commissioned as assistant-surgeons does it do so.

On the conclusion of the Peace of Amiens the following were reduced on English half pay in Great Britain.

Two chief physicians, three staff-surgeons, one inspector of health, four inspectors, one deputy-inspector, twenty assistant-inspectors, one field-inspector, sixteen physicians, thirty-four surgeons, fifteen apothecaries, eight deputy-purveyors, eleven hospital mates.

Half pay on the staff of the West Indies:—
One director of hospitals, two inspectors of hospitals, one assistant-inspector, four physicians, seven surgeons, four apothecaries, four purveyors, two deputy purveyors, and eighty-two other medical officers of various ranks belonging to later colonial garrisons or continental expeditions. Among the physicians occur the names of Sir Charles Blagden, Sir J. Fitzpatrick is inspector of health, and Sir J. Macnamara Hayes, Bart., inspector of hospitals.

On the 4th January, 1798, the following order regulating the dress of staff and regimental medical officers was issued from the Adjutant-General's office. "The uniform to be worn in future by the surgeons of regiments with cavalry and infantry; the assistant-surgeons and veterinary surgeons, is to be plain scarlet, with the uniform buttons of their respective regiments, but without epaulettes and lappels, a plain round red cuff and collar, white waistcoat and breeches, and plain cocked hat with the regimental button.

"The uniform of all officers of the Medical staff to be the same, excepting with regard to the button which is to have the King's coronet engraved on it, with the letters H. S. underneath.

"(Signed)   GEORGE HEWETT, Adjutant-General."
"Hospital Staff," had replaced the old designation of "Officers of the Hospitals."

On 29th March, 1803, the following Horse Guards General Order, directed the "Uniform of the Hospital Staff" to consist of a "plain scarlet coat lapelled with yellow buttons with the words 'Hospital Staff' round the crown in the centre, white waistcoat and breeches, military boots, plain cocked hat, infantry regulation sword and knots, no feathers or epaulettes.

"(Signed)   HENRY CALVERT, Adjutant-General."
The gradation of rank was then as follows:—hospital mate; battalion assistant-surgeon; battalion surgeon, commencing on 12s. per diem, chargeable with the expense of keeping a horse, and increasing progressively to 15s. and 20s. a day. The additional pay was issued by warrant upon certificates of a definite number of years' service. The pay was drawn monthly, that for length of service quarterly; while that of the "Hospital Staff," and more especially in the case of the physicians, was rarely issued until a year or fifteen months after it had become due. It was also subject to some deductions, but as a matter of fact many officers entered the Service on the pay of battalion surgeons or physicians, and never served in the lower ranks.

On the 10th January, 1803, before the renewal of the war with France, the total number of medical officers on full pay amounted to 600 :—

Assistant-Inspectors of Hospitals . 3
Surgeon-Majors . . . 2
Garrison Physicians . . 3
Garrison Surgeons . . 26
Extra Surgeon . . . 1
Apothecaries . . . 4
Hospital Mates . . . 8
Surgeons' Mates . . . 1

Royal Artillery.
Surgeon-General . . . 1
Surgeons 8
Assistant-Surgeons . . 15

Cavalry.
Surgeons 36
Assistant-Surgeons . . 57

Infantry.
Surgeons 144
Assistant-Surgeons . . 251

Miscellaneous Battalions.
Surgeons 11
Assistant-Surgeons . . 10

West India Regiments.
Surgeons 9
Assistant-Surgeons . . 9

Royal Waggon Train.
Surgeon 1

Towards the close of the preceding century several important changes were made bearing upon the duties of medical officers. Fining soldiers afflicted with venereal disease was repressed in 1795. Commanding officers enlisting recruits abroad were to obtain sufficient "chirurgical testimony" as to their fitness, and when a new code of regulations was promulgated for the recruiting services in 1796, it was directed that an hospital mate should be placed under the orders of each field-officer of recruiting districts to examine the recruits brought to him for inspection. In 1799 a certificate to this effect was to be entered on the back of each attestation, and in 1802 a new class of medical officers were appointed, called "district surgeons," and employed in the several recruiting districts to examine men before being attested for the Army. Twenty-six of these officers were employed in 1808, replaced by staff-surgeons in 1810.

The Medical Staff was represented at the attack and defence of Toulon, when the "patience and fortitude with which the officers and men suffered fatigue, hunger, thirst, and the unavoidable inconveniences attending the difficult and pressing services to which they were suddenly called," drew forth the special commendation of the commander, Lord Mulgrave. At Guadaloupe, where on the 1st September, 1794, out of 1,764 British troops, 1,375 were on the sick list, and only 387 fit for duty. In twelve months the 2nd Queen's lost at this time in the West Indies six officers, thirty-one sergeants, nineteen corporals, six drummers, and 254 privates, from which facts may be easily imagined how arduous were the duties in the hospitals.

During the expedition to Holland in 1799, and subsequent retreat, several medical officers became prisoners of war to the French, including those of the 11th Regiment, who, after the attack on Ostend, remained for nearly a year in the hands of the enemy at Douai. Much hardship was also endured during the Maroon War in Jamaica in 1795, when some regiments were so reduced by disease that they were obliged to recruit with boys. In the expedition against the Caribs at St. Lucia, the medical officers shared in the "fatigue, privation, and exposure," which led to one regiment (31st), on disembarking at Barbadoes, going as a body into hospital, and ending in a loss of seventeen officers and no less than 870 men from disease. At the capitulation of a portion of the 19th Regiment at Candy, in Ceylon, in 1803, Assistant-Surgeon Hope, five other officers, and 172 men were barbarously murdered. After the victory of Assaye in the same year, we find Sir Arthur Wellesley writing to General Lake, " I have been much embarrassed by the difficulties of establishing an hospital for my wounded men; the Nizam's officers will not admit us into the forts which have any strength, and at last I have been obliged to place them at Adjuntes, a place of inferior strength upon the extreme frontier. However, I think they will be in security, and *I am now at liberty* to recommence my operations." Sufficiently indicative of the dangers through which the officers of the hospitals had passed throughout that short but decisive campaign, in common with their sick and wounded comrades in arms.

CHAPTER VII.

I must, for a moment, return to Ireland. In 1776 an Act was passed by the Parliament of that kingdom, regulating the status of those admirable charities, the County Infirmaries, by which it was enacted that no persons should be permitted to undertake the charge of the sick in them until their surgical knowledge was tested by an Examining Board, composed of the *Surgeon-General* and the surgeons of Stephen's and Mercer's Hospitals. This led up to the granting of a Royal Charter to the College of Surgeons in Ireland in 1784, one of the most important grounds on which it was given being, to use its own words, " the providing a sufficient number of properly educated surgeons for our Army and Navy." Dr. Renny, then surgeon to the Royal Hospital and Military Provost, and the Surgeon-General, Mr. Stewart, were the most active promoters of this important scheme; in recognition of which, and their efforts in obtaining the Royal Charter of Incorporation, the College placed a handsome full length portrait of the former, and a marble bust of the latter (as lasting memorials), in their Halls.

At this date most of the barracks and hospitals attached to them had been allowed to fall into decay by the Irish Parliament, who were then by no means enamoured of a military force, and had just voted £20,000 for the clothing of the newly-raised Militia, first embodied with the view of training to arms men of a proper description, and, so far as it went, counteracting the dangers of a standing army! which from the date of the departure of William III. had been fixed at 12,000 men on Irish Establishment pay. This body was entirely under the control of the Irish Government, and its medical concerns supervised principally by the medical officers attached to the different regiments entering into its composition. The Surgeon-General and joint Physicians-General resided in the Metropolis, and were connected with the Army through the "King's Royal Military Infirmary," situated in the Phœnix Park, and of which they were consulting medical officers. It being intended that a considerable part of the Army in Ireland should be encamped in the summer of 1795, and it being thought necessary that steps should be immediately taken for forming a Medical Staff, a letter was addressed by command of His Excellency the Lord-Lieutenant, to "Doctor Charles Guinn, Doctor William Harvey, joint Physicians-General; George Stewart, Esq., Surgeon-General; George Renny, Esq., Surgeon to the Royal Hospital," requesting that a "Medical Board of Controul" should be established, as in England, consisting of the Physicians-General, the Surgeon-General, and the Surgeon of the Royal Hospital, Kilmainham; Mr. Renny to be appointed Director-General of Hospitals, his duty to be to visit the different encampments as often as occasion might require, and carry into effect those orders and regulations which, as a Member of the Board, he had assisted in forming. The number of physicians and surgeons upon the Staff was to depend upon the number of encampments and their extent. The new Board was to have the superintendence of all hospitals, general as well as regimental, and the surgeons of each were regularly to report weekly or monthly, so that not only the number of sick, but the nature of their diseases might be known, and the Board be able to anticipate any epidemic, distemper, or camp fever which might be expected in the young regiments that were then about to take the field (encamp), the several duties of the Board being under the direction of the Commander-in-Chief in Ireland. In compliance with these instructions, the Irish Army Medical Board was formed on the 1st June, 1795.

They were directed immediately to issue such orders and instructions to the commanding officers and surgeons of the different regiments then on the establishment as were necessary for carrying out His Excellency's desires notified on their appointment. The following list of regiments, proposed to be encamped in different parts of Ireland, being enclosed for their information :—

Dublin Encampment.—Breadalbane Fencibles, Parkin's Fencibles, and the Downshire, Drogheda, Fermanagh, Londonderry, Longford, North Mayo, Sligo, and Westmeath regiments of Militia.

Southern Encampment.—Antrim, Armagh, Donegal, Dublin County, Galway, Leitrim, South Mayo, Monaghan, and Waterford Militia.

Northern Encampment.—Clare, South Cork, Limerick County, and Wexford Militia.

Tarbert Encampment.—A regiment of Fencibles.

The Board, on its formation, submitted, for the approval of His Excellency the Lord Lieutenant, a short set of rules for the future guidance and direction of regimental surgeons and mates, a principal feature of which was the establishment of a frequent and accurate system of reports by which means they would be enabled with facility to control and direct the whole of the medical and surgical business of the Irish army. The staff medical and surgical establishment proposed for the several encampments, formed on a reduced model as was consistent with the safety of the troops, could, in the opinion of the Board, be only ensured "by the employment of efficient and experienced physicians and surgeons who would not relinquish their professional prospects unless sufficiently paid." For each of the county encampments was appointed one physician, one surgeon, one apothecary, one purveyor, one hospital mate, in addition to nurses. A physician was permanently stationed in Cork during the war. A general hospital was opened at each of the encampments in addition to the smaller regimental dispensaries, to contain 100 beds at least, and attended by the staff physicians, surgeons, apothecary, and hospital mate. The physician and surgeon were to visit daily the regimental hospitals, and report weekly or oftener to the general officer commanding the district on their condition. Wooden buildings were recommended as most suitable for the camp hospitals.

The following gentlemen were recommended for employment as peculiarly fitted from their professional abilities and experience to fill the stations of staff hospital physicians, and surgeons, the physicians at 20s. per diem allowance and half pay, and the surgeon 10s. 3d. a day and half pay as in England, viz.: Doctors James Clegborn, Thomas Egan, Francis Hopkins, William O'Dwyer, Surgeons Ralph Smith O'Bre, Francis McEvoy, Clement Archer, William Moore Peile, and Dr. John Haig, the latter to be permanently stationed at Cork, where regiments usually assembled previous to embarking for foreign service, and where a general hospital had been formed in 1790.

The apothecaries, purveyors and mates were to be specially brought forward, as they were required, at a salary of 10s. a day each to the two former officers, and 5s. to the latter (afterwards increased to 7s. 6d.) gentlemen, and without half pay to either as was then the custom. The following allowances for medicines were recommended. To each of the nine Militia regiments encamped, not exceeding 500 men, twenty guineas; ten regiments not exceeding 700 men, thirty guineas; three Fencible regiments of 1000 men each, forty guineas; Downshire Militia, 840 men, thirty-five guineas; Drogheda Militia, 210 men, £11 7s. 6d., a total of £671 2s. 6d.

These propositions were sanctioned with some minor alterations in detail, by the Lord-Lieutenant, Viscount Camden, who desired that in "selecting the surgeons for this service, such persons should be recommended as had been acquainted with the practice of an army surgeon, and also had had the advantage of medical knowledge." The commander-in-chief in Ireland directed the Board to take the necessary steps for carrying into execution " my Lord-Lieutenant's pleasure," and so originated and was formed the Army Medical Board in Ireland. Previous to its formation, and until May, 1797, surgeons of regiments received the Irish establishment commuted allowances in full of all medical and hospital expenses, and were amenable to no other authority except that of their commanding officers. The Act of Parliament conferring these allowances was commonly known by the name of " Burke's Bill," viz. :

Commuted allowances for bedding, nurse hire, &c.	£30	0	0
Ditto for hospital rent	20	0	0
Ditto for medicaments at £12 10s. a company when consisting of sixty men and upwards . . .	125	0	0
Total	£175	0	0

When regiments consisted of less than 500 men, the medicament money was reduced to £75 per annum. The copy of the original rule which governed the allowances for medicaments was as follows: "And whereas His Majesty has been pleased to cause repayment to be made to the non-commissioned officers and men of his Foot Forces of the stoppages made for the use of the paymasters and surgeons; and whereas it is proper to make provision for the paymasters and surgeons in lieu thereof. Be it enacted that from the 25th day of December, 1783, an unusual allowance of £120 shall be made to each of the said paymasters and surgeons when the establishment of their companies is fifty private men or upwards, and an allowance of £70 annually after the companies shall be reduced within establishment below the said number of private men."

The inefficiency of this system had been long felt and complained of, as the sick of the army in regimental hospitals had few comforts, and the want of adequate medical control placed these establishments too much in the power of individuals, many of whom thought themselves authorised to appropriate a part of the medicament money to their use. These and other abuses were shortly afterwards remedied, so that notwithstanding that the price of medicines had greatly risen, and an additional expense of some £20 per annum had been incurred by a Regulation issued in 1811, allowing officers and the wives and children of soldiers to have medicines from the regimental chests, a privilege not previously permitted, the expense at the conclusion of the great war in 1816 was less than the commuted annual allowance granted by Government prior to 1797. The regimental hospitals were now provided and furnished by the barrack departments. The annual expense of medicines for regiments consisting of 800 men and upwards, during the twelve years ending 1816 had amounted to about £90, and the contingent charges to about £88 10s., the entire of which last mentioned expense had been liquidated by the savings which are recapitulated below.

Abstract of savings in General and Regimental Hospitals in Ireland for twelve years, ending 24th June 1816.

	£	s.	d.
General Hospitals	21,034	14	3½
Regiments of the Line	34,409	2	3
Irish Militia	20,841	2	5¼
British Militia	5,054	13	9½
Total	81,339	12	9¼

A few months after the formation of the Board, General Cunningham, Commander of the Forces in Ireland, was directed to express the thanks of His Royal Highness Field-Marshal the Duke of York, for the first returns of the sick of the Army in Ireland forwarded to him, and also that he considered the forms " so well adapted to the purpose for which they were intended," that the Army Medical Board in England had been ordered to adopt them. It was afterwards ordered that three copies of these monthly Reports on the Health of the Army in Ireland should be furnished. One for His Excellency the Lord-Lieutenant, a second for the Commander-in-Chief, and a third for His Majesty ; a practice continued for many years, during which period the able officers who administered the concerns of the Army Medical Department in Ireland received the constant support and approval of succeeding commanders and governments. About two years previous to its formation, viz , 1793, when the Militia and Fencible Regiments were raised in Great Britain and Ireland, His Majesty had been pleased to allow surgeons and mates to hold military commissions, principally because their pay and allowances under the old Medical Regulations of the Army were insufficient to induce professional men to accept of such situations. In April, 1796, an order was issued, on recommendation of the Army Medical Board, restricting surgeons and mates appointed subsequent to that date from holding military commissions, giving in lieu a slight increase of pay, but the government in both countries were obliged tacitly to depart from the letter of this order, and to allow matters to return into the old channel in which they remained for a number of years. As late as 1857, a paragraph in the Queen's Regulations and Orders for the Army will be found stating that, when medical officers of militia regiments hold double commissions, they shall only be employed in their medical capacity. The text of the original Order in Ireland forbidding the practice is given below:—

"Adjutant-General's Office, April 1, 1796.

"It being contrary to His Majesty's regulations that any officer in the Army should hold the commission of surgeon or warrant of surgeon's mate, it is His Excellency's the Lord-Lieutenant's pleasure that the same be observed in the regiments of Cavalry, Infantry and Fencible Corps in this Establishment, and the Commander-in-Chief also desires you will issue the necessary orders directing such surgeons or mates in the regiments of cavalry or regular infantry, under your command, as may hold other commissions to make an election prior to the first day of June next which of these commissions they will vacate conformable to these orders.

"(Signed) J. HEWIT, Adjutant-General."

During the several affairs in the East Indies, one of these officers who was captain and surgeon of his regiment, had led the corps out of action, and as only surviving senior officer commanded it on its return to England. The objection to these double commissions was that when the junior medical officer held one and not the senior, he might in virtue of his combatant rank command the former, and because in the heat of the fight or during the pursuit of the enemy, the hospitals and sick were oftentimes left to shift for themselves—hence the recommendations of the Army Medical Boards. Such objections would of course not have held good when medical officers assumed command of their own subordinates in the hospital or the ambulance, a necessity in the interest of humanity, good order and discipline.

On the 16th of June, a code of Military Medical Regulations was submitted for approval to the Commander-in-Chief in Ireland, and subsequently printed and distributed to the different regiments in the command. The meetings of the Board were first held in the King's Military Infirmary, now No. 1 Station Hospital. In the commission appointing Dr. Renny a commissioner of this hospital, reference is made to the ancient charter in the following terms:—

"By His Excellency the Lord Lieutenant-General and General-Governor of Ireland.

"Cornwallis,

"Whereas John Earl of Cartaret Lord-Lieutenant and Governor-General of Ireland did by his order, bearing date the 20th day of April, 1728, constitute and appoint the General and Commander-in-Chief of the Army under the Government of this Kingdom, the Lieutenant-General, the Major-General and Brigadier-General of the Army, in this Establishment for the time being. The Muster Master-General, the Quartermaster-General, the Adjutant-General, the Surveyor-General of His Majesty's fortifications and buildings, the Deputy Vice-Treasurer, the Physician-General of the Army, and the Surgeon-General for the time being, or any three or more of them to be Commissioners to supervise and govern the Infirmary or Hospital erected in Dublin for the relief and cure of sick and wounded soldiers, now called the King's Royal Military Infirmary in Dublin.

"And Whereas since the date of the said Order an Army Medical Board has been established in this Kingdom consisting of the Physician and Surgeon-General of the Army and the Director-General of Military Hospitals in this Kingdom, for the time being should be appointed one of the Commissioners to supervise and govern the said Royal Military Infirmary. We have therefore thought fit to constitute and appoint Dr. George Renny, Director-General of Hospitals in this Kingdom for the time being to be one of the Commissioners to supervise and govern the said Royal Military Infirmary accordingly with the like powers, privileges and pre-eminences as are enjoyed by the Commissioners of the said Infirmary appointed under the Order of the Earl of Cartaret of the 20th April, 1728, before recited. For all which this shall be sufficient warrant and authority. Given at His Majesty's Castle of Dublin, the 5th day of February, 1801.

"By His Excellency's Command,
"E. B. LITTLEHALES."

The foundation stone of the present building was laid on the 17th August, 1786, and completed in 1788, at a cost of £9000 and for some years afterwards the upper story of Stephen's Hospital was rented at £500 per annum. The expenses of the Royal Infirmary in 1818, amounted to a sum of £8,554 per annum, nearly £4,600 of which was supplied by a Parliamentary grant, and £3,954 by a stoppage of tenpence a day for each sick soldier admitted, the average expense of supporting each patient (salaries of officers included) was £33 per annum. All soldiers of the garrison inflicted with fever and other acute diseases were by order sent to the infirmary within twenty-four hours.

Medicine chests were supplied by the Governors and Directors of the Apothecaries Hall from the date of the formation of the Army Medical Board.

It was the usual practice to allow of soldiers suffering from venereal and other chronic complaints to sleep two in a bed, single beds being reserved for acute cases of disease, which occurred in about the proportion of one to six in well selected summer encampments. Owing to the difficulty of obtaining proper houses as hospitals, the Board suggested to the Commander-in-Chief, the advisability of attaching infirmaries to each of the barracks in Ireland. These and many other improvements were from time to time suggested, and carried out by the military executive. Before the breaking up of the camps in the following year, the staff-surgeons were continued in these districts by His Excellency's commands. For the purpose of being obeyed and consulted by regimental surgeons in these districts, assistant-inspectors were added in after years.

Many of the Militia regiments having materially suffered from the non-attendance of their surgeons, the Medical Board were requested, in 1796, to express an opinion as to the " best and most effective method of enforcing their attendance in future." The Militia of Ireland was first embodied in 1793, on the motion of Sir John Parnell, made in the Irish House of Commons 6th February, which he estimated would produce a force of 16,000 men. The surgeons and mates appointed by the several colonels were for the most part practitioners in medicine and surgery in their respective counties, and as the first Militia Bill afforded no prospect that the appointment of surgeon would be permanent, collegiate qualification was not required, and strict attendance at the quarters was very generally dispensed with; as had it been insisted on, it was highly probable that few militia regiments could at that time be supplied with any medical attendants whatever—the enrolment and other advantages being too inconsiderable to tempt professional men to quit for any time their settled residence. In 1795 an Act passed the Irish Parliament by which it was enacted that the pay of Militia surgeons should be made permanent, and that previous to the 11th of November of that year every Militia surgeon should be qualified in the same manner as surgeons of the Regular Forces, *i.e.*, by obtaining a certificate from the Examiners of the Royal College of Surgeons in Ireland. Militia surgeons declining to offer themselves for examination were permitted by their colonels to dispose of their commissions to qualified persons. Attendance was now regularly enforced on pain of dismissal. At this date the regular troops in Ireland were too feeble to cope with the insurrectionary risings which were constantly taking place. The best troops had been sent abroad and their place had been supplied by Invalid and Fencible regiments, and even of these there were only 10,000 present in the country. As the pay of a labourer was only sixpence a day, the soldiers on the whole were better off. About the close of 1796, more than 30,000 Yeomanry were added to the permanent force in Ireland, 19,000

Militia were under arms and some 10,000 Regulars, over the whole of which the Medical Board exercised a general supervision.

In 1796 the French, under General Hoche, threatened a descent upon Ireland and immediately it became necessary (in order to obtain the requisite number of gentlemen) to increase the pay of hospital mates from 5s. per diem to 7s. 6d., " with 20 guineas advanced to each as a douceur." The form of appointment to the Medical Staff in Ireland is given in the following Warrant :—

"Medical Board Room, Dec. 26, 1796.

" Sir,—We have to acquaint you that you were this day appointed Hospital Mate to the Forces in this Kingdom.

" You will receive an immediate douceur of twenty guineas and seven shillings and sixpence per day, pay to commence from the date of this letter.

" And you are forthwith to repair to head-quarters in the Southern District there to receive the special orders of the Physician-General, Director-General or Hospital Staff.

" C. W. Guinn.
" C. B. Hippax,   " W. Harvey.
   Secretary.   " Geo. Stewart.
                          " G. Renny.
" To Mr. Robert Hamilton, Hospital Mate."

General hospitals were now formed at Belfast, Kilkenny, Bandon, New Geneva, Duncannon, Waterford, Kilcullen (for the Curragh) Limerick, Phœnix Park, Athlone, Cork, Fermoy, Clonmel, Drogheda, in addition to the various regimental infirmaries. The contingent expenses of the former for the year ending 31st March, 1801, amounted to £10,000, which sum had been received in instalments from the Treasury by the Director-General and expended under his supervision. In addition, £4,000 was expended for bedding and other articles of hospital service; and £1,750 5s. 5½d. for medicines. The total cost for medicines amounting to a sum of £3,613 11s. 7½d., not including the Fencible and Yeomanry Corps, but the following regiments of the Line then on the Establishment and the General Hospitals, viz., 6th Dragoon Guards; 9th, 22nd, 23rd, 24th, 28th, and Hompech's Dragoons; 1st and 3rd Battalions Coldstream Guards; 1st and 2nd Battalions 15th Foot; 16th Foot; 1st and 2nd 20th Foot; 21st Foot; 1st and 2nd 46th Foot; 56th Foot; 1st and 2nd 62nd Foot; 71st, 72nd, and 82nd Foot, and four Battalions of Dutch Infantry, who were in charge of their own medical officers. The Royal Irish Artillery, principally occupying the forts, were under the supervision of their surgeon-general in Ireland, and had separate medical officers and hospitals belonging to the Ordnance Department.

On the 12th of January, 1797, the new Regulations which His Majesty had been pleased to make for the improvement of the situation of surgeons and mates belonging to the Regular Army, and for the better management of regimental hospitals, was by the Order of His Excellency, the Lord-Lieutenant, promulgated in Ireland.

By this Warrant (which had become necessary, as young men of professional merit had been deterred from entering the Service by the inadequacy of the income and their indifferent stations in the Army), the pay was increased from 6s. to 12s. per diem, in the cavalry, and from 4s. to 10s. in the infantry, with quarters, carriage of baggage, &c., as captains, with a half-pay of five shillings a day after twenty years' service on full-pay as surgeon and mate. The pay of assistant-surgeon from 3s. 6d. to 5s. per diem when at home, and 7s. 6d. when at foreign stations; a King's commission, quarters, &c.

Each regimental surgeon was supplied with a medicine chest instead of a specific sum in money, and a yearly allowance for the purchase of wine for the sick was allowed to regimental surgeons. Four sets of hospital bedding for every hundred men on home service, for the care of which the surgeon was held accountable to the Director-General of Hospitals. The twenty pounds per annum allowed by the Barrack Board to each regiment for the hire of a regimental hospital was to cease, and the buildings to be supplied by the Ordnance Department. Each surgeon on the Establishment was to supply himself with a set of capital instruments (the average cost of which was fifteen guineas) and within a radius of ten miles the regimental surgeon was to take care of the sick of any other regiments, recruiting parties, soldiers on furlough, &c., travelling expenses incurred thereby being allowed. The charge for apothecaries' bills was to be defrayed by the public.

The surgeon of each regiment raised during the war then being carried on was, when reduced to half-pay, allowed £36 10s. per annum, "subject to the usual deductions," unless entitled to five shillings per diem by a service of twenty years, a rate of pension which it was thought "would supersede every possible plea for the sale of the surgeon's commission." A practice, we are informed, "which had prevailed to the present hour in defiance of the most positive regulations to the contrary."

In February, 1797, between twelve and thirteen thousand men were stationed in the South of Ireland, ready to be collected in four days to any point, in order to defend Cork, Limerick, or Waterford. Clonmel was the central "Hospital Depôt." Three physicians, six surgeons, and twelve hospital mates, besides apothecaries and purveyors were attached to the troops to move along with them on any appearance of the enemy. An ambulance staff was superadded to the regimental establishments. *Twenty spring carts* were provided by the Ordnance Department, on the recommendation of the Director-General, for the purpose of removing sick and wounded soldiers—a mode of transit in use in Ireland contemporaneously with those introduced into the French service by

Baron Larrey. These and other excellent arrangements, too numerous to refer to, drew forth the following letter from the Government of Ireland:—

"Dublin Castle, Nov. 23, 1797.

"Gentlemen,

"His Excellency has read with peculiar satisfaction the last report from your Board, and concurs in opinion with you respecting the merits of the Staff-surgeons at the different hospitals. He desires that you will communicate to them His entire approbation of the diligence and attention with which they have discharged their duty. His Excellency has, at the same time, commanded me to say, that without diminution of the merit which is due to the Staff-surgeons he cannot help considering that the success of this important department of the Military Establishment is to be attributed to the judicious regulations and the unremitting zeal and assuidity of your Board, and His Excellency confides in a continuance of their exertions.

"I have great pleasure in communicating His Excellency's commands, and having personally observed the great advantage of your superintendence in the different hospitals I have visited in the south of Ireland.

"I have, &c., T. PELHAM."

"The Medical Board."

In this short sketch it would be impossible to delay further in following the most interesting history of the Army Medical Staff in Ireland, and of the Army with which they were so intimately connected. The leading spirit who presided over them for so many years was the Director-General of Hospitals—George Renny. He entered the 67th Regiment in June, 1775, as surgeon's mate, when just 19 years of age, on the pay of £63 17s. 6d. per annum. His corps had been raised in 1756. The regiment returned from America to England in 1771, and proceeded to Scotland in 1773, where it remained until 1775, when it embarked under the command of Colonel Edward Maxwell Brown for Ireland, to replace the 42nd on the establishment of that kingdom, embarking for the East Indies in 1785. Dr. Renny succeeded to the surgeoncy of the regiment in January, 1780, and previous to its departure for the East Indies was, in 1784, appointed surgeon to the Royal Hospital and also to the Military Provost, and in addition to these offices, Director-General of Hospitals in Ireland in 1795. He retired from the superintendance of the Department in Ireland in 1847, after unprecedented services as a medical officer of seventy-two years on full-pay and in the active performance of his duty, forty-nine of which in the office of Director-General of Hospitals. Previous to his retirement he was presented with an address and handsome testimonial from the medical officers of the command, and the following General Order was issued, a testimony of the esteem in which he was held.

General Order.
"Adjutant-General's Office,
"Dublin, July 27, 1847.

"The Lieutenant-General Commanding in announcing to the troops serving in Ireland the retirement of Dr. Renny, Director-General of Hospitals, feels that he would be wanting in what was due to that old and meritorious officer, were he to permit Dr. Renny to relinquish his important office, one which he has filled for more than half a century with so much advantage to the public interests, without placing on record the high sense he entertains of his valuable services, and of the Lieutenant-General's unqualified approbation of his conduct during the long period he has been under his more immediate command.

"By Order of the Lieutenant-General Commanding.
"W. COCHRANE.
"Deputy Adjutant-General."

He died in November of the following year, and was buried in the Royal Hospital, where he had resided from the date of his appointment to the surgeoncy of that Institution in 1784. He was succeeded by Sir James Pitcairn, Local Inspector-General of Hospitals, who had early joined the Irish Staff, after having served in the 'Helder' in 1779, and the campaigns in Egypt in 1801. The principal events in the life of Dr. Renny were the inauguration of the Medical Staff; the formation of General Hospitals in Ireland; the medical arrangements in view of the French invasion, and during the troublous times of 1798; the recommendation for the erection of the various hospitals now attached to the different barracks in Ireland; the improvements in the military provost prisons, and the substitution of separate confinement for the more degrading corporal punishment of the day. Dr. Renny was also largely concerned in the arrangements for the erection of the Lunatic Asylums in the different counties, and was one of the Members of the Board of Control placed over them. Sir James Pitcairn had been for many years principal medical officer of the Cork district, when he had succeeded Dr. Haig, Physician to the Irish Forces. He retired on half-pay August 24, 1852, and was succeeded by Deputy Inspector-General, afterwards Sir Charles Maclean, who was the last Local Inspector-General in Ireland.

On the death of Dr. Guinn, the office of Joint Physician-General merged into that of Physician-General of the Forces. Dr. Cheyne succeeded Dr. Harvey, and Sir Philip Crampton, Bart., Mr. Stewart the Surgeon-General. On the deaths of these officers, both offices ceased to exist. For a long period the officers of the Irish Medical Staff were entitled to rent and forage allowance, lodging money and soldier grooms for the invalid battalions. The device of the Department was a harp surmounted by a crown, encircled by the words Irish Medical Staff.

In 1802, second assistant-surgeons were added to regiments of the Line. The surgeon remained attached to the hospital at head-quarters, the first assistant was placed at the cantonments where there was the greatest number of men, and the second assistant with the next in succession in point of magnitude.

The following interesting extract from a memorial of a regimental surgeon in this year gives a graphic picture of the Service as it then existed.

"To His Royal Highness the Duke of York.
"The Memorial of Francis Fraser, M.D., Surgeon 36th Foot.
"Humbly sheweth—
"That memorialist has served in the Army as regimental surgeon from September, 1787. That he purchased his first Commission in the 5th Royal Irish Dragoons, for which he never received any sort of compensation. That memorialist has been a great deal upon actual service during all the late war, that besides performing all the duties of surgeon in the 18th Dragoons when in St. Domingo, he also acted and did duty as subaltern, which Commission he also purchased, and was afterwards promoted by General Simcoe to the rank of captain-lieutenant of that regiment, in which capacity he had the honor to command the regiment for many months, to draft it into the 21st Dragoons, and to bring home to England the remains of the 18th and 14th Light Dragoons. That upon his coming to England he found his promotion not confirmed, although he had been previously recommended for a troop by the commanding officer of the regiment, Colonel Grey, and the General Commanding at that time, namely General Forbes. That in the year 1802, when in Minorca, your memorialist had a severe paralytic stroke which has rendered him unfit for the actual duties of the regiment. That such being the helpless and unhappy situation of the memorialist he is induced to hope that Your Royal Highness will be pleased to take it into Your Royal Highness' consideration, and to allow him to enjoy his full pay for the few remaining years of his life, or, if more agreeable to Your Royal Highness, to give him a Company of Invalids or any adequate situation in the Invalid Corps in which he may continue to be useful to the utmost extent of his abilities."

Powerfully supported by the officer commanding his regiment, this touching memorial was not received adversely by the Commander-in-Chief, who at once granted it.

In this year also passed the "Irish Militia Act," which contained the following paragraphs relating to the medical officers of the Force:—

1. Colonels to appoint surgeons possessed of the qualification from the Royal College of Surgeons in Ireland.

2. Surgeons to have four shillings a day pay when disembodied with £20 per annum Irish currency in full for supplying medicines and necessaries for the sick when actually residing at the head-quarters of their Corps.

3. When the Militia are called out to exercise during peace, the surgeon's pay during the above period to be ten shillings per diem. He providing medicine and necessaries for the sick during the time they are so called out, from said pay.

4. No Militia surgeon to hold military commissions, nor at any time the appointment of surgeon to a County Infirmary.

5. Militia surgeons to attend to examine the men if within reasonable distance from their respective homes, if otherwise, a competent surgeon to be employed for such purpose. An allowance of ten shillings per day to be given to the surgeon who actually examines the men. An Inspector of Hospitals, Dr. Williams, had been attached to the British Militia during the period they were serving in Ireland. One of these regiments serving in Dublin had the following return of sick December 8, 1800:—35 acute, 15 chronic, 28 convalescent, 51 venereal; total 129. Fever and dysentry were the common acute diseases. Chronic and acute opthalmia were also very prevalent.

The following copy of the Hospital contingent expenses of the 1st Battalion 15th Foot for one month, ending 25th March of the same year, affords an idea of the medical arrangements of the day :—

1. Orderly sergeant	£ 0 15	8¼
2. Nurse	0 15	8½
3. Orderly man	0 9	8
4. Medicines, &c.	5 5	7½
5. Wine, porter, spirits	1 13	4½
6. Fuel	1 13	4¼
7. Horse hire	0 14	4
8. Sundries	1 8	11
Total	12 5	7

It was now becoming extremely difficult to fill up the appointments of surgeon's mates in the various Fencible corps embodied throughout the Kingdom, owing to the utterly inadequate rate of pay offered to these officers of four shillings and sixpence per diem. In forwarding the resignation of one of these officers in the Manx Fencible Regiment, the officer commanding, Lord Henry Murray expresses a wish that whoever may be appointed (he being unable to find a candidate) " may hold the double commission, as it was hardly worth the while of any young man of any professional abilities to hold the situation of surgeon's mate alone in a Fencible Corps." Most of these regiments were reduced at the Peace of Amiens, and very large reductions proposed in the Medical Staff, which were being carried out when hostilities were renewed with France in 1803. A few months before, a General Order had been issued from the Horse Guards, directing commanding officers of regiments to be very circumspect in the leave of absence granted to medical officers, applications being only proper when the regiment was assembled in "one or two quarters, and remarkably healthy." (Horse Guards General Order February 3, 1803.)

The following was the gradation on the British Medical Staff in 1803 :—

Surgeon to the Forces	. 10s.	per diem.
Field Inspector	. 15s.	,,
Assistant Inspector	. 20s.	,,
Assistant Inspector-General	. 30s.	,,
Inspector	. 40s.	,,
Inspector-General	. 60s.	,,

With some deductions for poundage, &c., &c.

At the Peace of Amiens it had been reduced to the following establishment in Great Britain.

	£	s.	d.
1 Inspector of hospitals	518	12	0
2 Assistant Inspectors at £345 15s. each	691	10	0
3 Physicians at £345 15s. each	1037	5	0
1 Purveyor	432	3	9
10 Surgeons at £172 17s. 6d. each	1728	15	0
6 Apothecaries at £172 17s. 6d. each	1037	5	0
5 Deputy Purveyors at £172 17s. 6d. each	864	7	6
6 Hospital Mates at £136 17s. 6d. each	821	5	0
40 Hospital Mates £91 5s. each	3650	0	0
	£10,781	3	9

The foregoing was exclusive of the regimental establishments.

The Irish Staff was reduced to two joint physician-generals, one surgeon-general, one director-general of hospitals, ten staff-surgeons, seventeen hospital mates, two apothecaries, three deputy-purveyors. In a peace establishment of 21,000 infantry and 4,000 cavalry of the Line.

A Horse Guards Order, dated 14th August, directs the second assistant-surgeons of regiments of cavalry and infantry to be retained "as at the present strength of these corps the medical duties could not be properly executed by one assistant-surgeon, but also with a view to avoid the necessity in many instances of having recourse to the assistance of country practitioners, whose charges against the public were found frequently exorbitant." This order in the sequel proved of the utmost importance, as on the outbreak of hostilities the greatest possible difficulty was found in filling up the medical cadres, bounties being actually offered as an inducement to enter the military service. The Medical Board in Ireland were appealed to by their *confrères* in England, "as great difficulties had been experienced in procuring young gentlemen of proper qualifications to fill up the vacancies which had lately occurred in regiments of the Line on that establishment."

The Inspector-General, Mr. Knight, had written through the Director-General to the professors of the various schools in Dublin, requesting their "influence to send over as many qualified persons for this service as could be procured, as he had a great call for medical officers to complete the staff of the regiments on the English establishment. There are several vacant assistant-surgeons, and the gentlemen first arriving will have the chance of early promotion, and should any of them be ordered to the West Indies they are on that station entitled to the commission of assistant-surgeon to the Forces with half-pay, and the further provision of a pension to the widows of such as may die who are married. The expense of the passage is defrayed, and they are allowed ten guineas outfit money." Such were the inducements to enter the service in the commencement of the century.

The surgeons of existing corps at this date could not be legally placed on half-pay as long as their corps were on the establishment, nor could they be provided for by the sale of their commissions, this being abolished. The retirement of five shillings was solely calculated as a provision for such cases of worn out surgeons of twenty years' army service.

The Army Medical Office was at this time at 4, Berkeley Street, Piccadilly.

The pressure of service in the field, and the difficulty of obtaining a due proportion of Medical officers under the conditions offered as inducements to enter the Army, led to the promulgation of the Royal Warrant of May 22, 1804. The preamble of the Warrant commences "Whereas we have approved of an arrangement for increasing the advantages, and improving the situation, of the Medical officers of Our Army, with the view of encouraging able and well educated persons to enter into, and continue in, that line of Our Service; Our Will and Pleasure is that from the 25th December last inclusive, the following Regulations do take place on the above head."

By this Warrant, hospital mates for general service were appointed by commissions and given a full-pay of 6s. 6d. net at home and 7s. 6d. while employed on foreign stations, with half-pay on reduction of 2s. a day, "subject to the usual deduction." Widows of hospital mates dying abroad on full-pay were allowed a pension of £16 per annum, and their children allowed from the Compassionate Fund. Hospital mates appointed for temporary and local service were not to receive commissions or half-pay.

Assistant-surgeons received 7s. 6d. a day, and when reduced to half-pay of 3s. Assistant-surgeons of Dragoon Guards and Dragoons a further allowance of 1s. a day for a horse, as at present.

Apothecaries to the Forces and surgeons attached to recruiting districts 10s. a day with a half-pay of 5s. a day. The pay of surgeons of Regular Infantry was increased to same rate as allowed to surgeons of Cavalry, 11s. 4d. per diem net; the surgeon in both cases being required to keep a horse at his own expense. His half-pay being increased to 6s.

Regimental surgeons, after seven years' service as such, or ten years in the Army, "the whole in a medical capacity on full-pay," had their pay augmented to 14s. 1d. per diem. After twenty years in the whole on full-pay, 18s. 10d. a day. If retired on grounds of ill-health, "certified by the Army Medical Department," a half-pay of 10s. Every regimental surgeon after thirty years' service on full-pay had the unqualified right of retiring on 15s. a day.

After twenty years' service, the widows of regimental surgeons were not to be precluded from pension on account of the retirement of their husbands.

Pay of surgeons of Militia Corps when embodied was increased, as in the Line, to 11s. 4d., under the same obligations to keep a horse.

Surgeons to the Forces had their pay increased to 15s., with a half-pay of 6s., with same increase after twenty and thirty years' service as given to regimental surgeons.

Physicians, purveyors of hospitals and deputy-purveyors to continue on the same rate of pay as heretofore.

Deputy-inspectors of hospitals to receive a full-pay of 25s. a day, and a half-pay of 12s. 6d. After twenty years' full-pay service, 30s. a day, and 15s. a day half-pay.

Inspectors of hospitals a full-pay of £2 a day and half-pay of £1.

"The general appointments undermentioned," the Warrant ends, "shall be hereafter discontinued in Our Service as superfluous and embarrassing, and holding out the idea of distinctions in rank and duty not easy to be defined, viz.:—Field-inspector, assistant-inspector, deputy inspector-general, inspector-general, superintendent-general."

On the 11th April a Horse Guards General Order was published stating that it was "His Majesty's pleasure that in future officers serving upon the Medical Staff of the Army shall respectively wear the uniforms undermentioned:—

"The Inspectors, scarlet coat, single breasted, with black velvet collar and cuffs, slashed sleeves and skirts, yellow hospital staff buttons, two epaulets embroidered with gold or black velvet, with two gold embroidered button holes on the collar, two on each cuff, and two plain on the sleeves. Cocked-hat with black feather, black button and black gilt loop, blue pantaloons and half-boots, black sword-belt (for the waist) Regulation sword and sword knot, as approved for officers of infantry.

"Deputy-inspectors and physicians the same uniform, with some minor alterations. Staff-surgeons were to wear only one epaulet on the right shoulder, as did also the staff-apothecaries and hospital mates. The purveyors the same uniform as the apothecary, with the exception of silver epaulettes and buttons of gold, Regimental surgeons and assistants the uniform of their regiments without facings, one epaulet on the right shoulder."

From an Order issued by the Horse Guards 10th October of the following year (1805) forbidding the use of the sash, it would appear that the latter was, up to that date, worn by medical as well as combatant officers, probably owing to the fact that many of the former had held combatant as well as medical commissions. Afterwards the rank of physician was distinguished by a double gold scroll on each side of the collar.

On 30th January, 1804, a letter emanated from the Horse Guards, stating that His Royal Highness the Commander-in-Chief was "thoroughly impressed with the conviction that it was indispensable that the surgeons of regiments should have a complete knowledge of pharmacy, and should be equal to the treatment of medical cases, particularly as nine-tenths of those who came under their care were medical not surgical, "and directing the Army Medical Board in England to make it a rule not to recommend for the surgeoncy or assistant-surgeoncy of a regiment any person who did not upon examination appear to possess a complete knowledge of pharmacy and the treatment of medical cases."

Mr. Rollo was at this time Surgeon-General of artillery at Woolwich, and Mr. Jameson, Senior Surgeon of artillery in Ireland. On 14th May, 1804, medical officers of artillery were informed that they were to afford medical aid to soldiers when there was no army surgeon present, and to admit them into their hospitals.

District staff-surgeons of recruiting were allowed 2s. 6d. per diem for the keeping of a horse, provided effective, which sum was charged in the Pay List of the "Royal Army Reserve." I may remark, in passing, that the earliest notice of the grant of forage allowance to officers of the Medical Staff dates from the German campaigns of the middle of the eighteenth century.

On 23rd June a circular letter was addressed by order of the Lord-Lieutenant of Ireland to colonels of Militia, informing them that " His Excellency had observed of late, with some concern, advertisements in the public papers for the sale of appointments of surgeons, and of commissions of adjutant of Militia," and directing that for the future the recommendation for these appointments was to contain a certificate from the colonel, " that no pecuniary consideration had directly or indirectly taken place according to the practice of regiments of the Line."

Assistant-surgeons of Militia in England at this date seemed not to have been noticed by Act of Parliament, or were they acknowledged by the Militia Regulations. They were paid from a contingent allowance made for this purpose to each regiment, and continued on the old establishment with a military commission as well as a professional warrant.

Early in the year 1804 the India Board had under consideration the medical arrangements proper for India. Lord Castlereagh, the President, wrote to Dr. Renny, the Director-General of Hospitals in Ireland, on 28th May, asking for a copy of the rules and regulations then in force, for the purpose of "guiding the judgment of the Board in deciding upon those which should be applied to the regimental and general hospitals in India." He had been intimately associated with the Director-General when secretary to the Lord-Lieutenant. Under the regulations issued some time afterwards, the surgeon of a European infantry regiment drew each month 415 rupees, a staff allowance of 300 rupees, and head money 25 rupees per 100 men. Total pay and allowances for a regiment 1000 strong, 965 rupees. The Hospital Establishment consisted of the following—one apothecary, Rs. 146; one assistant-apothecary, Rs. 70; two apprentices, Rs. 66; one head compounder, Rs. 10; one compounder, Rs. 8; one head-dresser, Rs. 8; one dresser, Rs. 6; two slop-coolies, Rs. 10; one steward, Rs. 126; one apprentice, Rs. 33; one native writer, Rs. 35; two steward's servants, Rs. 12; one head bheestie, Rs. 6; six bheesties, Rs. 30; one head sweeper, Rs. 6; eight sweepers, Rs. 32; one head coolie, Rs. 5; twenty coolies, Rs. 80; one head cook, Rs. 6; four cooks, Rs. 20; one clothier, Rs. 8; two tailors, Rs. 12; one barber, Rs. 6; one head washerwoman, Rs. 6; four washerwomen, Rs. 20; one nurse, Rs. 6; one female sweeper, Rs. 4;—total 778 rupees per month.

On the 25th June, 1804, the Army Medical Staff in Ireland was constituted of the following officers in addition to the Board Staff:—

Assistant-Inspectors.

Robert M. Peile,	September 25, 1803.	Dublin.
James Pitcairn,	October 22, 1803.	Athlone.
William Comins,	December 8, 1803.	Belfast.
Heeson Biggar,	December 8, 1803	Cork.

Staff-Surgeons.

Ralph S. O'Brie,	July 1, 1795.	Dublin.
Matthew Poole,	October 1, 1797.	Waterford.
Alexander Graydon,	October 1, 1797.	Limerick.
Edward Eagle,	May 13, 1798.	Clonmel.
Samuel Banks,	June 20, 1798.	Kilcullen.
Henry Purden,	do. do.	Belfast.
Joseph Stringer,	do. do.	Banagher.
Thomas L. Whistler,	do. do.	Galway.
Perkins Crofton,	September 25, 1803.	Kildare.
James Rodgers,	November 12, 1803.	Cork.
Peter Ormsby,	January 5, 1804.	Enniskillen.
John O'Connor,	do. do.	Mullingar.
Simon Rawling,	March 10, 1804.	Londonderry.
James Dalzel,	April 28, 1804.	Armagh.

Hospital Mates.

John O'Donel,	December 26, 1796.	Cork.
Hugh Power,	March 27, 1796.	Cork.
John S. Thwaites,	do. do.	Limerick.
M. E. Palmer,	May 24, 1798.	Cork.
William Harrison,	June 17, 1798.	Cork.
James Burkitt,	do. do.	Waterford.
Richard Packe,	July 7, 1798.	Kilkenny.
Roger Dockery,	August 4, 1798.	Dublin.
Lodge Hall,	November 9, 1799.	Cork.
Edward Kent,	March 2, 1801.	Dublin.
Samuel McAlpee,	May 4, 1801.	Cork.
John Stewart,	May 13, 1801.	Belfast.
Hugh Wilden,	June 25, 1803.	Naas.
John McFadden,	do. do.	Armagh.
Daniel Grim,	do. do.	Kilcullen.
Thomas Crawfurd,	do. do.	Londonderry.
John Barlow,	do. do.	Limerick.
Richard Brady,	September 21, 1803.	Athlone.
Thomas Little,	December 1, 1803.	Cork.
Abraham Collis,	December 5, 1803.	Dublin.
John Woodrooffe,	January 1, 1804.	Cork.
John Barker,	July 16, 1804.	—
Richard Geoghegan,	do. do.	—

Staff-Apothecaries.

George Alley,	August 28, 1804.	—
John Briscoe,	September 14, 1804.	—
John Cowen,	October 1, 1797.	Kilcullen.
Edward O'Brien,	June 20, 1798.	Cork.
Henry White,	April 14, 1804.	Kildare.

Purveyor

Thomas Loughlin,	April 14, 1804.	Cork.

Deputy Purveyor.

James Mould,	December 5, 1803.	Kilcullen.

Assistant-inspectors were allowed horse money at 7s. 6d. per diem each for three effective horses and lodging money £1 2s. 9d. a week. Staff surgeons 5s. horse money for two effective horses, and 15s. a week lodging money. The total pay and allowance of the Irish Medical Staff amounted to a sum of £18,882 6s. 8½. There were then on the Irish Establishment forty-six battalions of infantry, eight regiments of cavalry, forty-one battalions of Militia, ten general hospitals, and recruiting was actually progressing in the active army. The great majority of these regiments on leaving Ireland proceeded abroad.

Heretofore, in England, the hospital baggage had been guided by no fixed laws as to its limits, and had often swollen to an unnecessary and enormous magnitude, ill-adapted to the movements of a marching regiment. In one ponderous magazine every article was packed promiscuously ; a small chest was now contrived for 250 men with trays above this depôt to receive the more essential articles, with each of these chests a canteen of utensils was sent, and twelve sets of bedding packed in bales of waterproof cloth. On foreign stations these were issued from the general hospitals :—

In Great Britain the duty of providing medicine and equipment for regiments going on foreign service fell to the lot of the surgeon-general.

In 1805 a large encampment was formed at the Curragh of Kildare. The medical staff attached to the troops consisted of the following officers :—

Deputy-Inspector.—James Pitcairn,		Kilcullen.
Staff-Surgeons.—Samuel Banks.		Camp.
,,	Perkins Crofton.	Kildare.
,,	Peter Ormsby.	Castle Martin.
Staff-Apothecary.—John Cowen, M.D.		Castle Martin.
Hospital Mates.—John Woodroffe		Kildare.
,,	George Read.	Kilcullen.
,,	Joseph Young.	Castle Martin.
,,	Garner Champion.	Castle Martin.
,,	John Burke	Kilcullen.
,,	William Campbell.	Castle Martin.
Deputy-Purveyor.—James Mould.		Castle Martin.

The County Infirmary at Kildare and the General Hospitals at Kilcullen and Castle Martin, received the greater part of the sick. Two regiments of cavalry, and twenty-two battalions of infantry were encamped. Two shillings and sixpence per diem was now allowed to medical officers examining volunteers from the Militia, not the Line.

On the 12th November of this year, the 30th Regiment had the following sick list when quartered at the Royal Barracks, Dublin :—

In Royal Military Infirmary	. . 50
Regimental hospital	. . . 44
In quarters	 29
Total	123

A not uncommon sick list at this date in the garrison. Typhus was then the prevalent disease of the army, more especially in the new levies.

The Medical Board in England looked almost solely to fiscal concerns at this time. The most minute attention was exacted in such particulars ; an error even in fractional parts brought down the animadversion of the Board upon the unfortunate offenders and a protracted correspondence, the duties of a regimental surgeon and his assistant were chiefly those of clerks, as accountants to the public for their expenditure upon each sick man. In order to carry this system into effect, the class of inspectional officers was established, viz., inspectors of hospitals, and deputy-inspectors ; the former for the large and very extended districts, an army in the field, &c., and the West Indies ; the latter for smaller, as the various military districts. One of the first of these officers appointed, subsequent to the reorganization of the department in 1798, was Sir James McGrigor. This most distinguished officer and most able man was a contemporary and intimate friend of Fergusson, Jackson and Renny. He entered the Army in 1794, and purchased his surgeoncy in the 88th Regiment, through the intervention (as was then the custom) of the regimental agent. Shortly afterwards he served in the expedition to and retreat through Holland. Disease, particularly typhus, became general. The hospitals were filled to overflowing, and he tells us in his interesting biography that the " mortality among the medical officers in particular was great." He next served in the expedition to the West Indies under Sir Ralph Abercrombie. In 1798 he embarked at Portsmouth with his regiment for India. He alludes to the difficulty experienced this time of obtaining medical officers, which continued for many years afterwards, and was the occasion of many unqualified and uneducated persons being introduced into the Service ; but from the increase of pay and other advantages which Government found it necessary to concede from time to time, the encouragement held out induced likewise many men of finished education and great endowments to enter, " who redeemed the character of the medical officer with the Army in general." " It is not only," wrote Sir James McGrigor, " in the sense of humanity, but in that of a sound policy and real economy, that the State should provide able medical and surgical advice for the soldiers when sick or wounded. I look upon it to be an implied part of the compact of citizens with the State, that, whoever enters the service of his country as a soldier to fight its battles, should be provided with the same quality of medical aid, when sick or wounded, which he enjoyed when a citizen." Sir James McGrigor next served as head of the medical staff under Sir David Baird, in command of the troops destined for the expedition to Egypt, holding a company's commission for that purpose, being the first king's officer so employed as " Superintendent of the medical concerns of an army in the Indian Establishment. Dr. Shapter, was Inspector of Hospitals and head of the medical staff of that part of the expedition sent from the Cape. Mr. Young, who had been Chief of the Hospitals in the West Indies, was Inspector-General of the Hospitals of the English Army. The predominant disease in hospital at this time was fever which ran its course very rapidly, and terminated with the appearance of typhus. The dreaded plague also made its appearance, necessitating the erection of pest-houses, houses of observation and suitable quarantine regulations. Ophthalmia was also very prevalent and imported with the regiments which returned into the various home garrisons. During this expedition Dr. Buchan, Physician to the Forces, nobly volunteered his services in the pest hospital at a time of general consternation, and when several medical officers had died. On his arrival in England Sir James McGrigor published his "Medical Sketches of the Expedition from India to Egypt."

The force which assailed Egypt from the direction of the Red Sea consisted of 3,750 European, and 4,127 Native troops, who landed in Cossir (Kossier) Bay in three divisions, on the 16th and 19th of May, and 4th of June, 1801, with 6,815 lascars and camp followers. They marched by the old track route across the Thebes desert to Keneh on the Nile, a distance of 120 miles, the great difficulty being water, although General Baird had succeeded in procuring 5000 camels to carry *mussuks*. Many soldiers nevertheless died of thirst. The whole force proceeded down the Nile in boats, and assembled on the 27th August at the Isle of Rhonda, two miles from Cairo. After landing at Cossir, the troops having recovered from diarrhœa, induced by the water containing much Epsom salts, were uncommonly healthy, chiefly owing to the wise sanitary precautions adopted during the voyage; good water, fresh provisions and vegetables having been freely provided, as well as suitable clothing according to the season, and enforcement of bathing whenever practicable. The diet of the European troops was also made to conform as much as possible to that of the Hindoos: light Greek wines were supplied in the hot, and spirits in the cold weather, and for the Natives a portion of animal food and wine during the cold weather. The march to the Nile was completed with a few cases of ophthalmia and day blindness, and the army arrived at Giheh, 400 miles down the Nile with only a few cases of slight fever, but now sickness began to increase. In the first week from a twelfth to a tenth of the force were in hospital; in three weeks the sick exceeded 1000 nearly, by the end of the month 1,200, when embarked at Rosetta. The prevailing fever was rarely fatal, ophthalmia abounded, and there was some dysentery and liver disease. In spite of efficient means of purification and isolation, it proved fatal to thirty-eight European and 127 Native soldiers. The following were the deaths from disease, per 1000 per annum

	Europeans.	Natives.
Dysentery	52	7
Liver disease	23	2
Plague	13	24
Fevers	7	14
Other diseases	14	13
Total death rate	109	60

If to which is added the loss from invaliding, 41 per 1000 per annum for Europeans and six for Natives, the total loss to the Service was for Europeans 150, Natives 66 per thousand.

In 1804 after a service of eleven years in the Connaught Rangers McGrigor joined the Blues, after a short service in which he was promoted Deputy-Inspector of Hospitals, thus passing over the ranks of Staff-Surgeon and Physician to the Forces. He was posted to the Northern district where he introduced many improvements, and stimulated the zeal of his brother officers by his courtesy, friendly criticism, and advice. In the army at that period, he tells us, that with a very extensive field of experience medical officers were not taught to take advantage of and treasure up facts. They kept no regular registers or records; and the great evil with the regimental officer was, that his professional work was not considered the most important of his duties, or that which recommended him to his superiors—defects he was mainly instrumental in remedying in the English establishment; so that in a few years he had the satisfaction of stating that there was comprised in the body of the medical officers of the army not fewer men of literary attainments and University education than in the ranks of civil life. He was next transferred to Winchester, the head-quarters of the South Western District, of which H R.H. the Duke of Cumberland was in command, whose adjutant-major, afterwards General Foster, had entered the army as a medical officer. This district was then a most extensive one, including Portsmouth and the Isle of Wight, where was placed the great depot for ophthalmia and other eye diseases, often containing 1000 cases. The health of the troops in the district was generally bad, and the sick list high. On the return of the remains of Sir John Moore's gallant army, hastily embarked at Corunna, and which had suffered extremely from hunger, fatigue, and all the privations incident to war, he had to make arrangement for the overwhelming number of sick and wounded, suffering mainly from typhus, the mortality from which was considerable. On the return of Sir John Webb, head of the medical department of the unfortnate Walcheren army, he was appointed to succeed him. A terrible mortality had occurred amongst the medical staff of this expedition, necessitating a large call for professional assistance. On arrival he found the number of sick immense, and with the wounded officers and men, both together, nearly equalled that of the men in health. The apothecaries' and purveyors' stores were drained of many articles of the most essential description. The overwhelming sickness and mortality induced the Government to order two of the oldest medical officers to go out to Walcheren. Dr. Borland, Inspector-General of Hospitals, and Dr. Lempriere, Physician to the Forces, with whom was associated Sir Gilbert Blane, an eminent physician in London, who had been in the navy and volunteered his services. These three gentlemen went out as commissioners, and recommended the removal of the remainder of the unfortunate army to England.

Forty thousand men had been conveyed to Walcheren in 245 vessels in the sickly season of 1809, with only one hospital ship attached and a wholly insufficient store of medicines and comforts for the sick. The Physician-General, the President of the Medical Board had not been consulted in these respects until six weeks after the departure of the expedition. The force left in July; by the middle of August 3,000 men were down with fever. The water rose in the Island of Walcheren, flooded the British lines, and put out the fires. The men had to stand in water and sleep on damp ground. Several thousands were up to their breasts in water during a whole night. On the 14th September 8000 men were on the sick list. By 22nd October only 4000 men were left fit for duty. Sir Eyre Coote wrote, "The sick must be abandoned if the enemy attempt anything." Such was briefly the wretched experience of the Scheldt expedition. Sixty years before, Sir John Pringle, Physician-General to the army beyond the seas, had pointed out with a minuteness of detail the nature of the diseases of the country, and the means of preventing their advent and ravages, but his admirable work appears to have been altogether forgotten. Two companies of the Hospital Corps, employed as orderlies in the hospital, suffered severely. The remains embarked on board the 'Asia' hospital ship under the command of Captain Walker, one of their officers.

As the result of this expedition, an important change was made in the constitution of the Army Medical Department. The Board was dissolved and replaced by a Director-General, Dr. Weir and two principal inspectors. Dr. Weir, the Director-General, had served much abroad and was then very advanced in life. He was associated with Sir Charles Ker, who had long served in the East and West Indies, and Dr. Gordon, who in addition to a long and varied service, was looked upon as one of the most judicious and talented officers in the Medical Department of the army. The latter was shortly replaced by Sir William Franklin.

Previous to the expedition to Walcheren, Dr. Nisbet addressed a letter, in 1808, to His Royal Highness the Duke of York, on the Medical Department of the Army. He called attention to the fact that "the life of a soldier, like every other life of irregular exertion and hardship, predisposed him to disease, while from the nature of the service, the treatment of military diseases differed from common practice, and required peculiar experience, both in preventing the attack and also in rendering their cure speedy and complete." To remedy this defect, he prepared a military work, showing at one view all those peculiarities : " A Code of Military Medicine and Surgery for the British Army." In a second letter he gave the outline of a proposed code of medical regulations, which would embrace—1st. The education of military practitioners; 2nd. Inspection of men in order to judge as to their fitness for service and freedom from disease; 3rd. Outline of practice in prevention and cure of disease; 4th. Hospitals and regulations appertaining to 5th. Camps, their site, proper accommodation, &c., " Having it in mind that military practice requires bold and energetic measures; and that the absence from duty on the day of actual service is, perhaps, an irreparable loss to the country —hence the necessity of a medical officer possessing superior professional knowledge to others, much decision, and a great deal of acquired experience." The value of each soldier to the State at this time may be seen from the fact that the bounty to men enlisting for limited service was eleven, and for unlimited, sixteen guineas.

I have now arrived at a period the most interesting to medical officers of the British Army, the Peninsular War. In April, 1809, Sir Arthur Wellesley landed with reinforcements in Portugal. Dr. Frank was appointed principal medical officer of the expedition. At its commencement the precarious and insufficient food, bad clothes, head-gear, shoes, want of shelter while lying on damp ground, and crowding, had led to the development of much sickness, especially typhus and dysentery. In the valley of the Guardiana, in 1809, the army sat down on the wet sands of the locality, had 7,000 men admitted almost at once into hospital, nearly two-thirds of whom died. The sick throughout this war were a greater burden to the Commander-in-Chief than the wounded, averaging during the whole war twenty-one per hundred soldiers, and occupying the attention of hundreds who could ill be spared. The largest proportion of these sick were the Walcheren convalescents from the hospitals at home, who sank at once wherever the cause of fever was present; next to these the new levies; thirdly, the Peninsular convalescents. Fever, inflammation of the lungs, rheumatism, sore throat, catarrh, hospital gangrene, and tetanus were the prevailing affections. It was observed that whenever the troops were in an improved condition, they had food, rest, clothes, blankets, and active exertion in the open air. Large numbers had got into the habit of " shirking ;" 600 bayonets were received in the Second Division in one month by clearing the hospitals and depôts of malingerers prior to the battle of Vittoria.— (Napier.)

During the marches in the Peninsula, the guard following the column took up all stragglers and lodged them in the guard-room, except such as had received permission to fall out. Each man received a pint of wine daily. When a division (6,000 bayonets) arrived on the ground at the termination of each march, the site for a temporary division hospital was pointed out to the surgeons. At an appointed hour the sick reports were gathered from the different companies, and the sick paraded for the surgeon's inspection, who reported to the staff-surgeon, who in his turn forwarded his report to the General commanding the division, rendering his own report to the Inspector-General of Hospitals. When the sick and wounded were detached to the rear, they were generally in charge of a subaltern, a duty, we are told, undertaken with anything but satisfaction by the latter. The eternal screeching of the ungreased wheels of the Portuguese bullock-carts, too often irritated the sick men into a fever, if they had not one already. In the earlier sieges there were no tents, but the men often hutted themselves with boughs of trees. Tents were first used at the siege of St. Sebastian.

Several General Orders were issued during these campaigns which are of interest to medical officers. On the 1st September, 1809, the allowance of forage-money (6d. each animal) on foreign stations, from hospital-mate to general commanding, was published at Merida. Inspectors of hospitals were allowed thirty; deputies, fifteen; physicians, twelve; purveyors, fourteen; deputy-purveyors, six; surgeons, eight; apothecaries, six; assistant-surgeons, two: hospital-mates, two; regimental surgeon, five (same number as allowed to captains), assistant-surgeons, one.

The ratio at first, 1 lb. of bread and 1½ lb. of meat for each individual, was increased to 2 lbs. of beef when no bread was obtainable. Latrines were dug in certain spots and lime thrown into them every second day; ground intervening between encampments was swept daily, and strict orders issued as to surface conservancy. As the war progressed, spring waggons and mules were used when practicable for the conveyance of the sick and wounded. One spring waggon or other cart was allowed to each battalion for this purpose, and the carriage of twelve sets of hospital bedding. Twenty-five pounds were advanced to the regimental surgeon to provide a bat-horse for the carriage of the field medicine panniers or chests; these last and the pack-saddles being obtained from the Inspectors of Hospitals. Men falling sick on the march and dropping from the ranks were immediately examined by a medical officer, and, if necessary, sent to the rear in charge of a non-commissioned officer, who conducted them to the nearest town or village, when they were given in charge to the magistrates or placed in the nearest general or other hospital. Hospital subsistence money was paid weekly to the surgeon; slight ailments were treated with the regiments, and no men were sent to the general hospitals without the previous inspection of the senior medical officer or staff-surgeon of the Brigade, who forwarded, weekly and monthly, a return of sick to the Deputy-inspector of the Division, abstracts of which were sent to the principal medical officer, and on the 20th of each month to the Horse Guards and Medical Department in London.

On the 16th September, 1809, Lord Wellington, in a General

Order, called attention to the fact that " officers of the army were much mistaken if they supposed that their duty was done when they had attended to the drill of their men and to the parade duties of their regiment—the order and regularity in camp and quarters, and the subsistence and comfort of the soldier being of equal importance." General hospitals were formed on the principle that "all men likely to continue sick for any length of time," were to go there. By a subsequent Order, "All men unable to march on account of sickness," were to be sent to the general hospitals immediately (March 16, 1811), as otherwise " whole transport arrangements for supply were being deranged by being pressed to carry sick soldiers." (General Order, Treneda, Oct. 5, 1811.) Already the inconvenience of carrying large numbers of sick with their regiments was being felt during the more rapid marches of this period of the war. During its continuance, the annual loss by deaths amounted to 12,356; discharges, 3,618; desertions, 4,679, or 20,553 in all.

Next to Lisbon, the largest hospital establishment was at Coimbra. When the proposition was first made to the Duke of Wellington to provide conveyances for the hospital establishment of each regiment and brigade, he objected to have such an interruption to the movements of the army, which such plans would clog. Such hospitals appeared afterwards to have become a necessity, there being no adequate arrangements for the formation of the more mobile field-hospitals of modern times. In these were treated in the first instance all slight cases of disease and wounds, and under the able administration of Sir James McGrigor, they were brought to a state of perfection never since observed. " They were frequently established in the face of the enemy, and nearly within reach of his guns." At the assault of Badajoz in 1812, the medical officers discharged their onerous duties, often under circumstances of personal danger. Lord Wellington said to Sir James McGrigor that " he himself had witnessed it." On the day of the successful assault, Sir James McGrigor urged upon Lord Wellington their claims to a public acknowledgment of their services in his despatches as an incentive to further exertion. Lord Wellington assented at once, and when the *Gazette* appeared announcing the victory, the Medical officers in England saw *for the first time* the merits of the brethren publicly acknowledged; an example followed after every subsequent great action.

The following fact is proof of the zeal and ability which directed the medical concerns of the Army of the Peninsula:—

" During the ten months from the siege of Burgos to the battle of Vittoria inclusive, the total number of sick and wounded which passed through the hospitals was 95,348. By the unremitting attention of Sir James McGrigor and the medical staff under his orders, the army took the field preparatory to the battle, with a sick list under 5,000. For twenty successive days it marched towards the enemy, and in less than one month after it had defeated him, mustered, within thirty men, as strong as before the action; and this, too, without reinforcements from England, the ranks having been recruited by convalescents."—(Napier.)

In these campaigns the English veterans " had killed, wounded, or captured 200,000 enemies, losing of their own number 40,000, whose bones whiten the plains and mountains of the Peninsula." —(Idem).

Dr. Somers was Physician-in-chief in the Peninsula, and Dr. William Fergusson, Inspector-General of Military Hospitals, and principal medical officer of the Portuguese army under the command of Marshal Beresford. He joined the army in 1794 at Ghent, accompanied it on the retreat through Holland, his commission as surgeon of the 2nd Battalion 90th Regiment having been antedated to the date of the Letters of Service for raising the regiment. He afterwards served with the 67th at St. Domingo in 1796; in 1801, accompanied the expedition to the Baltic as staff-surgeon of the troops embarked, and was present in the attack upon the Danish line of defence before Copenhagen, after which he was entrusted with the conveyance of the British wounded to Yarmouth, when he received the thanks of the " Sick and Hurt" Office on delivering up his charge. In the Peninsula he was principal medical officer at the taking of Oporto and passage of the Douro; was present at Talavera, where Assistant-Surgeon Walker (afterwards Physician to the Forces) was left with the wounded on the field of battle, and captured by the enemy. In 1815 Dr. Fergusson accompanied the expedition against Guadaloupe. In 1817 he quitted the army, receiving the thanks of the Commander of the Forces in General Orders. In his "Notes and Recollections of a Professional Life" may be found many interesting facts relating to the medical service during the period he was an active member of it. Dr. Fergusson deplored the want of a proper head-quarters for the Medical Staff of his day, and of "an ambulance with the British Army at which the young medical officer might find a home, and an hospital corps to furnish him with means of conveyance and assistance."

As a result of his experience in the Peninsula, Napier wrote: " The British soldier is more robust than the soldiers of any other nation; this can scarcely be doubted by those who observed his powerful frame, distinguished amidst the united armies of Europe; and notwithstanding his habitual excess in drinking, he sustains fatigue, and wet, and the extremes of cold and heat with incredible vigour. When completely disciplined, and three years are required to accomplish this, the whole world cannot produce a nobler specimen of military bearing, nor is the mind unworthy of the outward man. He is observant and quick to comprehend his orders, full of resources under difficulties, calm and resolute in danger, and more than usually obedient and careful of his officers in moments of imminent peril."

Lord Wellington made evident reference to the Medical Staff and Hospitals of the army in his earlier dispatches (Gurwood), in one of these he wrote: " in all times and places the sick list amounts to at least ten men per 100, or 3000 upon 30,000 men. .... It is besides very necessary that some effectual measure should be taken to increase the medical staff, not with gentlemen of rank, but with hospital-mates. The duty of the general hospitals in every active army ought to be done by the General Medical Staff, and the regiments ought to have their surgeons and assistants entirely disengaged for any extraordinary event in sickness that may occur. We have not now one surgeon or assistant with each regiment, instead of three, the others being employed in the hospitals instead of the hospital-mates, and we have always been equally deficient. Indeed one of the reasons which induced me to cross the Tagus on 4th August, instead of attacking Soult, was the want of surgeons with the army, all being employed with the hospitals, and there being scarcely one for each brigade; and if we had had an action we would not have been able to dress our wounded." In a late dispatch he writes, "It is quite impossible for a large army to carry on extended operations without military hospitals. We have had nearly thirty for wounded upon this frontier." (St. Jean de Luz, 24th June, 1814). At this date portable huts were brought from England as temporary field hospitals, described as " a great relief." In the last action of the war, the battle of Toulouse, the labours of the medical officers were exceedingly great, not only on the day of action, but for some weeks afterwards, for the duty devolved on them, not only of dressing the wounds and attending to the British, but also of performing similar offices for the allies, the Portuguese and Spaniards, owing to the inadequacy of their own surgeons, both of whom and the wounded French prisoners expressed their sympathy in many affecting ways. Speaking of the Peninsula in which he served, Guthrie said, " Nothing could be more inefficient than the Medical Department of the army during the first two-thirds of the war. It was only when it reached the summit of the Pyrenees that its medical department approached perfection, and when the army moved from Toulouse, the medical officers who accompanied it were equal to the charge of the wounded of another battle, if one had taken place. The French and English surgeons visited each other, every case of interest was thoroughly investigated, and the surgery of the British army and the Empire dates much of its improvement from the facts elicited or confirmed on those occasions. And why was this so ? Simply because the necessary means of every kind were at hand, and the medical men were numerous, young and efficient." " The confidence the Duke of Wellington reposed in

Sir James McGrigor, the Inspector-General of Military Hospitals in the Peninsula, in giving him the uncontrolled management of the department, enabled him to enforce military discipline amongst us on the one hand, whilst he encouraged ability, excited emulation, and rewarded merit in the other. Every officer of the department endeavoured, by a zealous discharge of his duty to deserve his attention, and by keeping the army effective in the field, to prove to their brethren at home, that although they were less profitably, they were not less honourably employed in the service of their country." He goes on to allude to the fact that although military surgeons during the Peninsular war had not given many observations on military surgery, " their opinions were none the less widely promulgated and used by authors without acknowledgment." He dedicated the first edition of his work on gunshot wounds to the junior members of the department, "but very soon, young men sent out to the Peninsula incapable of performing any operation in military surgery, became able operators in a short time from the practical lessons inculcated in the dissecting room, hospitals, and fields of battle."

After the battle of Toulouse, Sir James McGrigor visited the French hospitals, and although he saw " very little to copy from them, as an improvement on his own," he expressed an opinion that one part would have been an improvement, " the ambulances for the transport of their wounded and sick, particularly the former." On his return to England in 1814, he was presented with a costly service of plate from the physicians, surgeons, apothecaries, and purveyors who had served with him during the Peninsular war, a warm recognition of his professional merits and services. Crosses, medals and clasps for the actions in the Peninsula were conceded to the chiefs of the military departments, their deputies and assistants, having the rank of field officer.

At the conclusion of the Waterloo campaign, Dr. John Hennen published his principles of Military Surgery. He was born 21st April, 1779, at Castlebar, county Mayo, Ireland, and after a career of nearly thirty-one years spent in active employment and entirely devoted to the public service, died at Gibraltar, of yellow fever, on 3rd November, 1829, in the fiftieth year of his age, having entered the service in his nineteenth year. After some years' service in the Mediterranean and Ireland he accompanied the 30th Regiment to the Peninsula in 1809. On the retreat of the French from Portugal in 1811 he accompanied the 5th Division as Senior-Surgeon, acting as principal medical officer in its various advances, retreats, skirmishes, and ·actions until October, 1811, when he was promoted to the rank of Surgeon to the Forces, when eleven years in the service and thirty-two years of age. Owing to his dexterity as an operator, and incessant zeal in the cause of suffering humanity, the charge of some of the most important surgical hospitals in the Peninsula was given to him. Upon the peace of 1814, he returned with the army to England, and was placed for a short time on half pay. On the return of Napoleon from Elba in 1815, he was again called into active service and ordered to Belgium, being placed in charge of the Jesuits' Hospital at Brussels. After the battle of Waterloo he had had sole superintendence of the wounded General Staff, and continued to direct the duties of the Jesuits' Hospital until September, 1815, when he was promoted to the rank of Deputy-Inspector of Hospitals. In the winter of 1820 he delivered a course of lectures on Military Surgery, and, in co-operation with Professor Thompson, gave weekly clinical reports on the cases in the Military Hospitals, as did Mr. Guthrie at the York Military Hospital, then at Chelsea, during the two years following the victory of Waterloo. In this hospital many of the worst cases had been admitted from Antwerp and Brussels. When it was broken up, the men were transferred to Chatham. Mr. Guthrie early suggested the appointment of a "Military Professor of Surgery," capable, "from his previous experience and civil opportunities, of teaching all things in the principles and practice of surgery connected with his office," and very properly remarked that when a young surgeon is sent in the execution of his duties to distant climes where he has few, and sometimes no opportunities of adding to the knowledge he had previously acquired, it is apt to be impaired, and he may return to England, after an absence of several years, less qualified, perhaps, than when he left it. To such persons," he writes, " a course of instruction is invaluable, and should be open to them, as public servants, gratuitously, and conveyed by a person appointed and paid by the Crown—leave of absence for three months being granted to officers in turn for the purpose of attending these lectures, the Professor certifying to their time being well employed." On the termination of the Peninsular War, several of the large number of medical officers, placed upon half pay, availed themselves of such opportunities in attendance, with the advice of Sir James McGrigor, the effect of which exceeded his most sanguine expectations.

"The great and peculiar care of the medical officer, on commencing a campaign," wrote Hennen, as the result of his experience, "should be carefully and minutely to examine his medical and purveyor's stores, with a view to their completion in every respect. Whether in charge of a corps of the army, of a regiment, or of a detachment, so much of the success of the surgical campaign depends upon this, that too great pains cannot be bestowed upon it. The skill and experience of a medical officer are in few particulars more strongly evinced than in making his requisitions on the great depots for his field and hospital supplies with judgment and selection." He praises the *ambulance volante* of the French armies, " found so useful," and thought " that an establishment of that kind, duly remodelled, would be of important service in our field arrangements." The then "improved plan" of the British equipment not recognizing the carts and waggons for the carriage of a field hospital on the line of march, " only a proportion of spring waggons for the use of each division being allowed to accompany the army, and that solely for carrying the sick and wounded."

In the following extract he gives a brief description of the preparations for the casualties of a battle in Peninsular days:— " We will suppose that the army has taken the field, or opened the trenches, each of its divisions furnished with a due proportion of the General Hospital Staff, with their stores, the field-panniers of the regiments and of the staff-surgeon complete, their surgeon and assistants present, and an arrangement made with the commandant for the transport of the wounded to the fixed hospitals in the rear. The usual and most rational plan for providing against the casualties that will naturally succeed to the opening of the fire on the field is that laid down by Ranby—viz., to form in small parties, at a convenient distance in the rear, out of the immediate range of shot and shells, where the field-panniers are fixed as a sort of table, and where some of the regimental non-combatants, the drummers, band, &c., are prepared to act as orderlies. When, however, it can be conveniently done, especially at a siege, two, three, or more points of rendezvous, at a house, farm, church, or marquee, ought to be appointed to carry the wounded to in the first instance. In either of these situations the first dressings should be applied, and the primary operations performed; here, also, the wounded should be selected for conveyance to the receiving hospitals in the rear, those who can walk selected from those who require mules, horses, or waggons, and the whole sent off under a proper escort, with a careful assistant, with a due supply of rations, in such proportion as the nature of circumstances may point out. Every article, however, of this kind, particularly with 'spirits,' is to be kept in a separate waggon, or mules, and never entrusted to soldiers."

At the conclusion of the war in 1814, the Medical staff are shown at the commencement of the Army List after the General staff of the army, and taking priority of the regiments as an appanage of the Staff:—

Director-General—John Weir, 24th February, 1810.

Principal Inspectors—Charles Ker, M.D., 24th February, 1810; William Franklin, M.D., 12th July, 1810.

Ten Inspectors—Robert Jackson, M.D., 28th April, 1795; Lewis Versturm, M.D., 25th November, 1795; William Moore, M.D., 13th March, 1799; John Wright, M.D., 16th January, 1800; James Borland, M.D., 22nd January, 1807; James McGrigor, M.D., 25th August, 1809; Gabriel B. Raymond, 3rd September, 1812; William Ferguson, 18th February, 1813; Sir James Fellowes, M.D., 29th April, 1813; Ralph Green, 26th August, 1813.

Thirty deputy-inspectors, 2 with local rank; 29 physicians; 137 surgeons, 25 surgeons with local rank; 22 surgeons of recruiting districts; 21 assistant-surgeons; 9 purveyors; 38 deputy-purveyors; 27 apothecaries, and 1 apothecary with local rank.

Large additions had been made to the establishment in 1813— viz., 4 inspectors, 12 deputy-inspectors, 9 physicians, 45 surgeons, 11, assistant-surgeons, 1 purveyor, 11 deputy-purveyors, and 11 apothecaries. The total number of medical officers on full pay before the reduction of the army after the Peninsular War was as follows:—

Medical Staff	362
Regimental Surgeons	313
Regimental Assistant-Surgeons	573
Garrison Surgeons and Assistant-Surgeons	16
Miscellaneous Appointments	8
Ordnance Medical Department	102
Foreign Artillery and Ordnance Train	3
Total	1,477

The Ordnance Medical Department head-quarter staff consisted of the following officers:—

Director-General—Sir John Webb, 20th November, 1809.

Surgeon-General and Inspector—Gustavus Irwin, 27th December, 1809.

Assistant Surgeon-General and Deputy Inspectors—MacMelhan Jameson, 27th December, 1809; Joseph Kenedy, M.D., 11th November, 1811.

Resident Surgeons—Wm. Wittman, M.D., 13th March, 1811; Nicholas Hornsby, 5th August, 1813.

Twenty-two surgeons, 1 apothecary, 26 assistant-surgeons, 47 second assistant-surgeons, and 3 chaplains.

In the Peninsula the hospital system of the Guards and Ordnance Department were on a different footing from the rest of the army, these corps not reporting to the chief of the medical department in the field.

Irish Medical Department.

Physicians-General—C. W. Guinn, 1st June, 1795; William Harvey, 1st June, 1795.

Director-General—George Renny, M.D., 1st June, 1795.

Surgeon-General—Philip Cranpton, 10th June, 1813.

Deputy-Inspectors—R. M. Peile, M.D., 28th September, 1803; James Pitcairn, M.D., 22nd October, 1803; William Comins, 8th December, 1803; H. Riggar, M.D., 8th December, 1803.

Fourteen staff-surgeons, 3 staff-apothecaries, 2 deputy-purveyors, 5 purveyors' clerks, and 12 hospital-mates.

Such was the Medical staff of the army at the close of the great war, numbering in all some 1,600 officers of all ranks. The deaths of 41 medical officers occurred during the year—viz,, 7 regimental surgeons, 25 assistant-surgeons, 3 physicians, 2 surgeons to the Forces, 1 assistant-surgeon to the Forces, and 1 apothecary.

In the Provisional Battalion of Militia are shown the following among the officers—Lieutenant John L. Parker, assistant-surgeon; Lieutenant Thomas Luby, assistant-surgeon.

John Charlton, Surgeon-Major 1st Foot Guards, is senior-surgeon in the army, his commission dating 21st July, 1790, or twenty-four years before. The mean strength in the Peninsula of officers and men for forty-one months ending May, 1814, was 66,772; the deaths during the same period numbered 35,525, of which only 9,948 fell in battle or died of their wounds; 225 per thousand of the 61,511 men was on an average on the sick list, and their annual mortality was at the rate of 161 per thousand.

In 1813 Regulations had been issued by the Army Medical Board in Ireland revising those published on formation of the Department. They contained very good rules as to the cleanliness, isolation of contagious cases, &c. The hospitals were under the direction of their respective surgeons, and subject to the Director-General of Hospitals and officers of the Medical staff. Civil practitioners were to be employed for detachments without assistants, and sufficient intercourse was to be kept up with them by the surgeon to enable him to compile his monthly report. Weekly or fortnightly health inspections were ordered, and, if a regiment was sickly, special reports were to be made as to the cause, &c. Punished men were to be treated in separate wards. Recruits registered and inoculated with vaccine matter. Diseased and disabled men examined and certified by staff-surgeon or deputy-inspector of respective visitations, certificates of unfitness to be forwarded with their monthly reports. Medicine chests were supplied, and medicine, but not stimulants, allowed to women and children. The barrack department supplied beds and equipment, and each surgeon was allowed two *cars* for carriage of hospital stores of each regiment; three *cars* for private baggage, and one to each assistant. A table of dietary was to be hung in the wards, and not altered without permission of deputy-inspector or staff-surgeon. Weekly tables of disbursements were to be kept in each hospital and certified by staff medical officers at inspections. Surplus of hospital savings to form part to go towards liquidation of general medical expenses of corps, and to be credited to public half-yearly. Each hospital being allowed a hospital serjeant, one or two orderly men, and a nurse. Stimulants were to be previously mixed with food or medicine, monthly returns of which were to be forwarded to Medical Board. The quarters of the medical officers were to be as near the hospital as possible, and, when encamped, one of them was to sleep there. Sick men, when recovered, were to rejoin their regiment by march route.

Staff-surgeons, when permanently stationed in a quarter, were to take a certain extent of country and certain number of troops under their medical superintendence, and were invested with authority to call for frequent reports from regimental medical officers, and advise with them when necessary. The hospital staff in Ireland then had four districts, each in charge of a Deputy-Inspector—viz., Leinster, Connaught, Ulster, and Munster, the head-quarters of which were in Dublin, Athlone, Belfast, and Cork. Superintending staff-surgeons were in addition stationed at Dublin, Naas, Kilkenny, Athlone, Birr, Limerick, Galway, Tullamore, Belfast, Strabane, Sligo, Armagh, Cork, Clonmel, and Waterford. The King's Military Infirmary was used for the treatment of fevers and all other acute diseases of soldiers in the Dublin garrison, and all accidents or other cases requiring immediate surgical assistance, as well as serious cases from country quarters, who were, if subsequently invalided, discharged the service upon the certificate of the surgeon or physician-general and resident staff-surgeon. The hospital stoppage, which had been 4s. a-week in 1799, was now 10d. per diem. Shortly after the appointment of Sir James McGrigor as Director-General, a memorandum was issued by the Army Medical Board in England, laying down the qualifications, &c., required from medical aspirants to commissions. It is dated 30th September, 1816, and commences—"The Army Medical Board, solicitous for the improvement of the Department in its various branches, and considering the present a favourable opportunity for the selection and encouragement of well-educated persons, have thought it advisable to promulgate the course of instruction, and the qualifications required from gentlemen entering the Medical Department of the Army, and during the progress of advancement in the service."

Candidates for first commissioned appointments were to produce certificates of regular study at an established school of eminence in surgery, anatomy, practical anatomy, practice of medicine and chemistry during a full period of twelve months; materia medica and botany during six months, and the practice of medicine and surgery in a hospital or infirmary during at least one year, with a regular apprenticeship, or three years without an apprenticeship, in which case a certificate of having studied practical pharmacy was required. Regimental medical officers were to be acquainted with midwifery, and it was considered an additional recommendation to gentlemen entering the service to have attended public establishments for the treatment of diseases of the eyes and mental derangement. "A liberal education is indispensably requisite," the memorandum goes on to state, " and the greater the attainments of the candidate are in the various branches of science, in addition to competent professional knowledge, the more eligible he will be deemed for promotion; as selections to fill vacancies will be guided more by reference to such requirements than to seniority. By the established regulation, every gentleman must have served five years at least in the junior appointments before he can be promoted to the rank of regimental surgeon, and he who gives the best proofs of diligent exertion in the performance of his public duty, and of attention to the requirement of practical knowledge will be voted as the most eligible candidate for advancement."

" Gentlemen already in the service are earnestly recommended to avail themselves of every opportunity of adding to their knowledge by attending universities or schools, for which purpose every facility will be afforded by the Director-General, and every gentleman must be prepared for a recent examination, if called upon, before he obtain further promotion."

" Medical officers are encouraged and recommended to look forward to the appointment of Surgeon to the Forces and of Physician to the Forces, and to endeavour especially to qualify themselves for either, ascending to the rank of their inclinations, and to their previous study."

This excellent stimulant to the medical virtues produced, according to the testimony of Sir James McGrigor, results far more favourable than he could have anticipated, although subsequent to the war promotion had become very slow, averaging after some time, fifteen or sixteen years ; no new appointments being made until the effective officers on the large half-pay list had been absorbed.

The men also owed to the exertions and forethought of the Director-General the foundation of the Army Medical Officers' Benevolent and Friendly Societies, which should be joined by every officer of the Department, and the valuable library and collection subsequently formed at Fort Pitt, and brought together at York Hospital. Sir James McGrigor had succeeded to the place on the Medical Board, vacated by Mr. Weir through ill-health, and had as colleagues Mr. Charles Kerr and Sir William Franklin. Dr. Kerr shortly afterwards retired, and was succeeded by Dr. William Somerville, who remained only a few months, the Government being determined to reduce the number to two. In 1816, Dr. Thompson, Surgeon to the Forces and Regius Professor of Military Surgery in the University of Edinburgh, published an interesting Report on the state of the wounded after the Battle of Waterloo, and Dr. Mulligen, in 1819, his " Army Medical Officers' Manual," which contains several facts, illustrating the general practice of the Department at that time. Sir George Ballengal succeeded Dr. Thompson as Regius Professor of Military Surgery in the University of Edinburgh, and published his excellent " Outlines," which went through several editions as a standard professional work, and even now may be perused with interest and profit.

In 1825, Mr. Samuel Cooper, also a late Surgeon to the Forces, incorporated many of his surgical observations in his Dictionary and First Lines, a standard work, for many years, and largely read in the medical schools. He had served in military hospitals in Holland, Belgium, and France. Shortly after his appointment as Director-General, Sir James McGrigor " organized a system of returns and' reports, by which he was kept informed periodically, not only of the extent of sickness and mortality prevailing in the army, both at home and abroad, but also of the diseases by which these were occasioned," as well as " detailed information as to the sites of the barracks and cantonments, the physical geography of the surrounding country, the rations and diet of the troops, and such other circumstances as might be deemed likely to exert any influence upon their health; with remarks upon the diseases, and abstracts of the more interesting cases, from which an opinion could be formed, whether the professional duties of the department were conducted in a satisfactory manner."

In 1830, and again in 1840, new regulations were issued, granting some additional advantages to the officers of the Medical staff, who, after the first-named year, ceased to enter the army as hospital assistants. In the interval between these dates and the termination of the Peninsular War, the Medical staff had accompanied the troops in the repulse of the attack on Canada, the expedition against the Pindarees in 1818, the first Burmese War of 1824-5, when the army had to traverse a great alluvium, covered with jungle and inundated with floods during the worst season of the year, and where a terrible mortality resulted from sunstroke, fever, dysentery, and cholera, sixty-seven per cent. of the troops perishing from disease in the two years of the war. In the war of the succession in Spain a contingent of officers served with Sir De Lacy Evans, one of whom Mr., afterwards Sir Rutherford, Alcock gave a very graphic account of the demoralising effect resulting from the want of an hospital corps, where he says that he had seen " in less than an hour, a whole battalion tail off after some fifty wounded."

In commemoration of Dr. Hennen's efforts to arrest the epidemic yellow fever at Gibraltar in 1828, a monument was erected to his memory at the expense of Sir George Don, the Governor, and many of the inhabitants. On it were cut the following words: " Erected by his personal friends—not with a view of perpetuating his name, for that lives in the more imperishable memorials of his own genius, but as a testimony of regard for a man whose zeal was indefatigable, and who, in the day of general calamity, sacrificed all consideration of his safety for the public weal."

Between 1819-28, the annual ratio of mortality in the British Army was at home fifteen, and abroad fifty-seven per thousand; increased at home in 1832 by the serious epidemic of cholera which swept through the United Kingdom. Only 108 cases and forty-two deaths occurred amongst the troops, numbering 21,761 men. "We are disposed," wrote Sir James McGrigor and Mr. William Franklin, " to attribute this comparative exemption of the military from this dreadful disease to the strict and exemplary manner in which we believe the regulations were enforced by commanding officers, and to the zeal and attention with which the inspections were performed, and the promptitude and judgment with which all incipient symptoms were detected and arrested by the medical officers in charge." (Report of Army Medical Board.)

In 1833, Dr. John Cheyne, Physician-General to the Forces in Ireland contributed to the Cyclopædia of Practical Medicine and Dublin Hospital Reports some admirable papers illustrating the diseases and habits of soldiers as observed by him in the King's Military Infirmary, and in 1835, Mr. Marshall, Deputy-Inspector of Hospitals, was appointed by Lord Howick, in conjunction with Lieutenant Tulloch, 45th Regiment, to prepare a report on the sickness and mortality among the troops in the West Indies. In the following year, Dr. Balfour, afterwards head of the Statistical Branch, was associated with Mr. Tulloch, and in 1841 had completed a statistical report, in four volumes, upon the health of the army at home and abroad, exclusive of that portion serving in India and Australia, which were afterwards presented to Parliament by command of Her Majesty.

On 25th March, 1836, a very important letter (afterwards published in General Orders, by direction of the General Commanding-in-Chief, Lord Hill) was addressed to the Adjutant-General of the Forces by Sir James McGrigor, on the subject of the selection of men about to embark for foreign service, as he had " grounds for believing that many men were permitted to go with their regiments, who, labouring under particular forms of disease, were little suited for the efficient performance of their duty." He expressed his opinion that no man with active tubercular disease in existence, active or chronic diseases of the bowels, chronic diseases of the eyes, chronic ulcers, asthmatic complaints, and rheumatism (especially old soldiers) should be allowed to embark, involving as it did " the expense of sending useless men to foreign stations, crowding the hospitals with them while abroad, and again giving rise to the expense of sending them back, which was considerable." He also recommended that in the case of young men embarked with a delicate frame, and whose constitutions were not sufficiently formed, " much care should be had in not over drilling them, more especially in full marching order: the weight and drag on the shoulders and chest being more than such were equal with impunity to bear."

The next campaign in which the medical officers took a part was the march through the arid plains of Beloochistan in 1839, into Affghanistan, penetrating the Bolan Pass, a gloomy defile of some fifty miles ; the occupation of Cabool, attack on Julgar, where the scaling ladders were hastily constructed from the poles used for carrying litters for the sick, and also at the memorable defence of Jellalabad. At the close of the campaign in 1841, the late Dr. Bryden alone remained to tell the tale of that horrid massacre during the retreat towards Jellalabad.

Again, in the first China war of 1841-2, under Sir Hugh Gough, and the Caffre outbreak of 1847-48, and 1850-53, during which Sir John Hall was Principal Medical Officer, and where the savage enemy frequently plundered the hospital waggons, and, if opportunity offered, rushed upon the wounded and beat them to death with their clubs. In the Sikh War of 1845, when the officers and men underwent very great hardships. On 12th December, the 31st left Umballah, mustering thirty officers and 842 men, marching twenty-five or thirty miles a day—the severe nature of which it was impossible to describe—they arrived at Moodkee on the afternoon of the 18th, halting about two miles from the scene of action, when scarcely fifty men were left with the colours, for miles in the rear they might be seen staggering forward through the soft sand in an exhausted state for want of water and rest. Scarcely had they halted, when they had to rush to arms and advance under a heavy fire of grape and musketry to a complete victory. After Ferozeshah, nearly 1,500 wounded, mostly from the effects of artillery, were thrown upon the hands of the surgeons, whose hospital marquees had on many occasions been under the fire of the enemy. At Moodkee, Ferozeshah, Aliwal, and Sobraon 315 officers and 4,570 men were received into the hospitals wounded; after Chillianwala ninety-four officers and 1,057 men. After Sobraon, the British saw with indignation the enemy hacking and barbarously mangling the unfortunate wounded who for the time had fallen into their hands. "I bivouacked," wrote Viscount Hardinge, after Ferozeshah, "with the men, without food or covering; our nights were bitter cold, a burning camp in our front, our brave fellows lying down under a heavy cannonade continuing the whole night, mixed with the wild cries of the Sikhs, our English hurrahs, the tramp of the men, and groans of the dying." In such scenes as these did the Medical officers of the army participate in the Punjab.

The war had not concluded, when on the 1st July, 1848, another Royal Warrant was issued, regulating the pay of military surgeons. The ranks of assistant-surgeon and Surgeon to the Forces were replaced by those of first and second class staff-surgeons, the latter, as Sir James McGrigor expressed it, "a fillip to the senior assistant-surgeon," only obtained after an arduous struggle of two years on the part of the Chief of the Department. Assistant-surgeons entering on 7s. 6d., increasing to 10s. per diem after that number of years' service. Regimental, or second-class staff-surgeons were given 13s. above ten, but under twenty years' service, 15s.; above twenty but under twenty-five years' service,

19s.; and over twenty-five years' service £1 2s. per diem. Staff-surgeons of the first-class, under twenty years' full-pay service, 19s.; above twenty but under twenty-five years' service, £1 2s.; above twenty-five years' service, £1 4s. Deputy-inspectors, who had become deputy inspectors-general by the Warrant of 1830, under twenty years' service, on full pay, £1 4s.; above twenty but under twenty-five years, £1 8s.; over twenty-five years' service, £1 10s. Inspectors-general, under twenty years' service, £1 16s.; above twenty but under twenty-five years, £1 18s.; over twenty-five years' service, £2 per diem, with the usual allowances. The relative rank was—Inspector-general as brigadier, deputy inspector-general as lieutenant-colonel, staff-surgeon of the first class as major, regimental surgeon and surgeon of the second class as captain; apothecary as captain, but junior of that rank; assistant-surgeon as lieutenant, deputy-purveyor as lieutenant, medical clerk on the establishment as ensign.

In 1848 were erected several of the present Military Prisons. To each of them was attached a medical officer from the half-pay list, whose exertions in the advancement of prison hygiene have borne abundant fruit in the more humane and natural treatment of military offenders. To their continued efforts in these directions the late Sir Joshua Jebb bore a warm tribute of praise, as have also each of his successors.

Sir James McGrigor retired from the office which he had held for thirty-five years in 1851, carrying with him into private life the good wishes of the officers who had served for so long under him. On the 31st of May a deputation of medical officers presented him, through the hands of Dr. Skey, Inspector-General of Hospitals, in presence of a large circle of friends, with a farewell address signed by more than five hundred of their number, and indicating many of the benefits which he had conferred on his brother officers. "The urbanity of his manners, the benevolence of his disposition, and the simplicity of his heart," we are told by his biographer, drew round him for the remaining years of his eventful life a large circle of friends. He died in London on the 2nd of April, 1858, in his eighty-eighth year, having spent nearly fifty-seven years in the active employment of his country.

In bringing forward the Army Estimates in the year 1851, the financial head of the army thus noticed his retirement: "In the Army Medical Department the Service has lost by the retirement, not, I am happy to say, by the death, of Sir James McGrigor, an officer to whom the public is much indebted;" and the Lords of the Treasury in fixing his pension expressed their high approbation of his "long, able, and most meritorious services."

During the period while Sir James McGrigor was Director-General, the salary attached to the office was £2,000 per annum, a sum barely adequate to the chief of a department numbering so many scientific officers, and involving so great responsibilities. The relative rank was that of major-general only.

Sir James McGrigor was succeeded by Doctor, afterwards Sir Andrew Smith. The emoluments of the office which he held were reduced to £1,200 per annum, with the title of "Superintendent of the Army Medical Department." Scarcely had he assumed the reins of office when the Crimean War broke out. Forty years of peace had dissipated the experience acquired during the Peninsular War, and the system of administration, when strained by the stern lessons of actual hostilities, proved wholly unsuitable.

Prior to the outbreak of hostilities the late Sir David Dumbreck, M.D., K.C.B., was, early in 1854, sent on special service to the expected seat-of-war, traversing on his mission Servia, Bulgaria, and part of Roumelia, crossing the Balkans in his journey. He was subsequently for a short time principal medical officer with our army, and served with it in the field as Senior Deputy Inspector-General.

One chief cause of the misfortunes which befel the army shortly after its landing, was the inadequacy of the preparations for a sudden and great war, and a timid adherence of the heads of the departments to the "regulations," where self-reliance, prompt decision, and independent action for unprovided emergencies was imperatively demanded, to which were added the unfortunate selection of the camps in Bulgaria, manœuvres for hours in a broiling sun in heavy marching order, nearly suffocated by stocks and patent leather shakoes, the difficulty of persuading many officers to relinquish their antiquated customs, and the extraordinary nature of the wet and tempests in November in the Crimea, acting upon an army already weakened by attacks of diarrhœa, dysentery and cholera. The sufferings of the British Army from sickness during the first five months of the war filled the country with grief and indignation, and the French Medical Organization, then thought to be altogether superior, was specially recommended for instant adoption!

On the outbreak of the war there was no ambulance-corps in existence, or land-transport. The old pensioners sent out with the ambulance-waggons dropped off fast, and there were none of those necessary adjuncts to a manœuvering army at the Battle of the Alma. The bandsmen of each regiment were allowed eight stretchers for carrying off the wounded, many of whom, from a want of a sufficient number of surgeons, remained for hours unattended to. The hospitals were fearfully over-crowded, and all the evils pointed out so forcibly by Brocklesby, Munro, McGrigor and Hennen as a result of such a state of things soon became manifest in a great mortality. Untold of difficulties were experienced by the English regimental surgeons during the winter of 1854 before Sebastopol, from the defective supplies of drugs and sick comforts, the result of stores mis-sent or improperly stowed on board-ship—men died starving in the midst of plenty. The Staff-Surgeon of the 3rd Division, Mr. Price, reported to the

General commanding :—" It is just a mathematical calculation, the strength of the Division is 3,000 men, so many die daily from over-work, want of fuel and clothing, short living, bad food, and no medical comforts. I calculate on the utter annihilation of the 3rd Division of your army before spring, unless something is done to preserve life."

On the 30th of November, 1854, 10,000 men were sick and non-effective before Sebastopol. The sick of the Royals on the 10th of February numbered no less than 356 men, an example of the overwhelming work thrown upon individual medical officers. Many of these evils had been anticipated by the chief of the Medical Department of the Army, whose officers were made the scapegoat for evils they were powerless to prevent. At home such a feeling was of short duration, and was followed by the conviction that "no branch of the Service, military or civil, displayed higher intelligence and heroism, or answered the calls of duty more satisfactorily than did the Medical staff of the British Army. How urgent were these calls, how self-sacrificing was the medical devotion to duty, was proved by the fact that a larger proportion of military surgeons lost their lives during this war than of any other officers of the army."—(Bryce). Out of 93,959 non-commissioned officers and men sent to the East, 1,761 died of their wounds, 16,298 from disease, 12,903 were invalided, and 2,658 killed in action, a total of 33,649, leaving 60,312. On the 31st of December, 1855, so greatly improved had become the health and efficiency of the army, owing to the energetic measures taken to remedy the evils which had brought it to the brink of destruction, that out of a strength of 59,045 non-commissioned officers and men, only 3,326 remained in the general and regimental hospitals, 1,490 of whom were in the hospitals on the Bosphorus and Dardanelles, &c., and the sick to strength for the five months ending the 31st of March, 1856, had been reduced to 6·53 per cent. Hospitals were at Kertch, Scutari, Renkioi and Smyrna; which, while the army was warmly clad, comfortably hutted, well rationed, performing duties and fatigues moderate in amount throughout the winter of 1855-56, the deaths had fallen under that of the Household Cavalry in England, 2·81 per cent. Under opposite conditions, in January, 1854, an army of 23,000 soldiers had more than one-half its strength in hospital, where everything had been deficient but the "patience, bravery and discipline of the men."

"The improvement in the health and condition of the soldiers, and confusion and crowding of the hospitals, had ceased in great measure, owing to the urgent representations of the medical staff, and judicious measures were in full activity before the presence of any adventitious commission could have influenced the changes." —(Bryce.) So healthy had the army become in 1855-56, that at this point the regimental and general hospitals contained only a moiety of patients; Sir John Hall's reports for months showing the health of the troops to be as good as if encamped in England. It was found that the overwork in proportion to the quantity, quality and irregularity of the food supplied was more fatal than the cold and privations of the first winter. The young soldiers, unable to bear the hardships and fatigue, died off in numbers. After the termination of the war, Sir John Hall, Principal Medical Officer of the Expedition, compiled an elaborate history of the medical and surgical events, the first of its kind ever published by the Army Medical Department. After the action of the Alma, Lord Raglan alluded in his despatch to the principal medical officer in the following terms:—" Dr. Hall, the principal medical officer, was in the field the whole time, and merits my approbation for his exertion in discharging his onerous duties."

Dr. Thompson, surgeon, 44th Regiment, and his servant remained in the field, after the departure of the army, to attend upon more than 200 wounded. He died afterwards of cholera at Balaclava, a bright example of true heroism. After the battle Her Majesty, with her usual thoughtfulness, telegraphed through the Duke of Newcastle to Lord Raglan, expressing " the sincere sorrow which she experienced from the perusal of the long list of gallant officers and men who had been either killed or severely wounded." In his despatch following the sanguinary action of Balaclava, Lord Raglan again alluded to the services of the medical officers. " It is due to the principal medical officers of the several divisions, Doctors Alexander, Cruikshank, Forest, Linton and Humfrey, to report that their able exertions have been strongly represented to me, and deserve to be most honourably mentioned, and the arrangements of the Inspector-General of Hospitals, Dr. Hall, for the care of the wounded merit the expression of my entire approbation." In Lord Raglan's despatch mention is also made of the " spirited exertions of Assistant-Surgeon Wilson, of the 7th Hussars, who at a critical moment rallied a few men, which enabled them to hold the ground until reinforced." Mr. Russell wrote of this officer that " with the greatest gallantry and coolness he assembled a few men of the Guards and led them to the charge, and utterly routed and dispersed the Russians threatening the Duke's life, whose horse was killed under him. At the close of the day Mr. Wilson was called to the front of his regiment and publicly thanked for saving, in all probability, his life." More than one of the medical officers who served in the Crimea exchanged their medical for combatant commissions, and some of these ultimately succeeded to the command of their respective regiments.

In bringing to the notice of the Major-General Commanding the names of the officers who distinguished themselves at the assault of the Redan, Major Danbeny mentions specially the services of Assistant-Surgeon O'Callaghan, attached to the 62nd Regiment, " who accompanied the regiment as far as the fifth parallel, and volunteered to remain behind after the regiment went back to camp, to assist in attending to and bringing in the wounded from the front at dusk." The name of Assistant-Surgeon Sylvester was also brought to the notice of Sir William Codrington, for going "to the front under a heavy fire to assist the wounded," for which act of bravery he was rewarded with the Victoria Cross, an honour obtained by the surgeon of the 6th Dragoons, and Assistant-Surgeon Hales, 7th Fusiliers, for similar acts of gallantry under fire during the siege.

M. Baudens attributed the greater relative health of the English Army, towards the end of the Crimean War, when the French were decimated with disease, to the fact that "the English hospitals were remarkable for cleanliness, partly due to the higher and more independent military position which the English surgeons held, and which entitled and enabled them to exercise greater authority in hygienic measures, and the ordinary sick diet being more ample and varied than the French one. During most of the time occupied by the siege, assistant-surgeons gave the first attention to the wounded. But at the periods of the assaults, staff-surgeons were advanced to the ravines, and performed such operations as were necessary on the spot, and attended to the transmission of the wounded to the hospitals. The peculiar shape, great velocity, and rotatory motion of the conical balls, then coming into use, gave a peculiarity to the wounds not before observed, rarely deviating from their direct course after entering the body; they produced great comminution of the bones, and when impacted were more difficult to remove. Chloroform was also for the first time extensively used. The hospitals provided for the reception of the sick and wounded in the Crimea were 141; the regimental hospitals within the lines 161; a general hospital at Balaclava; 101 hospitals or sanitaria on the neighbouring heights, and larger general hospitals at Scutari and the shores of the Bosphorus, were under the management of Dr. Linton, and Dr. Parkes was medical chief of the Civil Hospital at Renkioi. To the office of superintendent of the Renkioi Hospital was attached a salary of £2,000 per annum, quarters and table money. The following staff served under Dr. Parkes, viz.:—two physicians and two surgeons at two guineas a day each; twenty-three assistant-surgeons at twenty-five shillings; and one apothecary with the same daily rate of pay; four dispensers at seven and sixpence per diem each, and one clinical-assistant at ten shillings. The number of patients at no time exceeded 500.

Mr. Robertson was purveyor-in-chief; while peace with Russia was obligatory on France in the spring of 1856; because of the sanitary state of her army, the British had been restored to a state of sanitary efficiency rarely exceeded. A "Medical Staff Corps" had been organised for the service of the hospitals, clothed in a grey uniform with scarlet facings. In the French hospitals in fifty-seven days 603 out of 840 orderlies had been attacked with typhus, and of the whole French Medical staff seventy-two out of 350 fell victims to their professional duties. Sixty-one officers of the Army Medical Department succumbed from the effects of disease or wounds.

Towards the close of the Crimean War a Royal Commission was appointed to inquire into the causes of the disasters which had befallen the army, and to suggest appropriate remedies against their recurrence in future. It appeared to them that the weakest point in the Medical Department of the Army was the want of prestige, to give the officers that due importance among their brethren " so essential to the efficient performance of military duties." That this was the feeling of the medical officers themselves, was proved by the following passage from their Memorial to the Secretary of War, " We submit that we ought to be classed amongst the purely military branches, and reap our share of the honours accorded to them, the exclusion from which, in all campaigns, we deeply feel."

The united colleges of England, Ireland and Scotland, in their Memorial to the Secretary of State for War, expressed the opinion that "The existing regulations of the Service did not appear to hold out sufficient encouragement, either by present or prospective remuneration and rank, to induce students of the higher order, as to education and attainments, to seek for these appointments," and "that considering the valuable services which, by *universal acknowledgment*, were rendered by the medical officers during the late campaign, their self-sacrifice, moral courage, and devotion to their arduous duties, under trying circumstances, the present seemed a suitable opportunity for the recognition of the claims of this important branch of the Service to higher status and emoluments."

Upon the evidence presented to them and these memorials, the Royal Commission made the following remarks, " These are the opinions of men forming the Councils of the most eminent medical and surgical bodies in this country ; and it appears to us to be impossible to combat these statements. It is not, however, by money alone, that the ablest and most accomplished men will be attracted to the Army Medical Service, the rank, the position, and the honors which are to be obtained, constitute perhaps the stronger inducements to the higher class of minds." As a result the Committee recommended " That the Army Medical Department be held entitled to the same share of honours and rewards as combatant officers of the same rank." And that as the medical officers had been proved to have been embarrased by having to add to the abounding cares and anxieties of their own profession, the inconsistent duties of steward and purveyor, they should be relieved of these. Attention was also called to the total insufficiency of the administrative staff, and the haphazard system of trusting to convalescent and other soldiers to care and nurse the sick and wounded, instead of trained attendants; men attached to the hospitals because they were unfit for military, not because they were fit for hospital, duty. " Each division and each brigade," wrote His late Royal Highness the Prince Consort, "ought to have its staff, commissariat, medical department, ambulance and baggage-train attached to it. By keeping these commands and appointments filled up, we alone can get the means of judging of the fitness of men for command, and give them the means of fitting themselves to it."

The Medical officers who served in the Crimea have every reason to be proud of the Report of the Committee on the Medical Department, and of the testimony borne by the best and highest authorities to the uniform zeal, energy and courage displayed under the most trying circumstances that men could be placed in. After the Review of the Crimean troops, before General Lüders, had terminated, General Codrington wrote to Lord Panmure:— " The steady, the good, the healthy appearance of the Army; its apparent efficiency in every branch; the order, quietness and regularity, with which every regiment passed by, was a subject of pride to us all to feel that such was the appearance of the Army of England in the Crimea." Forty-nine battalions, thirteen batteries of artillery, eighty-six guns, and two regiments of land transport had defiled before the Russian commander on the 19th of April, 1856. In the preceding week only sixteen deaths had occurred, the rate of admissions to strength was only 1·81, the deaths ·02, and the sick to well 3·87 per cent.

On the 25th of May, 1855, the Commander-in-Chief assumed the command of the Royal Artillery and Royal Engineers from the Board of Ordnance, and Sir Andrew Smith became " Director-General of the Army and Ordnance Departments." Deputy Inspectors, Drs. Halahan and Ogilvie, superintended the affairs of the Department. These officers were absorbed in 1859, when the designations of senior surgeons, junior surgeons and assistants merged into those accorded by the Royal Warrant of 1858, viz., surgeon-major, surgeon and assistant-surgeon. In the Guards, £158 5s. 6d. was given to defray the cost of hospitals, recruiting and various miscellaneous expenses, by which allowances, granted in lieu of the profits of the hospitals; the pay of captains nominally £282 17s. 6d. per annum, was made up to £450—that of captain and lieutenant-colonel. In 1858 the estimates for the hospital expenses, medicines, and treatment of the sick amounted to a sum of £92,945, which was nearly covered by the hospital stoppages from the soldiers, which returned £89,719 to the Exchequer. To give an estimate of the field of observation open at the Central Invalid Depôt of the British Army, it may be mentioned that the number of soldiers who arrived and were disposed of at Chatham during the two years of the Crimean period, 1855-56, amounted to 14,700, and that the average number for the eighteen years, from 1839—1856, was considerably above 3,000 per annum. During the Crimean War a large number of acting assistant-surgeons were appointed for the first time, many of whom were afterwards assorted into the ranks of the Department. During the last year of the war the annual estimates had risen to £34,998,504, falling in the following year to £11,225,533.

While these events had been occurring in the Crimea, one regiment of British troops, the 64th, with its medical officers, served throughout the Persian campaign of 1856-7. On one of their marches against Soofa-vol-Moolk at Bocangoon, 3rd February, each man carried his great coat, blanket, and two days' provisions, but without tent or other equipage. The rain fell heavily and the nights were bitter cold. The position was reached on the 5th. On the return march the enemy was defeated; the troops bivouacked on the field of action, and during the following night marched twenty miles over a wet country, rested six hours, and continued the march to Bushire, which was reached at midnight, a distance of forty-four miles having been traversed within fifty hours, carrying with them sixty-two wounded, the casualties in the action of the 8th. The field hospital was under the direction of Superintendant Surgeon-Major Mackenzie, and the "Result" accompanied the expedition.

At this time there were only 757 officers and 22,741 men, (four cavalry and twenty-two Queen's regiments) in India, and no British Medical Staff in accordance with the exclusive policy of the Company, who conferred all staff appointments to their own officers. The success, witnessed after Ferozeshah, and the other Sikh campaigns, had so conclusively proved the want of such assistance that the Viceroy, Lord Hardinge, after what he had seen in the field-hospitals of the Punjab, desired to send a Medical staff to India but was foiled in the attempt, it being well-known that the numerical strength of the Company's officers was inadequate to supply all the numerous demands made upon it; many instances occurring of stations, including two regiments and a large staff with several detachments, being in charge of one surgeon. Under these circumstances excessive sickness and mortality was scarcely to be wondered at.

By the close of 1857, the whole of the acting assisting-surgeons taken on during the Crimean War, had been absorbed or left. Upon the outbreak of the Indian Mutiny, this establishment was again largely increased, 103 assistant-surgeons, and 32 acting assistant-surgeons being brought into the department. The latter were exclusively employed in Great Britain.

Few at the present time remember the hardships underwent, and the gallantry displayed by our brave men during the Indian Mutiny. "The heat of the day, intense as it was in the open plains, was deadly so in the jungles, all circulation of air being there prevented by the density of the vegetation. Water! water! was the cry of men and officers, and now became evident" (wrote an officer with the Azinghur Field Force) "the precaution taken by our considerate commander to have skins of it brought on upon camels and elephants. At almost every step soldiers and their officers had to stop and have their heads drenched. Many felt so giddy as to stagger and fall, others gasped for breath, considerable numbers had to be brought on in dhoolies, and not a few would have dropped behind the column were it not for the fear of the enemy. Large numbers of the 6th regiment, which preceded the infantry, were so fatigued, that elephants, carts, and dhoolies had to be sent out to bring them into their own camp; the boys sent out to fill vacancies being physically unfit for the severe exposure and fatigues they had to undergo." The want of vegetables was felt severely.

The outbreak had commenced at Meerut on May 10th, 1857, and by the end of May 1858 the British force had been increased to 3,102 officers and 78,437 men (including four troops of Royal Horse Artillery, nineteen Field Batteries, and six companies of Garrison Batteries) with a detachment of the Medical Staff Corps.

At the siege of Delhi, which lasted from May 30th to September 14th, the fighting was continuously day and night, and the men being constantly on the alert caused great fatigue. The 8th and 61st regiments suffered severely from cholera, attributed to their long marches during the height of the rainy season. The 52nd who were 680 strong with six sick on September 14th, shortly after their arrival from the Punjab were reduced by the ravages of fever and cholera to 240 effectives. At the defence of Lucknow the strength of the garrison on July 1st was 18 officers and 1,600 men fit for duty, with 80 sick and wounded. None within the walls of the Residency were safe; wounded soldiers, ladies and children were shot in the hospital. For eighty-seven days and nights the officers and men stood or slept under arms. Cholera and small-pox added to the loss sustained by the enemy's fire; delicate women, in their earliest grief for the loss of their husbands, assisted in nursing the sick and wounded. By September 26th the brave garrison had lost 140 officers and men killed, and 190 wounded, in addition to 72 Natives killed and wounded. During this period the relieving force had been marching under a perfect deluge of rain, irregularly fed, and badly housed in the different villages, their sick and wounded being constantly exposed to the attacks of the rebels. In one of his despatches Sir Hugh Rose stated that when a wing of the 71st were prostrated by " sun-sickness " during the attack at Banda, the only complaint heard in the field-hospitals from there was, that they could not rise and fight. Thirty-six cases of sunstroke occurred from the intense heat (rising in one day to 130° in the shade) and ten succumbed. Examples sufficient to indicate the nature of the duties falling to the lot of the Medical officers engaged, five of whom were decorated with the Victoria Cross. Surgeon Herbert F. Reade, 61st regiment, at the Siege of Delhi, where on September 14, 1857, "while this officer was attending to the wounded at the end of one of the streets of the city, a party of rebels advanced from the direction of the Bank, and having established themselves in the houses of the street, commenced firing from the roof. The wounded were thus in very great danger, and would have fallen into the hands of the enemy had not Surgeon Reade drawn his sword, and calling upon a few soldiers who were near, to follow, succeeded, under a heavy fire, in dislodging the rebels from their position; his party consisted of about ten in all, of whom two were killed and five or six wounded. Surgeon Reade also accompanied the regiment at the assault of Delhi, and on the morning of September 16, 1857, was one of the first up at the breach in the Mugaznee, which was stormed by the 61st and Belooch battalion, upon which occasion, he, with a sergeant of his regiment, spiked one of the enemy's guns." Assistant-surgeon Valentine M'Master, " for the intrepidity with which he exposed himself to the fire of the enemy, in bringing in and attending to the wounded on September 25." Surgeon Joseph Gee, C.B., " For most conspicuous gallantry and important services on the entry of Major-General Havelock's relieving force into Lucknow on September 25." Surgeon Anthony Dickson Home, 90th Regiment, "For persevering bravery and admirable conduct in charge of the wounded men left behind the column, when the troops under Major-General Havelock forced their way into the Residency of Lucknow, September 25, 1857; and Assistant-surgeon William Bradshaw, " For intrepidity and good conduct when ordered with Surgeon Home to remove the wounded men left behind the column that forced its way into the Residency of Lucknow, on September 26, 1857. The bearers had left the dhoolies, but by great exertion, and notwithstanding the close proximity of the Sepoys, Surgeon Home and Assistant-surgeon Bradshaw, got some of the bearers together, and the latter with about twenty dhoolies becoming separated from the rest of the party, succeeded in reaching the Residency in safety by the river bank." Assistant-Surgeon Boyd, 90th Foot, officiated as Medical officer in charge of the European Garrison Hospital during the siege of the Residency at Lucknow, for which he was promoted and given a year's service.

There were several other instances of individual gallantry on the part of the medical officers during that momentous period. At Mussel Aboo, Surgeon Tooth, in the absence of the officer commanding the 83rd detatchment, was thanked in General Orders for having defended the station by means of the convalescents when attacked by the mountaineers of the Joudpore Legion, thereby saving the lives of 136 women and children. Surgeon-Major

Swettenham, who was wounded at the assault and relief of Lucknow; Surgeon Patterson in action at Sirthova; Assistant-Surgeon Veale, severely at Lucknow, on its relief by Lord Clyde. At the action of the Hudun, Assistant-Surgeon Moore was killed, and Dr. Innes was wounded and had a horse shot under him. Senior Surgeon Graham was killed at Sealkote; Dr. Kirke at Gwalior, Dr. Hay at Bareilly, Dr. McEgan at Jhansi, Surgeons Garrett and Collyer, Dr. McAuley, Assistant-Surgeon Rawling and others at Cawnpore, Lylle at Patna, Dopping at Delhi, Janies at Augur, Hawkins at Bareilly, Knight, Anthony, Douglas, Joseph, Fell, Tirsa, Ferns, Graham, Collin, Harris, Macdonald, Hayes, Winslow, Kirk, John Moore, Dempster, Chalvin, and Assistant-Surgeon Stack at Jhansi, whilst attending the wounded of the 84th. On no occasion did the Medical officers show themselves so deserving of the title of combatant officers, as during the Indian Mutiny.

These remarks are fully borne out by the history of the Medical staff, for in every war in which they have been engaged during the present century, some of their number have been either killed or wounded. At St. Lucia, in 1803, Mr. Hartle, who accompanied the storming party in the assault on Morne Fortunée; Surgeon Wilde, of the 87th, was killed at Monte Video; Assistant-Surgeon Buxton at Buenos Ayres; Assistant-Surgeon Edmunds, of the 31st, who was wounded and left in charge on the field after Talavera, died shortly afterwards; Power, of the 83rd, at the attack on Martinique in 1809. In the first expedition to Burmah in 1828, Sandford was taken prisoner at Ava, loaded with fetters and placed in a noxious dungeon until his profession was discovered, when he was removed to attend upon the king, whose life he saved; allowed to carry despatches to the general from his fellow-sufferers, and returning back, in accordance with his promise, he was given many presents by the royal patient for acting so honourably. In the Second Burmese War, Dr. Murphy was wounded at the taking of Prome; at Buddiwal Surgeon-Major Banon was chained to a gun and detained by the Sikhs for fourteen days; after the battle of Moodkee, Assistant-Surgeon Gahan, 9th Foot, died of his wounds; at the attack on Jellalabad in 1842, Barnes of the 13th, was wounded; in the burning of the "Kent," East Indianman in 1825, Graham, assistant-surgeon of the 31st, was in charge of his regiment; in the Caffre War of 1846-7, Assistant-Surgeon Howell, Rifle Brigade, was killed on January 11 near the Kei River. In the following war of 1850-3, Assistant-Surgeon Stuart, of the Cape Mounted Rifles, in action December 14, and Davidson, of the 43rd, in a night attack on February 14. In the Crimea, O'Leary, assistant-surgeon 68th, was cut in two by a cannon shot while in the act of assisting a wounded seaman. An officer who was present during the siege wrote home, "It is only to be wondered at that more casualties have not occurred among the medical officers, for during the heat of the fire they are constantly called from place to place, running along the batteries, through the line of fire, in quest of the wounded." Another, a general-officer, wrote after the attack on the Redan, " While balls and round shot were flying about, I was much pleased to observe on this occasion the zeal and fearless conduct of Assistant-Surgeon Hyde, who moved about the wounded, doing all in his power to assist them." During an outbreak of cholera in 1858 at Ceylon, Surgeon-Major Cogan, 2nd Queen's, was mentioned in General Orders by General Lockyer for services "most creditable to himself and honourable to his profession." And in the Second China War, when at the capture of the Taku Forts, August 20, 1860, hospital-apprentice Arthur Fitzgibbon earned the Victoria Cross, " For having behaved with great coolness and courage while accompanying a wing of the 67th regiment, when it took up a position within 500 yards of the forts, and having quitted cover, he proceeded under a heavy fire, to attend a dhoolie-bearer, whose wound he had been directed to bind up, and while the regiment was advancing under the enemy's fire, he ran across the open to attend to another wounded man, in doing which, he himself was severely wounded." These are only a few of the many instances on record, proving the absurdity of classing medical officers of the army among non-combatant departments who never serve in action with the enemy, or accompany the troops under fire.

Among the Medical officers who controlled the administrative arrangements were Dr. J. H. K. Innes, senior medical officer of Sir John Jones' force in Rohilcund. C. A. Gordon of Frank's force in the advance on Lucknow and relief of Azimghur; F. W. Innes of the force under Havelock and Outram until the fall of Lucknow, Barclay of the 23rd brigade, Saugaon Field Force, &c.

On November 1, 1858, India was transferred by proclamation from the Company to the Queen, and in the following year the Local Inspectors of Hospitals were gazetted Inspectors-Generals.

In the Gazette of August 26, 1859, Assistant-surgeons Fryer, Partridge, Greenhouse, and Reid of Her Majesty's Indian Forces had conferred upon them the brevet rank of surgeon, in recognition of their services during the Siege of Lucknow; and a General Order, dated Fort William, Calcutta, March 29, 1859, the Governor-General in Council expressed to Dr. Forsyth, Inspector-General of Her Majesty's Hospitals, Dr. Linton, C.B., and the medical officers employed in the field or who had elsewhere furthered the service by their exertions in providing for the welfare and wants of the troops, " the cordial acknowledgment of the Government of India for the important services rendered."

On the outbreak of the Second China War in 1857, a Medical staff was detailed for the expedition, comprising Dep. Insp.-General Dr. Dane, three first class staff-surgeons, eight second class, sixteen assistant staff-surgeons, one apothecary, three dispensers of medicines, three medical clerks, and eight purveyor's clerks, and a detachment of the medical staff corps. It had been intended to have a military force of four regiments, four companies of artillery, two of engineers, and one of the military train.

At the close of the Crimean War the Order of the Legion of Honour was conferred upon the following officers, in a Decree published in the 'Moniteur' of the 16th July, 1859. Sir John Hall, principal medical officer, Archibald Gordon, M.D., James Mouat, M.D., Thomas P. Matthew, M.D., Richard Coffin Elliot, M.D., Thomas Alexander, M.D., Assistant-Surgeons Thomas C. Brady, Thomas Legertward 40th Foot, Thomas Sylvester 23rd, George Fair, Charles O'Callaghan, William George Reeves 38th, William Alexander McKinnon 42nd, John Gibbons 44th, Surgeon Stanhope H. Fusser, R.A., William P. Ward, R.A., Thomas Parke, R.A., Arthur H. Taylor, R.A., and in a subsequent Decree of April 3, 1857, on Drs. Arthur Anderson, Ramsay Brush, John Wyatt, Ashton Bostock, R. F. Valpy de Lisle, 4th regiment, A. P. Lockwood, 7th, Thomas Longman, 19th, R. Mackinnon, 21st, D. G. Barlow, 28th, W. M. Muer, 33rd, John Frazer and J. B. St. Croix Crosse, 11th Hussars.

The Sardinian medal was conferred on Surgeon Davis 49th Foot, Assistant-Surgeon Clarke, 33rd, Burton, 77th, and Bowen, Royal Artillery—and on several others the Turkish Order of the Medjidie.

On June 22, 1858, Mr. Alexander succeeded Sir Andrew Smith as Director-General. The latter officer had entered the service as hospital-assistant, August 15, 1815, was appointed assistant-surgeon, October 27, 1825, staff-surgeon July 7, 1837, Deputy Inspector-General December 19, 1845, and Inspector-General February 7, 1851. Mr. Alexander had served with the 60th Rifles during the Caffre War 1851-53, was principal medical officer of the Expedition across the Kei, at the termination of which he was thanked in General Orders for his services. He proceeded with the first troops despatched to Gallipoli as principal medical officer, was in medical charge of the Light Division of the Eastern Army from its first taking the field, and until the division left the Crimea, without being absent a single day from duty. Was present at the Battles of the Alma, Inkerman, Balaclava, Siege and Fall of Sebastopol, sortie of 21st October, assaults of 18th June and 18th September on the Redan; was Principal Medical Officer of the Kertch Expedition, was specially noticed in Lord Raglan's despatch after the Battle of Inkerman "for his able exertions as deserving to be most honourably mentioned," and also in General Codrington's despatch after the fall of Sebastopol. Promoted Deputy and Inspector-General, C.B., and Knight of the Legion of Honour.

On the 1st October, 1858, was promulgated one of the most popular Warrants as well as the most important up to that date issued to the Department. The ranks were for the future to be four: viz., Inspector-General of Hospitals, Deputy Inspector-General of Hospitals, Staff or Regimental Surgeon—who, after twenty years' full-pay service in any rank, was to be styled Surgeon-Major—Staff or Regimental Assistant-Surgeon. Candidates for admission to this department were to hold qualifications to practice medicines and surgery before being admitted to a competitive examination, after passing through which they were to undergo a course of special instruction in the Army Medical School. Assistant-surgeons were to pass a professional examination before being eligible for promotion to the rank of surgeon. Assistant-surgeons entered on a pay of 10s. per diem, increased to 11s. 6d. after five years' service, 13s. after ten years' service; surgeons on promotion were entitled to 15s., increased to 18s. after fifteen years' service; surgeon-major, £1 2s., increased to £1 5s. after twenty-five years; deputy inspector-general commenced on a pay of £1 8s., increasing progressively to £1 10s. and £1 14s. after thirty years' services; inspectors-general, £2 per diem on promotion, after twenty-five years' services, £2 5s. In addition to the pay of their rank, officers at the head of the Medical Department at foreign stations were to receive allowances of 20s. per diem, with an army in the field of 10,000 men and upwards; 15s. with an army of 5,000; 10s. with an army of any less number. Half-pay was granted at rates commencing at 6s. per diem for assistant-surgeons placed on the ineffective list after five years' service on reduction of establishment, or on the Report of a Medical Board, in consequence of being incapacitated by reason of ill-health, caused by wounds, or brought on by the discharge of their duties, up to £1 17s. 6d. for inspectors-general after thirty years' full-pay services. With the view to maintain the efficiency of the service, executive medical officers were to be retired at fifty-five years, and administrative medical officers on reaching sixty-five years. Officers of twenty-five years' full-pay service were to have the right of retiring on seven-tenths of their daily pay—the relative rank of medical officers was to be that of lieutenant in joining, captain after six years' service, major on promotion, and lieutenant-colonel for persons of that rank on completion of twenty years' service; deputy inspectors-general as lieutenant-colonel, after five years' service as colonel; inspectors-general as brigadier, after three years' service on full pay as major-general. By clause 17 of the Warrant it was ordered that " such relative rank shall carry with it all precedence and advantages attaching to the rank with which it corresponds (except as regards the presidency of court-martials, when our will and pleasure is, that the senior combatant officer be always president), and shall regulate choice of quarters, rates of lodging money, servants, forage, fuel, and light, or allowance in their stead, detention and prize money. But when a medical officer is serving with a regiment or detachment, the officer commanding, though he be a junior in rank to such medical officer, is entitled to a preference in choice of quarters." By clause 18, "Medical officers shall be entitled to all the allowances granted by the Warrant of 13th July, 1857, on account of wounds and injuries received in action, as combatant officers of the same relative rank," and their families " to all the allowances granted by the Warrant of 15th June, 1855, to the families of combatant officers holding the same relative rank." Medical officers were all to be entitled to field allowances as granted by the Royal Warrant of 1st July, 1848, and surgeons and surgeons-major of infantry regiments were not in future to be subject to any "diminution of the alllowance of forage, nor to any stoppage out of their daily pay for any ration of hay, straw, or oats, supplied for the horse or horses kept by them for the public service." Staff-surgeons of the first class and the senior surgeons of artillery were to rank and to have the pay of surgeons-major; medical officers were to be entitled to the same honours as other officers of the army of equal relative rank, and a medical officer retiring after twenty-five years' full-pay service might be recommended by the head of his department to receive a step of honorary rank. Good-service pensions were to be awarded to the most meritorious medical officers in the army, and Her Majesty signified her desire that "six of the most meritorious medical officers of the army" should be named her honorary physicians, and six her honorary surgeons.

Such were the practical results of the recommendation of the Royal Commission appointed to inquire into the constitution of the Medical Department. The original warrant recommended by the Committee proposed to confer the rank of surgeon-major upon all surgeons after fifteen years' service, with a pay of £1, increased after twenty years' service to £1 5s., after twenty-five years' service to £1 10s.; deputy inspectors-general on appointment £1 10s., after twenty-five years' service, £2; inspectors-general on appointment £2 10s., after twenty-five years' service £3 per diem.

Contemporaneously with the Royal Warrant of 1858 was published Regulations distinctly defining the duties of the Medical officers, laying down scales of equipment for troops in the field, and the uniform to be worn by officers of the Medical staff. The conditions under which Medical officers who volunteered for service in Western Africa were also altered with the view of recompensing those officers who had the courage and endurance to risk the *désagréments* and deadly malaria of that trying climate. Each medical officer being allowed to count two years' service towards promotion and retirement for each year's service on the coast. Previous to this, as vacancies occurred, volunteers were called for from the general staff and given at once a step of rank in the army, or very shortly after arrival in Africa. In no country, or in no climate, did the officers of the Medical staff undergo greater risk to life, and nowhere were special rewards more honourably earned. Of 1,658 Europeans sent from England between the years 1822-30, 1,298 perished from climatic causes, 360 were invalided, 123 of whom died on the passage to England, fifty-seven of the remainder being discharged as unfit for the service on arrival —results frequently repeated until the general employment of Native troops. Between 1799, the date of the re-occupation of the settlements in Western Africa and the promulgation of the Royal Warrant of 1st October, 1858, the officers of the Department employed there had served through the yellow fever epidemics of 1807, '13, '16, '21, '28, '37, '47, and '51, in which each year three of their number died at the Gambia ; also at the defence of Freetown in 1801 ; Cape Coast Castle, 1807 ; capture of Goree and Senegal from the French in 1809 ; first Ashantee War and action at Essinmacow, 20th May 1825, where Mr. Tedlie, the senior medical officer, was killed ; General Turner's expedition to the Sherbro in 1825 ; action of Dodowah, in 1826 ; capture of Fort Bullen and action of Barra Point, 11th November, 1831; destruction of stockades on the Rio Nunez in 1844; second expedition to the Sherbro in 1849; and action in the Quenalla plains at the Gambia, where a medical officer, Mr. Kehne was wounded; defeat of the pirates on the island of Basi, Rio Jeba, by British and French naval and land forces; expedition to Malaghea, 22nd May, 1855 ; various actions on the Gold Coast and River Gambia, where, at the forcing of the pass of Baccow in 1855, Mr. Hendly, S.M.O., was wounded; and Governor Hill's and Commodore Wise's expedition up the Great Scarcias, January, 1858. The names of the late Deputy-inspectors of Hospitals, Drs. Barry and Nicholl, Dr. Lawson, Inspector-General of Hospitals, and Surgeon-General Gordon, C.B., are associated with the earlier and later history of the African Medical service.

On the 17th August, 1859, the following distinguished officers were gazetted honorary physicians and honorary surgeons to Her Majesty. Honorary Physicians.—Sir John McAndrew, M.D., K.C.B.; Inspectors-General Andrew Ferguson, M.D.; William Linton, M.D., C.B. ; John Forest, M.D., C.B.; J. B. Gibson, M.D., C.B. ; and T. G. Logan, M.D., C.B. Honorary Surgeons.—Thomas Alexander, C.B., Director-General; Inspector-Generals Andrew Melvin and J. B. Taylor, C.B.; Deputy Inspectors-General E. Bradford and Thomas Mostyn; and J. M. Bostock, M.D., Surgeon-Major Scots Fusilier Guards.

On the 10th December, 1859, monthly returns were abolished, and weekly sick returns substituted for all troops serving in the United Kingdom.

In August, 1860, took place the first competitive examination for entrance into the Army Medical School. The following gentlemen were the successful out of thirty-nine candidates, C. H. Y. Godwin, J. Walters, F. Gillespie, Albert A. Gore, F. Maunsell,

G. F. White, F. R. Wilson, W. H. Jones, N. Alcock. D. M. Davidson, R. E. Heath, R. Adams, B. J. Jazdowski, J. Thompson, C. S. Wills, R. de B. Riordan, S. Hope, T. Y. Baker, J. H. N. Bracken, F. Pont, P. C. Baxter, S. G. White, H. Lamit, H. O. Harvey, G. B. Grant, W. R. Wall, and T. B. Flynn. The first session of the Army Medical School was opened at Fort Pitt, Chatham, on the 2nd October, 1860, in the presence of the Right Honourable the Secretary of State for War, Mr. Sidney Herbert, Dr. Gibson, C.B., Director-General, (Mr. Alexander having died suddenly a short time previously), Major-General Eyre, commanding at Chatham, and several military and medical officers. Three professors had been appointed. Mr. Longmore, Deputy Inspector-General of Hospitals, who had served with distinction in the Crimea, professor of military surgery; Dr. Parkes, late Chief of the Renkioi Hospital, professor of hygiene; and Dr. Aitken, associated with Dr. Lyons as pathologist to the Crimean expedition, professor of pathology. The nucleus of a museum of Military surgery and hygiene had been already formed by the removal to Chatham of the collection brought together at the Royal College of Surgeons in Ireland by Mr. Tufnell, who had in the year 1846 commenced the delivery of a course of lectures on Military Surgery in Dublin.

In his opening lecture, Mr. Longmore gave a brief but interesting sketch of the new duties devolving upon the medical department, and during its delivery alluded to the valuable privileges conferred by the Royal Warrant of the 1st October, 1858. " My only object in alluding to this subject," Mr. Longmore went on to say, " is, that we may consider if, on the one hand, these are our advantages, what, on the other hand are our obligations, and to what results they should act as incentives. Passive enjoyment of benefits conferred, contentment with an indifferent transaction of the daily routine of business, the avoidance of reprimand and disgrace, will no longer suffice, if we intend to consult the satisfaction of our own minds, or receive advancement in our profession. There have always been many exceptions to success following such a line of conduct as I have just indicated, men who have risen by active, and not passive qualities, but what have hitherto been the exceptions must in the future become the rule. All the changes which have lately been made in the department have this purpose in view. For the said changes themselves we owe a deep debt of gratitude to the members of the Royal Commission, who recommended them, especially to the late Director-General, Mr. Alexander, who, as one of the members, worked so earnestly and so sincerely to obtain them, and to the present enlightened Secretary of State for War, Mr. Sidney Herbert, who by his influential position has since contributed so much to their establishment, and to the country, as represented in Parliament, for the support it accorded to them;

to His Royal Highness the Commander-in-Chief, and to the general and other commanders for their testimony in person of the medical officers as a body, and to our Most Gracious Sovereign who was pleased to order that the recommendations should take practical effect. These debts must be discharged; and I am confident I speak truthfully in saying that the surest way of doing so will be by each, in his particular sphere, contributing to solve the great problem of lessening the rates of sickness and mortality in Her Majesty's Forces; for by such means we shall best repay the country for its increased outlay in the medical establishment, and justify and gratify the feelings of those who have laboured in the cause of our improvement."

Mr. Sydney Herbert, after alluding to a letter from the Adjutant-General with the army in China, conveying the "most gratifying accounts of the excellent condition to health," of the Force, with which the present Director-General, Sir William Muir, acted as principal medical officer, and the great benefit which had arisen from the appointment of a sanitary inspector, first held by Dr. Rutherford, as acting indirectly in "rousing not only the regimental medical officers, but the combattant officers to pay increased attention to hygienic measures," expressed a hope, that the gentlemen assembled before him, as medical officers "would do their utmost to support the dignity of their profession, and by their example and conduct as scientific officers, direct the tendency of their young companions into a more useful sphere of action, profit to the greatest extent by the advantages afforded them in the establishment of the school, and by their incessant intelligence and zeal prove they were worthy of the advantages lately conferred upon them," concluding by wishing them every success and happiness in their new career. General Eyre bore testimony to the most exemplary conduct of the young gentlemen, who had been sent down to Chatham for duty in anticipation of the opening of the school, who he saw before him; and the Director-General, as the head of the department, informed his future officers that those amongst them who profited most by their studies "he intended to give the first and best appointments. They should be sent to the most popular stations, or to the regiments which were considered the best, as far as the exigencies of the service would allow." Sir James Gibson had entered the service as hospital-assistant 14th December, 1826, became assistant-surgeon, 12th January, 1829; surgeon, 2nd July, 1841; surgeon-major, 19th May, 1851, deputy-inspector-general, 1st May, 1855; inspector-general, 31st October, 1858; director-general 7th March, 1860. He had served with the army during the Eastern Campaign of 1854; and on the Duke of Cambridge proceeding to the East, was appointed by His Royal Highness as his personal attendant, was present at the battles of the Alma, Balaclava, Inkerman, and siege of Sebastopol. Under such happy auspices did the new organisation of the Army Medical Department come into existence.

On the 1st January, 1860, 1,075 medical officers were on full pay. During the year fifty-eight assistant-surgeons entered the service; thirty-two medical officers died; seventeen were placed upon temporary half-pay, from ill-health, seven resigned, and eleven retired.

The first of the Army Medical Reports was shortly afterwards published, since which date these volumes contain the more recent history of the Army Medical Staff, whose members in China, New Zealand, Abyssinia, and Ashantee have sustained with honour the ancient prestige of their corps, and added laurels to the many already gained by their predecessors. It only remains to add that it has been to me a great pleasure to place on record the story of their Services under the Crown, and my only regret is that it had not fallen to the lot of some abler hand than mine to picture so interesting a history.

THE END.

LONDON:
Printed by A. Schulze, 13, Poland Street.

APPENDIX.

Précis of the Report of the Committee on the Army Medical Services.
1878.

(BRITISH MEDICAL JOURNAL.)

In February last, a Committee consisting of Mr. Ralph Thompson, C.B., Under Secretary of State for War; Sir William M. Muir, Director-General of the Army Medical Department; and Mr. D. Robinson, War Office Actuary, was appointed by Viscount Cranbrook to inquire into the causes which prevent eligible candidates from coming forward for the Army Medical Department, and to point out the necessary remedies. The report of the Committee has recently been issued.

As a preliminary investigation, the Committee inquired whether there had really been a difficulty in obtaining candidates, and to what extent. They gave the result of their inquiries in a table, showing that while in 1868 the percentage of candidates to vacancies was 176, and in the two examinations of 1871, 158 and 242 respectively, it has fallen to 46 in 1875 and 1877, and 48 in 1878. This diminished supply has necessitated the employment of medical men lower and lower in the pass list; and even then the establishment has not been kept full. Such a result, they observe, is eminently unsatisfactory. They endeavour to explain the diminution of the number of candidates, not only for the Army, but for the Naval and Indian Medical Services, by the greater opportunities of employment offered to young medical men in the colonies, the mercantile marine, &c., and also by the reduction in the number of persons entering the medical profession, in consequence, probably, of the opening of the British and Indian Civil service to competition, and perhaps of the increasing attraction of the mercantile world. They refer to a report from the Medical School of St. Thomas's Hospital, in which it is stated that the ratio of medical practitioners to 10,000 of the population has thus decreased: in 1851, 7·2; in 1861, 6·4; in 1871, 6·0.

The Committee remark that, while it may not be necessary to draw to the Army the very *élite* of the medical profession, it is desirable that there should be a fair leaven of surgeons of a high class, and it is eminently necessary that the officers of the Army Medical Department should as a whole be at least equal to the average of successful medical practitioners. The problem then is to make military medical life attractive, so as to draw a sufficient number from the best or nearly the best class of students.

Proceeding to point out the causes which tend (or are represented as tending) to discourage candidates from coming forward for the Army Medical Service, the Committee first state that there is the element of prejudice engendered by the complaints of officers serving or who have served in the department, and whose dissatisfaction is reflected on their relatives and friends who happen to be students in the medical schools. Apart from this source of difficulty, there are others connected with the Army Medical Department itself which, in the opinion of the Committee, form obstacles to its success.

188   APPENDIX.

The difficulties to be examined are, therefore, arranged in two classes; viz.: 1. The alleged grievances of officers who are now serving or who have served in the Army Medical Department; 2. The direct discouragement afforded by the calculable prospects in the department itself.

Under Class 1, the Committee examine *seriatim* the alleged grievances so far as they have been able to ascertain them; viz: 1. Scales of pay and system of retirement; 2. Loss of forage; 3. Loss of a soldier servant; 4. Difficulties as to quarters; 5. Sick half pay; 6. Relative rank and honours; 7. The unpublished roster; 8. Non-discrimination between seniors and juniors in the assignment of duties; 9. Questions of leave; 10. Difficulty of exchanging; 11. Generally, that faith has not been kept by Government; and especially, that the Royal Warrant of 1858 has been departed from; 12. The abolition of the regimental system; 13. Increased difficulty in obtaining promotion to the rank of deputy surgeon-general.

1. The first complaint noticed is, that the pay is insufficient, and that retirement, except on inadequate terms, cannot be claimed as a right until after twenty-five years' service. On this, the Committee remark, in the first place, that successive warrants have raised the pay of army medical officers, so that none are serving on worse pay than that secured to them by the agreement under which they entered the service. But such a contrast cannot fairly be considered as life-long when the value of money decreases and payment of all sorts of services rises. Although the medical officers are treated within the legal letter of their contract, they have a moral right to have their position improved *pari passu* with that of civil practitioners. On the subject of retirement, the Committee are of opinion that medical officers should have as great facilities for retirement as are afforded by the Royal Warrant of August 1877 to combatant officers; and they recommend that a surgeon should be allowed to retire after ten years' service on a gratuity of £1,250; after fifteen years' service, on a gratuity £1,800; and after eighteen years' service, on a gratuity of £2,500. Every such gratuity accepted would be ultimately a saving to the State; and (presuming a sufficient number of candidates to be forthcoming) no officer would be serving who was unwilling to serve, while there should be a continued influx of candidates fresh from the schools. After twenty years' service, the retiring pay of a surgeon-major should be a £1 a day. after twenty-five years, £1 2s. 6d.; and after thirty years, £1 5s. a day. The Committee propose the abolition of grants of higher rates of retirement to officers retiring under the certificates of Medical Boards.

2. The next point examined is the loss of forage allowance. After an examination into the history of the matter, the Committee remark that the conditions under which the medical officer had forage and other allowances were the conditions laid down in the Royal Warrants regulating the issue of such allowances to all services. It has been carefully laid down in the Royal Warrants (1848, 1864, and 1878) that the horse to be foraged must be actually and *bond fide* kept for the public service; and now, if this can be certified, the forage is not withheld. They consider further, that it should be distinctly understood that forage is not intended to constitute an emolument of the officer; nor, in enabling him to maintain a horse, to add to his dignity or his pleasure. If a horse be required, the State contributes towards the expense of keeping it; but that is all. Moreover, the cessation of forage can scarcely be regarded as a pecuniary loss: for neither the forage in kind nor the money allowance covered the cost of keeping the horse. But, while not admitting the grievance respecting forage, the Com-

mittee remark that, when an officer holds an appointment which does not involve the maintenance of a horse, but requires him to undertake temporary duty for which he must be mounted, the State should relieve him from the necessity of buying a horse and probably selling it afterwards at a loss, or of hiring one at a cost which will in most cases exceed the forage allowance. To meet such cases, they think a sufficient number of horses should be provided at large stations for the use of officers requiring to be temporarily mounted.

3. As regards the complaint of the loss of a soldier-servant, the Committee admit that, by comparison, the medical officer (like other staff and departmental officers) is worse off in the matter of the servant than a regimental officer; but they consider that the difficulty is met by the increase of the pay of medical officers recommended in a subsequent part of the report. The provision of a servant from the Army Hospital Corps would remove all grievances, but would be costly.

4. The next matter considered is the complaint that, in the assignment of quarters and issue of fuel and light, medical officers are treated as regimental officers, although in other respects deprived of regimental privileges. The Committee recommend that a suitable quarter should be provided for the medical officer in barracks where it is indispensable that a medical officer should reside. At the same time, they suggest that as in the case of large institutions such as schools and colleges, the duties may be equally well performed by a non-resident medical officer.

5. The Committee next notice the dissatisfaction at the present rules for sick leave and sick pay. They observe on this that, when the unhealthy nature of an army surgeon's occupation is considered, as well as the high rate of mortality to which medical officers are found to be subject, he should be allowed, in case of ill-health duly certified as not caused by misconduct, leave on full pay up to a year, according to the necessity of the case—instead of six months, as at present. In case of non-recovery, they recommend that medical officers should be placed under the half-pay regulations applicable to combatant officers, who are granted temporary half-pay until they recover, and until opportunities occur for their re-employment.

6. The next point considered is the question of honours and relative rank. The Committee sympathise with the medical officers in their complaint that honorary distinctions do not, as compared with other corps, fall sufficiently to their share; and they think that the medical officers show good cause why, in the matter of honours, they should be associated with the combatant rather than with the administrative services. They make the following suggestion: *a.* That a new title be given to the Army Medical Service—such as "Royal Army Surgeons" or "Royal Medical Staff"; *b.* That the Army Departments should have no precedence *inter se*, but be arranged alphabetically; *c.* That honours and good service pensions be bestowed on the scale applicable to combatants; *d.* That the Honorary Physicians and Honorary Surgeons to the Queen have the letters Q.H.P. and Q.H.S. appended to their names in the seniority list; *e.* That the names of the Queen's Honorary Physicians and Surgeons be printed in the *Army List* immediately after those of Her Majesty's aides-de-camp (*i.e.*, in the first or second page instead of an obscure corner in the body of the work); *f.* That appointment as Honorary Surgeon or Physician raise an officer *ipso facto* to the rank of Deputy-Surgeon-General, to be borne as supernumerary in the rank until he would have been promoted to it in regular course; *g.* That surgeons-major rank with lieutenant-colonels, not as juniors, but according to the date of completing twenty years' service; *h.* That surgeons rank as captains (instead of lieutenants)

from the time of passing through the course at Netley; and that probationers at Netley have the rank of lieutenants.

7. With reference to the complaint of an unpublished roster, the Committee state that the surgeon-general in whose charge it is, will always permit to any medical officer making written application a statement of his position, and that the roster is open to the inspection of any officer applying personally.

8. The next complaint considered is that of the non-discrimination between seniors and juniors in the assignment of duties. The Committee remark that it is clear that medical duty of whatever kind must be taken by a senior if a junior be not available; but that, on the other hand, it ought undoubtedly to be so arranged by the principal medical officer in each command that the duties of this character should fall as lightly as possible on senior officers. They do not think it advisable to lay down any fixed rule.

9. Regarding leave of absence, the Committee remark that the complaint of having to find a substitute during leave is now obviated by the arrangements by which either military or civil substitutes are found from those absent. As regards the complaint that medical officers do not have the same (ordinary) leave as combatant officers, the Committee remark that, while the combatant officers' services are not always required, the medical officer is always wanted; and they think that, under ordinary circumstances, two months' leave in the year afford sufficient recreation.

10. In referring to the complaint of difficulty of exchanging, the report says that three years' service at home is considered as a rule the period after which an officer should be prepared to take another turn of foreign service ; but if he have had long foreign service, exchange is permitted.

11. In examining the allegation that faith has not been kept by Government with the medical officers, and especially that the Royal Warrant of 1858 has been departed from, the Committee inquire *seriatim* how far the recommendations of the Select Committee of 1856, of Lord Herbert's Royal Commission in 1858, and of the mixed Committee of Naval and Military Officers in 1866, have been carried out; and they also give summaries of the Royal Warrants of 1873 and 1876. The conclusion arrived at is, that the Royal Warrants of the last twenty years have progressively improved the status, pay, and promotion of Army Medical Officers ; the only points on which there are colourable grounds for the charge of breach of faith being: *a*. Partial loss of forage ; *b*. Substitution of the staff system for the regimental system; *c*. Increased difficulty in obtaining promotion to the rank of deputy-surgeon-general.

12. In speaking of the abolition of the regimental system, the Committee observe that, with the regimental system in force, reliefs were impracticable with any fairness, while the incidence of foreign duty now falls equally through the department. They further point out as advantages of the unified staff system the increase of allowances for lodging, fuel, and light; and the fact that, by being attached to station hospitals, medical officers have been relieved from the expense of providing their cases of capital instruments. They think, however, that the social losses to the medical officers might be made up. At a few large stations, a medical institute might be established as a club, library, and scientific resort; Government providing the building, fire, and light, and possibly making an annual grant towards the purchase of medical books, microscopes, &c. At smaller stations, also, officers of the several departments might be encouraged to combine for messing together, Government affording facilities.

13. Regarding the complaint of increased difficulty in obtaining promotion to the rank of deputy surgeon-general, the Committee remark that in 1867 the Indian Government made a rule requiring three years' previous service in India from every officer allowed to have administrative charge there; and a large proportion of administrative appointments are in India. They recommend that this rule should be officially promulgated, which does not appear to have been done.

II. The direct discouragements caused by the calculable prospects in the Department itself are considered under three heads: 14. The ten years' system of service; 15. The system of admission by half-yearly competitive examinations; 16. The low rate of pay and pension as compared with civil medical life and with other professions.

14. The Committee admit the failure of the ten years' system, by which it was supposed that an excellent career would be created for a small number of officers, while for the remainder the period when civil practice would be unremunerative would be bridged over. They consider it vain to struggle against the opposition of the medical schools. They recommend that, for all new entries, retirement after ten years be optional instead of compulsory—the pay for the first five years being £200 *per annum* instead of £250; and the gratuity on retirement being increased from £1,000 to £1,250; and that officers who joined under the the " ten years' rule," if allowed to come under the new system, retain their £250 a year; but, in case of their subsequent retirement on gratuities, be only eligible for sums less by £250 than those shown in Recommendation No. 1.

15. The Committee propose a modification of the system of entry by public competition. They recommend that one half of the vacancies be filled up without examination, but subject to the approval of the Director-General, by registered surgeons nominated and vouched by the medical schools of Great Britain, Canada, and Australia in rotation; that one-half of the vacancies be filled by half-yearly examinations in advanced practical subjects; that (admission in all case being on probations) probationers be sent to some great station for practical instruction in drill, ambulance duty, &c., until the Netley course begin; that probationers rank as lieutenants, and have pay at eight shillings a day; and that the maximum age for admission as probationer be reduced to twenty-eight.

16. Speaking of the low rates of pay and pension as compared with civil medical life, and with other professions, the Committee remark that, as a rule, combatant officers are not wholly dependent on their pay; but with medical men the case is otherwise, and the prospect of the greater pay will afford to them the greater attraction. They have endeavoured—though with but imperfect success—to obtain estimates of the earnings of civil medical practitioners; and they think that it may be assumed that, taken one with another a young man obtains £300 a year within five years of commencing practice: this rises to £500 after ten years, and goes on increasing to an average of £800. Comparing this with the rates of pay of army medical officers, they maintain that—especially after ten and fifteen years of service and in the later years of retirement—the State pay cannot compete with civil earnings, and is insufficient to draw to the department an adequate supply of medical men of the better class. They feel that an entire reconsideration of the rates of pay and pension is called for, so that the medical department of the army may fairly compete with civil practice for a considerable period. They recommend—with a view of increasing the medical officer's chance of obtaining a good pension—the interpolation, between the deputy surgeons-general and the surgeons-major, of

an executive rank of fifty brigade surgeons promoted by selection from surgeons-major, to form the body from whom deputy surgeons-general are to be taken. They recommend the following rates of pay and pension.

Effective.	Daily Pay.	Yearly Pay.	Relative Rank.	Estimated Pay and Allowances excluding Forage.	Present Rate (Warrant of 1873), excluding Forage.
	£ s d	£ s d		£ s d	£ s d
Surgeon, on appointment	. . .	200 0 0	Captain.	291 5 0	260 11 3
Ditto after 5 years	. . .	250 0 0	Captain.	341 5 0	306 3 9
Ditto after 10 years.	0 15 0	275 15 0	Captain.	365 0 0	365 0 0
Surgeon-Major, on appointment (at 12 years' service	1 0 0	365 0 0	Major.	483 12 6	365 0 0
Ditto after 15 years.	1 2 6	410 12 6	Major.	529 5 0	483 12 6
Ditto after 20 years.	1 5 0	456 5 0	Lieut.-Colonel	584 0 0	565 15 0
Ditto after 25 years.	1 7 6	501 17 6	Lieut.-Colonel	629 12 6	620 10 0
Brigade-Surgeon, on appointment	1 10 0	547 10 0	Lieut.-Colonel	675 5 0	no such rank
Ditto after 5 years in rank	1 13 0	602 5 0	Lieut.-Colonel	750 0 0	Maximum
Deputy Surg.-Gen.	2 0 0	730 0 0	Colonel.	876 0 0	803 0 0
Surgeon-General	3 0 0	1095 0 0	Maj.-General	1368 15 0	1186 5 0

Surgeons and surgeons-major to have the right of retirement as already stated in paragraph No. 1; brigade-surgeons to have the right to retire after twenty years' service on £1 7s. 6d. a day; after thirty years, on £1 10s.; deputy surgeons-general at any time, on £1 15s.; and surgeon-general, on £2. Retirement to be compulsory at the age of fifty-five for brigade-surgeons and surgeon-major, and at the age of sixty for surgeons-general and deputy surgeons-general. The Committee recommend that all medical officers retiring before the age of fifty-five be liable until that age to be called upon to serve in time of declared national emergency (at all events, for home service); that their names be in the meantime retained in italics, and that they be entitled to wear their uniform. As a set-off to the expenditure entailed by the recommendations, the Committee recommend that the number of surgeons-major and surgeons be reduced to 796, instead of 893, as in the present establishment.

In concluding their Report, the Committee say: "We believe that the time has fully come when the difficulty of obtaining medical officers for the army must be met in a liberal and comprehensive spirit. Their services are indispensable, and are recognised practically in the civil community by handsome remuneration. Government, to command those advantages, must supplement the certainty and the distinction of its service by pecuniary offers not seriously lower than those made by the civil community."

ERRATA.

Page	line	for	read
9	4	decimates	decimate
9	3	cause	causes
10	26	their	this
10	27	resnlt	result
12	48	Tungriac	Tungrian
17	7	nature	nation
17	20	Aranzoar	Avanzoar
18	12	house	honor
18	18	Petard	Pecard
19	20	Marodini	Morodini
21	21	Morte	Mort
25	26	oatmeal	ointment
28	6	klingeth	belongeth
28	14	men	man
28	43	whose	their
33	21	lease	leave
33	36	assail	assoil
38	28	repeated	rejected
40	18	lodging	leveying
41	7	joint	first
41	19	prisoners	pioneers
42	12	squared	squarest
42	13	harqueback	harquebus
43	2	their	the
44	10	rule	pale
44	43	ruff	buff
46	21	Dore said	aforesaid
50	11	Brayhill	Broghill
51	10	Luton	Ireton
54	34	improvement	impressment
59	27	musquethers	musqueteers.
61	25	when	where
62	38	of	or
65	9	staffs	staff
65	9	are	is
69	46	Clonmel	Connel
71	26	Downs'	Down's
72	2	troops	men
78	17	several	some
84	48	and	had
88	19	him	an
89	14	impunity	disability
90	21	Hora	Hore
96	31	Retechial	Petechial
102	30	Musket	Murket
104	36	his	any
106	4	the	their
113	31	peace	pence
114	23	exercise	orders

ERRATA.

Page	line	for	read
119	36	best	butt
120	1	the officers	these officers
123	10	writing	worthy
123	18	surgeons	majors
125	41	does	did
129	25	Guinn	Quinn
130	42	10s 3d	10s 6d
131	41	unusual	annual
136	18	Guinn	Quinn
138	26	they were	it was
139	39	Guinn	Quinn
139	40	of	to
139	44	rent	bat
139	45	for	from
143	37	allowed	allowances
143	41	to	a
145	30	Army Reserve	Army of Reserve
146	33	Heeson	Hewson
149	40	in	of
157	3	evident	frequent
157	24	for	thousand
158	16	but	who
158	39	accompanied	went with
159	33	attendance	accordance
161	36	Guinn	Quinn
164	25	men	service
172	29	141	1st
172	30	161	2nd
172	31	101	3rd
172	44	while	whilst
175	5	assorted	absorbed
175	28	success	scenes
175	41	this	the
177	17	Magaznee	Magazine
178	9	Janies	James
178	10	Augur	Saugur
178	13	84th	86th
179	29	Saugaon	Saugur
179	36	and	in
181	36	for	but
181	37	persons	junior
183	26	Kohne	Kehve
184	4	Lamit	Lamb
185	15	to health	of health
186	2	organisation	organization

www.ingramcontent.com/pod-product-compliance
Lightning Source LLC
Chambersburg PA
CBHW020922230426
43666CB00008B/1533